# Senegal Abroad

# AFRICA AND THE DIASPORA

## History, Politics, Culture

---

### SERIES EDITORS

Thomas Spear

Neil Kodesh

Tejumola Olaniyan

Michael G. Schatzberg

James H. Sweet

# SENEGAL ABROAD

## Linguistic Borders, Racial Formations, and Diasporic Imaginaries

Maya Angela Smith

The University of Wisconsin Press

The University of Wisconsin Press
1930 Monroe Street, 3rd Floor
Madison, Wisconsin 53711-2059
uwpress.wisc.edu

Gray's Inn House, 127 Clerkenwell Road
London EC1R 5DB, United Kingdom
eurospanbookstore.com

Printed in the United States of America

This book may be available in a digital edition.

Library of Congress Cataloging-in-Publication Data

Names: Smith, Maya Angela, author.
Title: Senegal abroad: linguistic borders, racial formations, and diasporic imaginaries /
Maya Angela Smith.
Description: Madison, Wisconsin: The University of Wisconsin Press, [2019]
| Series: Africa and the Diaspora: History, Politics, Culture
| Includes bibliographical references and indexes.
Identifiers: LCCN 2018014266 | ISBN 9780299320508 (cloth: alk. paper)
Subjects: LCSH: Senegalese—Foreign countries. | Senegalese—Language.
| Senegalese—Racial identity.
Classification: LCC DT549.42 .S65 2019 | DDC 305.896/63—dc23
LC record available at https://lccn.loc.gov/2018014266

# Contents

# Acknowledgments

During this several-year labor of love, many people provided unwavering emotional and intellectual support. I would like, first and foremost, to thank my partner, Rohit, my parents, Emily and Elton, and my brother, Jonathan, for being there for me and reminding me to breathe. I would also like to thank the numerous people who read various drafts of the manuscript and provided insightful, thoughtful, and detailed feedback: Louisa Mackenzie, Danny Hoffman, Rick Kern, Rich Watts, Livi Yoshioka-Maxwell, Jonathon Repinecz, Stan Thangaraj, Lynn Thomas, Laada Bilaniuk, Dorothy Kim, Jesse Shipley, María Elena García, Tony Lucero, and the anonymous readers contacted through the University of Wisconsin Press.

Several others provided a wide range of support, including mentoring, offering opportunities to discuss my project through invited talks, engaging in brainstorming sessions, providing a second pair of eyes for the foreign-language transcription and translation, suggesting where to get financial support, and writing reference letters for fellowships: Trica Keaton, Sarah Zimmerman, Paap Alsaan Sow, Keyti, Xuman, Binta Faye Gaye, Daniele Santoni, Beatrice Arduini, Denyse Delcourt, Nadine Amarelo, Lise Lalonde, Sabrina Tatta, Geoff Turnovsky, Mairi McLaughlin, Claire Kramsch, Stephanie Maher, Ralina Joseph, Manka Varghese, Frieda Ekotto, Martin Repinecz, Clorinda Donato,

Jeannette Acevedo Rivera, Deborah Thomas, Frédéric Viguier, and the women of WIRED at the University of Washington.

I am also grateful for the financial support and research leave that allowed me to complete this project: the Woodrow Wilson Career Enhancement Fellowship, the University of Washington Research Royalty Fund, and the University of Washington Society of Scholars.

I would be remiss if I did not thank my editor, Dennis Lloyd, whose enthusiasm for and support of my interdisciplinary project was a welcome relief. Dennis was a great interlocutor and demystified the publication process. He and the staff at the University of Wisconsin Press made the whole experience a delightful one.

Finally, but most importantly, I would like to express my gratitude for the numerous people who took time out of their lives to tell me their stories. The Senegalese throughout the diaspora interviewed in this book met my questions and inquiries with introspection, thoughtfulness, and humor. They provided perspectives that were both emotionally and intellectually stimulating. This book would not exist without them.

# Conventions of Transcription and Translation

## TRANSCRIPTION CONVENTIONS

| | |
|---|---|
| ::: | Colons indicate stretching of the preceding sound, proportional to the number of colons. |
| — | A hyphen after a word or a part of a word indicates a cut-off or self-interruption. |
| LOUD | All caps denote raised volume. |
| [*conduct*] | Paired brackets enclose descriptions of conduct. |
| [ | Separate left square brackets, one above the other on two successive lines with utterances by different speakers, indicate onset of a point of conversational overlap. |
| / / | Words between back slashes are transcribed with the International Phonetic Alphabet (IPA) for instances in which a language's writing conventions are inadequate. |

## NOTE ABOUT TRANSLATION

All translations are mine unless otherwise stated.

# Senegal Abroad

# INTRODUCTION

## Understanding Global Senegalese Identity Formation through Language and Movement

In the winter of 2009, I was sitting on a park bench in Rome, talking with two Senegalese migrants. Ndiaga, born in a small town in northeastern Senegal but raised in Dakar, had lived in Rome for eight years. By this point in my field-work in Italy, I had been meeting with him on a regular basis, and he seemed to enjoy our conversations about his life in Rome, his experiences as a migrant, and his relationship to the languages he spoke. On this day, he introduced me to his friend, a self-described studious man who went by the nickname Professore.[1] Born in the Fouta region of Senegal but raised in Saint-Louis, Professore had spent the last five years in Rome. Having agreed to Ndiaga's request to join us for the afternoon, Professore let Ndiaga do most of the talking while occasionally answering my questions with thinly veiled suspicion. However, halfway through the conversation, Professore warmed up to me somewhat and began participating in earnest.

The conversation was in both French, the official language of Senegal, and Italian, the official language of the country in which we all currently resided. Even though Professore was becoming more talkative as the time went on, which I owed to the natural camaraderie between Ndiaga and me, when I asked him about his experiences living in Italy, he seemed at a loss for words. Ndiaga responded for him in French by asking me if I had seen *The Color Purple*,

3

a film adapted from Alice Walker's novel of the same name that depicted the struggles of African American women in the United States. He then proceeded to relay his version of the main character Celie's defiant declaration, "Je suis *nero*, je suis *brutto*, *ma* je suis *vivo!*" (I am *black*, I am *ugly*, *but* I am *alive!*).[2] Ndiaga dexterously centered the conversation about his experiences in Italy around the topic of race by revoicing this marginalized character through multiple languages. By using the experience of an abused black woman as a medium to talk about his lived experiences, Ndiaga relied on this character's gendered and racialized positionality to amplify the marginalization that he and Professore faced in Italy. In addition to the meaning associated with these words, code-switching from French to Italian for the word *nero* further drew attention to his racialized positionality in Italian society and the exclusion it entailed. Paradoxically, by using descriptive adjectives in Italian, he also indicated that he was partially marking himself as Italian, and the force in which he landed on the word *vivo* suggested a defiant tone. He was not only commenting on racial formation in Italy but also turning it into a site of negotiation.

In addition to the creative use of language, Ndiaga and Professore also showed how cultural production in one part of the world could be used to articulate understandings of blackness and belonging in another part of the black diaspora. It is noteworthy that *The Color Purple* links and juxtaposes experiences in the United States and Africa because later in our conversation Professore confronted his racialization in Italy by remarking how in Africa he was never described as black but that he was made hyperaware of his blackness after arriving in Italy.[3] As both Ndiaga and Professore began to share their difficulties as black men in Rome, Professore remarked that because I, too, was black, I could understand what they were saying. Cultural production from the United States was allowing him not only to make sense of his current environment but also to forge a connection with me. Professore was relying on my identity as an African American to co-construct a narrative of black exclusion in white spaces.[4] In the chapters that follow, I analyze many such stories shared by my informants—Senegalese in Europe and the United States—in order to understand how languages function as sites for the negotiation of various identity formations.

Senegalese migration has captured the interest of scholars from a variety of disciplines. Most of the extensive anthropological research on global Senegalese communities relies on an economic lens to shed light on societal integration, transnational belonging, and racial/religious differentiation.[5] In addition, robust literary criticism on literary cultural production has examined the representation of Senegalese immigrant experiences abroad, particularly in France.[6] What is missing is the privileging of language that this book offers. On the one hand, my qualitative research on the Senegalese diaspora chooses an underutilized sociolinguistic framework in lieu of the more popular economic focus found in these anthropological texts to home in on identity formation in these sites. On the other hand, like literary and cultural studies, my sociolinguistic, ethnographic approach addresses issues of identity formation but grounds them in real-world linguistic experiences. In other words, through a critical examination of languages and multilingual practices, *Senegal Abroad* shows how language is key to understanding the formation of national, transnational, postcolonial, racial, and migrant identities among Senegalese in Paris, Rome, and New York. This book is about language attitudes, how they influence people's local and global interactions with the world, how they change through the experience of migration, and how in turn they affect migrants' language use. Senegalese are exemplary both in their capacity for movement and in their complex relation to language.

The multi-sited approach I employ makes clear just how mobile language and identity are. Many Senegalese migrants live and work in multiple cities with distinct languages over the course of their lives. What is more, their experiences highlight that not only national but also racial identities are expressed through language.[7] While the category "Senegalese" does not necessarily denote blackness, the experiences of Senegalese living as phenotypically black in majority-white settings bring race to the fore.[8] In asking the people I interviewed what it is like to be simultaneously a black immigrant, a postcolonial subject, a language learner, and a language user, I demonstrate how language is at the center of many other phenomena typically discussed in connection with migrants and immigration.

My fieldwork focused on Senegalese migrants and people of Senegalese descent ranging in age from seventeen to fifty-eight years old in Paris, Rome, and New York City. In each of these cities, I conducted interviews and participant observations with twenty-five to thirty participants over three-month periods.[9] Speaking with people from a variety of educational and linguistic backgrounds (whose time in the three different host countries varied from months to years to entire lives) raised many questions about the complexities of identity formation among migrants and their descendants: How do Senegalese communities outside Senegal relate to the languages they speak? How do migrants navigate language choices and ideologies in specific societal contexts, many of which specifically exclude the possibility of black-bodied migrants' belonging, especially if they speak a language that marks them as even further from the norm? How do diasporic Senegalese approach integration in each site as well as participate in transnational discussions of belonging in a postcolonial and racialized world? How do they understand their identity as comprising multiple languages and claim agency and symbolic capital by using these languages? It is not only *what* my informants say that conveys certain understandings of self and environment. It is also *how* they speak—the particular ways in which they switch between languages and structure their discourse—that shapes their identities.

## MULTILINGUALISM AND MOBILITY FROM A SENEGALESE PERSPECTIVE

### Navigating Languages

I first became interested in relations among language, identity, and context as a college student. While studying abroad in Paris and Dakar, I experienced the social nature of learning a language and how this social practice varied with context. For me, learning French in Paris was a more challenging experience than learning French in Dakar. Many Parisians seemed to have little patience with language learners, and I was often self-conscious about my French-speaking abilities—worried about making mistakes. By contrast, while learning French in Dakar, I felt less pressure to speak French perfectly, partially because I was simultaneously studying Wolof, the most widely spoken national language of Senegal. Senegal, however, represented a conundrum to me. While I did not sense the same imposition of standard French as I had when studying in France, there was still a reverence for the French language that surprised me. People I met in Dakar insisted that Senegalese spoke the best French in Africa and even better than many people in France. I had not expected an African country to take so much pride in a colonial European language, all the while enthusiastically championing the various national languages of Senegal.

The historical relationship between Senegal and France sheds light on current attitudes toward the French language, multilingualism, and migration patterns. The French arrived in West Africa by the early seventeenth century and set up trading posts along the Senegalese coast. By the nineteenth century, the Four Communes, which were the colonial towns of Saint-Louis, Dakar, Gorée, and Rufisque in present-day Senegal, made up the seat of the French colonial government. By 1848, those born in these four towns technically enjoyed the rights of full French citizenship, even if in practice very few could exercise these rights.[10] Regardless, France had more direct contact with Senegal than with any other colony in the region, and administratively some citizens of the Four Communes received a French education in order to help govern other parts of the French West African Empire.[11]

During the formation of Senegalese statehood, the French language took center stage. As Fiona McLaughlin notes, Léopold Senghor, the country's first president, "exhorted his people to speak French '*comme (des) bourgeois de Paris*' ('like Parisian bourgeois') and was subsequently (if not consequently) elected member of the Académie Française."[12] As such, Senghor defended the French language vigorously, and Abdou Diouf, who succeeded Senghor as president, continued extolling the virtues of the French language, serving as secretary general of the Organisation internationale de la francophonie (OIF; International Organization of La Francophonie) for over a decade after the end of his term. For many Senegalese, French offers a medium for interacting with France and other francophone countries. Business and education continue to tie Senegal and the other former French colonies to France.[13] In addition, speaking a Western language provides a certain kind of national intelligibility on a global scale and a way of navigating the nation's presence on the world stage.

Studying at the University of Cheikh Anta Diop (UCAD) in Dakar, I was immersed in French and marveled at how well my French-language abilities improved. However, this image of Senegal as a premier French-speaking space was constantly being challenged by my everyday interactions with people in various domains. What I learned in Wolof class was vital to my getting by. When riding the *cars rapides*, Dakar's chaotic version of mass transit, I hardly ever heard French spoken. Furthermore, I had to rely on my limited Wolof if I wanted to buy street food, such as mouth-watering *fataya* (meat-filled fried dough slathered with hot sauce). Even my highly educated host family spoke Wolof most of the time, usually only speaking in French when they wanted to include me in the conversation. The two live-in maids from a nearby village spoke no French at all, communicating with each other in one of the twenty-five or so indigenous languages of Senegal and communicating with my host family in Wolof.[14] The reality is that as little as 10 percent of the population in Senegal actually speaks French fluently, with another 21 percent of the population having partial command of the language. Meanwhile, more than 80 percent of the population speaks Wolof.[15] The diglossic situation in Senegal, where French is the "high" language of the elites and Wolof is the "low" language of the masses, illustrates the historical and contemporary importance of these languages, the societal attitudes about them, and the complicated power dynamics at play.[16]

While Senegal's special status in the French West African Empire necessitated the use of French, it was paradoxically Wolof, as the lingua franca, that spread most vigorously. During colonization, Wolof leaders cooperated with the French more than leaders from other ethnic groups did, giving Wolof special status. Subsequently, France established the colony of Senegal in Wolof territory. The Four Communes, in turn, attracted migrants from the interior who would then learn Wolof because it was an important trade language. Since independence, migration to these Wolof-speaking centers has only increased, further tipping the balance in favor of a Wolof-speaking nation.[17] Furthermore, Senegal's economic decline beginning in the 1980s resulted in less governmental hiring, providing little incentive for people to cultivate their French and paving the way for an increased use of Wolof and other local languages in a variety of domains.

From a sociopolitical standpoint, there has long been a move to validate traditional African languages instead of just capitulating to the global imposition of European languages. For many in Senegal, supporting a language such as Wolof is important for national self-respect. During the push for decolonization, scholars such as Cheikh Anta Diop began to promote African languages to combat the marginalization of African cultures and societies, and following this rhetoric Senegalese author and filmmaker Ousmane Sembène began using African languages in his works in the 1960s. Sembène's *Mandabi* (The money order) was shot in Wolof, becoming the first feature-length film in an African language.[18] Meanwhile, the intense politics of language was playing out in other parts of the African continent. Starting in the 1970s, Kenyan author Ngũgĩ wa Thiong'o published literary criticism on the importance of producing literature in African languages, and he began writing plays and novels in Gĩkũyũ and Kiswahili.[19] In a statement at the beginning of *Decolonizing the Mind*, he declared that in addition to his creative writing in Gĩkũyũ and Kiswahili, he would also no longer write explanatory prose in English. However, his subsequent prose publications have been in English, calling attention to just how difficult it is for African languages to stake a claim in the linguistic environment of the publishing world. More recently, in *Something Torn and New*, he theorizes the nuanced differences of how linguicide (linguistic genocide) plays out both on the continent and in the diaspora, locating this phenomenon on the global stage.[20] In other words, the cultural production of writers, filmmakers, and theorists as well as everyday people's use of African languages, both in Africa and abroad, demonstrate the ongoing push against European linguistic colonization and the complications that arise in doing so.

However, in the case of Senegal, making any sort of clear-cut statement regarding language and identity goes beyond the lingering influences of European colonialism. The linguistic and ethnic diversity that existed before the arrival of the French has present-day implications for language policy. Although Wolof is the most widely spoken language, replacing French with Wolof as the official language is complicated by the fact that there are other well-represented ethnic groups. The Fulani and the Toucouleurs, who speak Pulaar, comprise 24 percent of the Senegalese population, followed by the Sereer at 15 percent. Many Pulaar speakers, in particular, bristle at the idea of Wolof as the official language of Senegal because they view Wolof as a colonizing language in much the same way that some Senegalese view French.[21]

The decision of whether to champion Wolof as an official language is further problematized by the question, which variety of Wolof? According to Leigh Swigart, many different socioeconomic groups in the large cities, from the educated elite to middle-class families to the general population, use "Urban Wolof," which is heavily influenced by French vocabulary, whereas "Deep Wolof" or "Pure Wolof," the variety that can still be found in rural villages, is often perceived as backward.[22] At the same time, using too much French in many contexts in Senegal marks a person as a "too willing victim of the French civilising mission."[23] Therefore, the designation Wolof refers to a broad spectrum ranging from no French influence to a highly complex French-Wolof hybrid language, in which the amount of French present allows speakers to make certain identity claims.

Theorizing the nature of Wolof also highlights the difficulties of explaining linguistic phenomena in multilingual societies. In the case of Urban Wolof, at least two languages are present in conversation, denoting the occurrence of code-switching. However, one must ask whether Urban Wolof consists of two distinct languages or whether it has evolved into one language. Fiona McLaughlin argues that Dakar Wolof, the variety of Urban Wolof spoken in the capital, is a hybrid language with Wolof as the matrix language and French as the embedded language.[24] She demonstrates that plenty of people who use a heavily French-influenced variety of Wolof do not actually speak French, suggesting that in those instances only one language is used.

The intent of my book, however, is not to focus on defining and distinguishing between different types of multilingual phenomena but to show how people engage in a strategic balancing act when using multiple languages and how, with regard to identity formation, these linguistic choices constitute a potent means for situating oneself in any given context.[25] Senegal is marked by the prevalence of code-switching in the most general sense of the term, where the use of Wolof and French, alongside other local (e.g., Pulaar, Sereer) and global (e.g., English, Arabic) languages, is central to everyday communication and manifests itself in a variety of ways.

In other words, the linguistic situation in Senegal and the negotiation of these linguistic spaces are extremely complex. Even when harboring strong feelings about individual languages, most people recognize the value of being multilingual.[26] While Senegal is one of many multilingual nations dealing with the legacy of colonialism and its implications for current language ideologies,[27] it is also a country where migration patterns profoundly influence language attitudes and use. As McLaughlin notes, little research has addressed "the effects of migration on the Senegalese linguistic repertoire, but many returned migrants speak several European languages quite fluently."[28] Furthermore, Jan Blommaert calls for studies in multilingualism to analyze more vigorously the effects of mobility on linguistic repertoires.[29] Using Senegal and its diaspora as a case study, this book conveys the often competing and paradoxical attitudes toward language in the Senegalese imaginary and traces the transformation of these attitudes in the context of migration.

## Transcending Borders

When interacting with people in Dakar, I realized that most people had either been abroad, were planning to go abroad, or had family members abroad. Senegal thus was already a mobile space constructed and managed through various diasporic settings. Many of the students at UCAD had spent time studying in France or were planning to study in France, and I assumed that this mobility was tied to social class. However, I soon realized that people from all social classes had access to the world beyond Senegal. For instance, vendors at Marché Sandaga, Dakar's largest market, when they realized I was American, would tell me about their experiences living in New York City and about how many of their family members were still there. They would proudly show off the English they had learned. Others, when hearing of my travels to Spain and Italy, would talk about their time in these countries, and we would compare our experiences there. These were not isolated incidents. It seemed like everyone had a story from abroad.[30] These informal conversations I had with Senegalese thus became a point of departure for a more formal inquiry into language and migration in the Senegalese diaspora.

According to many of the people I interviewed, no one places more value on the learning of languages and freedom of movement than Senegalese. Although I interrogate this claim more thoroughly in the chapters that follow, Senegalese indeed have a robust history of migration both within and outside Senegal. In addition to the continual rural exodus to Senegal's capital and the importance of Senegal as a host country for intraregional migration within West Africa, there has been a steady flow of immigration to France since the colonial period. Many Senegalese arrived in mainland France as *tirailleurs sénégalais*, members of France's West African colonial regiments, who fought for the French army in various wars, most notably in World War I and II. In 1960, as West African countries were starting to gain independence, France's new policy allowed citizens from Senegal, Mali, and Mauritania to freely enter France. France's economic boom in the 1950s and 1960s increased the demand for unskilled foreign labor, attracting in particular Toucouleur, Fulani, and Soninke migrants from the northern part of Senegal. However, the economic downturn in the 1970s and 1980s led to increasingly restrictive and selective migration policies in France. Most of the migration at this time consisted of family reunions where wives and children joined their already-established husbands.[31]

The most recent statistics estimate over ninety thousand Senegalese reside in metropolitan France, a number that does not convey the full extent of the Senegalese community because it excludes French citizens of Senegalese descent who identify as Senegalese or Senegalese French. Many Senegalese are drawn particularly to Paris—France's largest city and the one with the highest concentration of immigrants—because it represents an important space in the Senegalese cultural imaginary.[32] For many Senegalese students seeking a francophone higher education, Paris is the pinnacle of educational opportunity. For those interested in trade and business, Paris provides economic prospects emanating from both a francophone and a European center. For those following a long tradition of migration, Paris is central to this narrative. And for those who grew up in various parts of France, Paris entices them just as it entices many other French citizens. In a country as centralized as France, Paris is a necessary stop for many.

While France in general and Paris in particular have a long history of attracting Senegalese, French restrictions on migration in the late twentieth century, in concert with more liberal policies in Italy and the United States, redirected migration flows. In addition to a change in destination, the demographics of those migrating also shifted. The majority of people going to places such as Italy and the United States in the 1980s and 1990s were predominantly Wolof men from the northwestern regions of Senegal. They enjoyed help from a very complex migration network organized by the Mouride Brotherhood, a Sufi sect of Islam, which also controlled the vast majority of trade at Marché Sandaga. The Mouride Brotherhood welcomed new arrivals to Italy and the United States by providing them training as vendors and access to their extensive trade networks.[33] Mobility is key to understanding this wave of migration. As Bruno Riccio argues, "The Wolof commitment towards male mobility . . . seems to be demonstrated by the fact that when settlement and family reunion seemed the only available model in France in the mid-1970s, they opted to move to Italy or the United States instead."[34]

The most recent data show that over one hundred thousand Senegalese currently live in Italy—a number that does not include undocumented immigrants. Numerically, Italy is on par with France as one of the most popular destinations for Senegalese migrants.[35] While Rome does not have the historical or linguistic allure of Paris for Senegalese nor does it boast the numbers that some of the northern Italian cities do, it attracts Senegalese in surprising ways.[36] A group of musicians and dancers I followed found Rome to be welcoming of their craft. This was most evident in the African dance classes I visited, which were attended by enthusiastic Italian women. Rome has become a jumping off place for those arriving on artist visas and then touring throughout Italy. Rome also proves useful for commerce with a very extensive network of Wolof traders setting up shop daily at the central rail station and around tourist attractions. Through word of mouth, Rome has been touted as a bustling city but without the logistical headaches of Paris—fewer passport controls, warmer weather, more laid-back people.

Meanwhile, according to the U.S. Census Bureau's 2015 American Community Survey 1-Year Estimates, there are around twenty thousand Senegalese in the United States.[37] The Senegalese community in the United States is concentrated in New York City—America's quintessential immigrant city known for its many specific immigrant enclaves that channel the spirit of migrants' home countries.[38] New York represents a sort of mecca for African diasporans that stems from interest in American and African American culture, global English, economic opportunities, and kinship networks. The interviewees in all three sites conceived of Harlem's Little Senegal as just that, a little piece of Senegal, and well-established trade networks provide people with anything imaginable from the home country, minimizing the ocean that separates the two lands.

Importantly, investigating the different relationships that Senegalese have in various global sites nuances postcolonial theorization that often assumes certain temporal and geographic notions. Calling into question the linear logic that reduces postcolonialism to simply the time after colonialism, Anne McClintock contends that "the historical rupture suggested by the preposition 'post-' belies both the continuities and discontinuities of power that have shaped the legacies of the formal European and British colonial empires." Furthermore, in order to illuminate what she calls "a *multiplicity* of powers and histories," McClintock argues for "a *proliferation* of historically nuanced theories and strategies . . . to engage more effectively in the politics of affiliation, and the currently calamitous dispensations of power."[39] In looking at Senegalese communities in Paris, Rome, and New York City, I show that one way to think about postcoloniality is not only to analyze the legacy of colonialism that emerges from the relationship between a former colonizer and a former colony but also to recognize the ability of migrants to travel beyond the migrant pathways shaped by empire. Italy and the United States certainly would have been very unlikely options for Senegalese prior to 1960. In some ways, this project acknowledges that the pull of the former colonial metropole, that is, mainland France, is weakening. At the same time, I illustrate just how prominent France and the French language remain in the Senegalese imaginary. In conveying the complexity of how Senegalese transnational migrants relate to these various global spaces, I argue that they simultaneously accept and reject claims of belonging to France and *la francophonie*. In addition, they forge complicated ties with newer destinations such as Italy and the United States as well as maintain links with Senegal and an ever-expanding Senegalese diaspora. Therefore, the patterns and experiences that emerge from Senegalese migration and diaspora are telling examples of the kind of phenomena McClintock describes. By considering the experiences that Senegalese have in various global destinations and the different ways in which they interact with the legacies of colonialism, this research offers insight into present-day articulations of postcolonialism.

Furthermore, my interviews with Senegalese in these three sites indicate simultaneous border crossings of all kinds. They never spoke of just the relationship between the host country and Senegal. They described multiple vectors—a constellation of different geographic places throughout the world and the various pathways used to reach them. Many of the people I interviewed in New York, for example, had spent time in Senegal but also in France, Italy, Spain, and other European countries. The same was true for the people I interviewed in Paris and Rome, who were able to enjoy the relatively porous borders within the European Union. In research on Senegalese migration between France, Italy, and Spain, Sorana Toma and Eleanora Castagnone note that many migrants reach one destination and then decide to move on to another in what they label as "onward mobility."[40] In my own research, I found that even if migrants had not physically gone to a certain place, they were well versed in the collective Senegalese experience in far-off lands and were keen to share the anecdotes of friends and family members.

Instead of "migrants" or "immigrants," "transmigrants" might be a more appropriate term for those people who seem not to be overly attached to living in any particular host country or in Senegal. Nina Glick Schiller defines transmigrants as "those persons, who having migrated from one nation-state to another, live their lives across borders, participating simultaneously in social relations that embed them in more than one nation-state."[41] However, this transcending of borders often clashes with the expectations that host nations place on migrants, especially with regard to integration. Through national discourses, receiving countries convey certain linguistic, racial, religious, and civic conditions that do not always align with how the Senegalese in my study view themselves or how they want to engage with these environments. Furthermore, many Senegalese I interviewed did not see themselves simply as bound to a host nation no matter how long they had lived there. Whether it is the physical crossing of national borders or the sending of remittances back to Senegal, Senegalese position themselves as much within borders as across them.[42] I argue throughout this book that these multilayered negotiations, claims, and refusals of national identity are performed as much through linguistic codes as through more typically studied anthropological archives.

## Linking Language Ideologies and Racial Formation in National and Transnational Spaces

As a sociolinguist, ethnographer, and African diaspora scholar in a French studies department, I take an approach that reflects my various disciplinary backgrounds and a desire to make them talk to one another. Whereas French studies analyzes literature, film, music, and other types of cultural production to provide insight into the human experience and how different cultures understand and represent themselves, it often looks at these experiences in highly mediated ways. For example, the authors, filmmakers, and musicians who convey these human experiences have access to the institutions that allow them to share their texts. In turn, cultural production often follows established conventions. My interviews with people cross more class and social divides and represent a much broader range of experiences.[43]

Literary and cultural scholars may also be interested in the language of texts, but this exploration is often limited to the text, not necessarily focusing on the implications of language in real-world scenarios. Very few linguists are housed in language departments, and if they are, a sharp distinction is usually made between linguistic and literary scholarship. However, I argue that there should be more interaction between these disciplines. The literary practice of bringing close textual readings to ethnographic interviews is instrumental in revealing something new about the human condition. At the same time, an ethnographic, sociolinguistic framework makes more salient the experiences often conveyed through cultural production. In other words, juxtaposing cultural production and lived linguistic experiences helps articulate identity formation in novel ways.

In particular, the multilingual focus of my research diverges from the monolingual bias inherent in French and francophone studies. As Christopher Miller elucidates, "The study of black African literature in French requires an approach that is sensitive . . . to the homogenizing effects of the French language."[44] Most Senegalese writers and writers of Senegalese-descent publish in French, which allows them access to a larger and more global audience but which also strips away the multilingualism that is central to Senegalese experiences. In addition to the flattening effect that publishing in French has on this multilingual dynamic, when African authors do include Arabic, Wolof, or other African languages in their French-language works, they often footnote the linguistic usage or add ethnographic footnotes to explain cultural traditions, effectively othering their cultures.[45] Even though the multilingual interviews found in this book are followed by an English translation in order to reach a wider audience and allow the reader to better understand the phenomena at play, my sociolinguistic/ethnographic approach renders the complex set of multilingual practices in a way that actively works to avoid othering or exoticizing my interviewees. The exploration of multilingualism in my research is a key component instead of an afterthought; this exploration, therefore, further nuances various kinds of identity formation that are often central to the experiences of characters in francophone literature but are sometimes made invisible in a French-only medium.

In addition to forefronting multilingual identity in French studies, my research answers the call of the *PMLA* special issue on comparative racializations coordinated by Shu-mei Shih. Shih asserts that humanities departments, particularly French departments, which tend to replicate the republican ideology pervasive in France, are often averse to discussing and analyzing race.[46] The contributors to this special issue address the dearth of humanistic scholarly work on race by bringing "as many conversations from different disciplinary locations as possible and by insisting that these conversations be not an option but a necessity."[47] The sociolinguistic perspective guiding my own research not only develops an underdeveloped dimension of French studies; it also directly converses with and provides valuable insight into the race and migration work of scholars in ethnic studies and African studies departments.

Scholarship that makes concerted efforts to cross these disciplinary divides is starting to emerge. In French studies, Denis Provencher explores how linguistic discourses in the French republican system simultaneously afford gays and lesbians equal rights while also silencing them by rendering them invisible.[48] His work *Queer Maghrebi French* furthers this foray into interdisciplinarity by looking at how those who identify as both queer and Muslim position themselves in discussions of immigration, integration, and citizenship. His ethnographic research on how language intersects with queer, national, and postcolonial identities helps inform how I analyze language to uncover the relationship between racialized and various other identities in *Senegal Abroad*.

Suresh Canagarajah's edited volume titled *The Routledge Handbook of Migration and Language* showcases how another field makes interdisciplinary overtures when a variety of scholars in applied linguistics reflect on the relationship between language and migration in their research. Canagarajah is quick to point out that while this is an interdisciplinary endeavor, the work of scholars from other fields in the humanities and social sciences does not appear in this volume.[49] I present *Senegal Abroad* as a way to push the interdisciplinary conversation forward even more. The fields of sociolinguistics, cultural studies, critical race theory, and African diaspora studies by themselves are not completely adequate for the stories that need to be told; however, combining these fields and the methodologies associated with them (e.g., textual analysis, ethnography) affords us the opportunity to understand people's perspectives regarding language and identity. My research is thus at the fulcrum of these various tendencies, and I argue it is through this interdisciplinary perspective that I can best tell the stories of the Senegalese in my study.

## Language and National Identity

I center my work on the notion of language ideologies: the sets of beliefs that speakers have about languages, the people who speak them, and the contexts in which they are spoken. Research on language ideologies sheds light on a range of issues from how societies view standard languages and marginalize the speakers of nonstandard languages such as African American Vernacular English (AAVE) to the attitudes that individuals develop concerning certain languages as we saw earlier through the research on Senegal and multilingualism.[50] Comparing Paris, Rome, and New York City (and by extension, France, Italy, and the United States) allows me to highlight how societal language ideologies—different historical and contemporary understandings of language and linguistic identities—not only influence the native populations of the respective countries but also impact the integration and linguistic attitudes of new populations.

France has a well-known reputation for being a nation that emphasizes a standardized linguistic norm, so much so that Einar Haugen's seminal work on standardization, which demonstrated the link between nationhood and a linguistic norm, focused on French within France. During the establishment of modern France, promulgation of a standard French language was a means to unify a fledgling nation-state. At the time of the French Revolution, only a small portion of the French population spoke French, while the majority of the country spoke regional languages or dialects.[51] Therefore, French citizens were encouraged to speak French as a sign of loyalty to the nation. Today, many French people conceptualize their language as a national treasure.[52] However, these expectations placed on the French language can lead to anxiety for language learners inside and outside the classroom and can have consequences for those who apply for citizenship.[53]

Meanwhile, Italy is often described as a place where the existence and use of a standard national language as well as the concept of nationhood arrived relatively late compared to other European nations.[54] Currently, throughout Italy, regional varieties are still spoken to a much greater degree than in France, and Italy remains somewhat linguistically fragmented even if the use of regional varieties is declining.[55] This linguistic diversity calls into question the notion of a coherent national Italian identity and eases the burden on language learners, who may not feel as pressured to speak standard Italian correctly. However, it can also complicate the language-learning progress of foreigners who want to communicate in the preferred language of the local population and are thus tasked with learning a local language or dialect along with Italian, the official language.[56]

The situation in the United States poses a different set of problems with regard to language ideologies. Unlike France and Italy, the United States has no official language at the federal level; however, English is the official language of over half the states, and the Official English movement has been gaining traction for decades.[57] Various waves of immigration and the xenophobic responses that ensue have contributed to the rise of an English-language consciousness. Questions surrounding language are thus at the very core of American identity formation.[58] At the same time, because of its particular linguistic identity, New York City represents an anomaly not just for the United States but also the world. New York has been dubbed the most linguistically diverse city in the world with an estimated eight hundred languages spoken there.[59] According to the U.S. Census's "2012–2016 American Community Survey: Quick Facts New York City," 49 percent of New Yorkers speak a language other than English at home. Spanish is the most commonly spoken language, with 25 percent of the general population speaking it at home. While New York City's multilingualism means that foreigners may not necessarily need to learn English to survive, those who want to learn English might not always have the opportunity to be immersed.

The people in my study are definitely influenced by the prevalent linguistic attitudes of the sites to which they have migrated. While Senegalese in the diaspora already possess highly formed opinions about their languages before they migrate, these attitudes continue to evolve in the various locales they inhabit. The discussions analyzed in this book show how these specific contexts contribute to linguistic identity formation and how this formation goes beyond language to also influence other types of formation such as racial formation.

## Racial Identity Formation
## through a Sociolinguistic Lens

While some Senegalese migration scholarship, such as Donald Carter's *States of Grace*, explores racial identity among other forms of difference (religion, nationality, citizenship status), *Senegal Abroad* prioritizes racial identity formation.[60] In the interviews I conducted, I did not broach the topic of race unless the interviewee specifically brought it up first in the course of talking about linguistic identity; however, as I soon realized, linguistic experience was key to the formation of racial identity.[61]

In order to situate my informants' racialized experiences, I build on Michael Omi and Howard Winant's theorization of racial formation. Describing racial formation as "the sociohistorical process by which racial identities are created, lived out, transformed, and destroyed," they introduce the concept of historically situated racial projects to explain how race is woven into any given society from macro-level social structures to micro-level personal experiences: "A racial project is simultaneously an interpretation, representation, or explanation of racial identities and meanings, and an effort to organize and distribute resources (economic, political, cultural) along particular racial lines. Racial projects connect what race means in a particular discursive or ideological practice and the ways in which both social structures and everyday experiences are racially organized, based upon that meaning. Racial projects are attempts both to shape the ways in which social structures are racially signified and the ways that racial meanings are embedded in social structures."[62] While Omi and Winant mention the organization and distribution of economic, political, and cultural resources, I demonstrate how linguistic resources are just as productive in understanding race. I reveal how Paris, Rome, and New York as linguistic contexts have bearing on racial formation both at a societal level and in the everyday linguistic experiences of my interviewees.

My sociolinguistic approach to understanding racial formation emerges from research conducted in the fields of linguistic anthropology and second language acquisition (SLA) that investigates the various ways that identity formation relates to language. Studies show how the social interactions people have with speakers in a particular setting are partially responsible for how they learn a second language and for the feelings they have regarding this experience. For instance, Bonny Norton emphasizes power relations, language ownership, investment in the target language, and the ability to claim the right to speak in explaining the successes and failures of migrant women learning English in Canada. Ben Rampton's work examines participants' social knowledge about ethnic groups and their interrelationships, which includes attitudes about prestige, legitimacy, and positions in society.[63] In a similar vein, research on cultural legitimacy in language production demonstrates how claims on legitimacy extend beyond language to include nationality, ethnicity, race, religion, and the color of one's skin.[64] Meanwhile, in the emerging field of raciolinguistics, Jonathan Rosa and Nelson Flores argue that a raciolinguistic perspective "seeks to understand the interplay of language and race within the historical production of nation-state/colonial governmentality, and the ways that colonial distinctions within and between nation-state borders continue to shape contemporary linguistic and racial formations."[65] I build on their U.S.-based work by showing how the phenomena they eloquently articulate in the American context play out in European sites as well.

Other scholarship more thoroughly pinpoints the connection between blackness and language ideologies. For instance, Awad el Karim M. Ibrahim's sociolinguistic research on predominantly West African francophone youth in Canada highlights the power of the *social imaginary*, which he describes as "a discursive space or a representation in which [black youth] are already constructed, imagined, and positioned and thus are treated by the hegemonic discourses and dominant groups, respectively, as Blacks."[66] In brief, he foregrounds how blackness is a social construct imposed on people who might not otherwise think of themselves as black. Ibrahim's research shows how this newfound affiliation with blackness influences the students in his study to make specific choices about the languages they learn. They cultivate a black identity by learning what Ibrahim calls Black Stylized English (BSE), emulating what they hear in rap music and other black cultural production.[67]

The multi-sited aspect of my work further theorizes the link between racial (particularly black) and linguistic identity formation by showing how these formations differ for Senegalese depending on the specific national contexts. I argue that the racial formation of the people in my study can be fully appreciated only against the backdrop of how each of the three nation-states understands race and blackness. In the cases of France and Italy, conceptualizations of race are rooted in the colonial period, albeit to differing degrees. Not only are there obvious differences in the relationships between the colonizer and the colonized, but the effects of colonization on the colonizer's construction of national identity differ between France and Italy as well. In particular, the people I interviewed in Rome objected to being racially othered because they found that this othering dehumanized them. In Paris, this racialized othering was even more problematic because in addition to dehumanization, it unexpectedly barred them from accessing French cultural citizenship or from claiming ownership of the French language. Meanwhile, discussions of race in the United States are rooted in the historical institution of slavery and its afterlives as well as understandings of the African diaspora. Informants in New York focused most of their attention on the cleavages in black identity formation and the tension between Africans and African Americans.

It is worth considering in more detail the specific histories of racial formation in each of these three national contexts. In the case of France, Frantz Fanon highlighted the historical implications of French colonialism from a linguistic and cultural perspective. One of the vestiges of colonialism is the internalized inferiority complex that is directly related to the imposition of French language and culture at the expense of local language and culture. In Fanon's discourse, the concepts of language and culture become racialized: "The Negro of the Antilles will be proportionately whiter—that is, he will come closer to being a real human being—in direct ratio to his mastery of the French language. . . . Mastery of language affords remarkable power."[68] Fanon equated whiteness with the acquisition of the colonizer's language. Here, the degree of whiteness refers not to skin color but to cultural and linguistic appropriation and the process of becoming "civilized." These understandings of race, culture, language, and power that were inscribed into colonial practices still persist long after colonization has ended and influence how France, its citizens, and its immigrants view themselves and one another today. These perceptions in turn affect how these groups construct and fit into a national identity.

Mainstream political discourse on the relationship between France and Africa maintains these lingering assumptions about inferiority and superiority. Former French president Nicolas Sarkozy's speech at Dakar's UCAD in 2007 struck a chord with many of the Senegalese I interviewed. After stressing the positive aspects of colonialism, Sarkozy argued that Africa had not sufficiently entered history: "Le problème de l'Afrique—permettez à un ami de l'Afrique de le dire—, il est là. Le défi de l'Afrique, c'est d'entrer davantage dans l'Histoire, c'est de puiser en elle l'énergie, la force, l'envie, la volonté d'écouter et d'épouser sa propre histoire. Le problème de l'Afrique, c'est de cesser de toujours répéter, de toujours ressasser, de se libérer du mythe de l'éternel retour, c'est de prendre conscience que l'âge d'or qu'elle ne cesse de regretter ne reviendra pas pour la raison qu'il n'a jamais existé." (Africa's problem—allow a friend of Africa to say—is here. Africa's challenge is to enter to a greater extent into History, to tap into its energy, strength, desire, willingness to listen and to espouse its own history. Africa's problem is to stop always repeating, always rehashing, to break free of the myth of the eternal return, to realize that the golden age that Africa is always recalling will not return because it never existed.)[69]

Patronizing and condescending, Sarkozy positioned himself as a friend of Africa in order to suggest that he had the right to criticize it. The capitalization of the word *histoire* found in the version posted on an official governmental website implies that the history of which he speaks is the main history, his history, the history of the first world, a history into which Africa has not entered.[70] Achille Mbembe, in his open letter, decried the speech for perpetuating the same racist attitudes from the nineteenth century, arguing that the postcolonial mentality of France is no different from its colonial mentality.[71] Just like Mbembe, the people I interviewed objected to what they saw as the perpetuation of racist discourses. In fact, many of them took direct issue with Sarkozy's speech. This book allows my interviewees' concerns, objections, and counter-arguments to be heard.

This forum is particularly important because those who understand the racial connotations in these discourses often find it difficult to have frank conversations about race and its effects in France since the topic of race is often seen as taboo.[72] The republican model, which was nobly constructed to ensure equality for all, makes it difficult to investigate the concept of race and how it affects individuals. Paradoxically, while blacks as a distinct social group do not exist in governmental statistics, many of the people I interviewed noted the visibility of their black bodies and the impact this visibility has on everything from housing and employment to claiming legitimacy as citizens.[73] The debate surrounding the conceptualization of race, and in particular blackness, plays out at the level of French discourse with the avoidance of the tiny, monosyllabic word *noir*.[74] It is as if pretending that race and blackness do not exist will mean the systemic problems that emerge from a racialized hierarchy will cease to exist as well. However, as the experiences recounted in this book demonstrate, refusing to acknowledge racial groups does not mean that members of these groups do not experience a racialized identity.[75]

In the past decade, some scholars and cultural commentators have begun to problematize the colorblind model and prioritize race, and blackness in particular, in discussions of French national identity.[76] In addition, the emergence of migration literature in francophone sub-Saharan African studies has allowed us to better understand how francophone African writers both throughout Africa and in France advance the conversation on race, migration, and belonging through literary production.[77] By approaching race and national identity through an ethnographic and sociolinguistic lens, my work provides a complementary perspective on these phenomena that focuses on language attitudes and use. The experiences analyzed in this book illustrate how linguistic competence is often determined by more than just one's ability to use a language; one's linguistic competence depends on the ability to prove cultural legitimacy, which is closely connected to conceptualizations of race. For instance, in proving the validity of Fanon's theorization on language and race, the Senegalese I interviewed in Paris lament the French language's association with whiteness such that no matter how well they speak, they will never be accepted as rightful owners of the language. Furthermore, I show how Senegal's particular relationship to the French language makes this exclusion sting even more.

Even countries that did not colonize or that had limited colonial holdings have highly racialized perspectives that influence linguistic experiences. Compared with France, Italy represents a very different context for understanding the interconnectedness of race, language, and nationhood. Nevertheless, the concept of race in Italy, and understandings of blackness and whiteness, firmly took root during the colonial period, even though the country was a minor colonial power.[78] As Ruth Ben-Ghiat and Mia Fuller contend, "Although Italian colonialism was more restricted in geographical scope and duration than the French and British empires, it had no less an impact on the development of metropolitan conceptions of race, national identity, and geopolitical imaginaries."[79] The colonial policy and the postcolonial aftermath in Italy attempted to create a national identity reinforced by imperialism and racism in order to combat the country's fragmentation, seen most clearly through a North-South divide.

Italy's North-South divide, also known as the Southern Question, is the historical and contemporary phenomenon in which the northern provinces have economically dominated the South, causing mass migration from the South to the North and engendering feelings of cultural superiority in northern residents. The existence of this North-South divide emerged most clearly during Italian unification. According to some in the North, Italy's southerners were not superior to the people of the African continent.[80] This rhetoric helped justify what Pasquale Verdicchio calls the first phase of colonialism: "the 'liberation' of the south."[81] In order to create a uniform, national identity that effaced the understood differences between the North and the South, Benito Mussolini had to convince Italians of their commonalities by eliminating any notion that southerners were related to Africans.[82]

This historical racialization of Italian identity has present-day repercussions. For instance, the xenophobia expressed by the Northern League uses racialized rhetoric.[83] Also, a growing number of Italians of African descent are writing about their racialized experiences.[84] While literature produced by blacks in Italy conveys an indispensable perspective on race, my research offers a linguistic entrée into this topic. I show how the Senegalese migrants in my study use code-switching and other discursive features to construct notions of blackness in a country where whiteness is the norm. Some use code-switching as a way to emphasize their exclusion from society, while others use language in creative ways such as my interviewee Idi, who, in chapter 4, playfully argues that he can change nationalities simply by changing languages. By highlighting the connection between language, race, and nationality, I depict identity formation as a contested space where even the most marginalized can negotiate their position.

Across the Atlantic, the United States engaged in a different type of colonization, relying on settler colonialism in the creation of its nation-state. This young country orchestrated the near-extinction of indigenous populations as well as the enslavement of Africans as one of the primary means of wealth production. In order to justify the inhumane treatment and killing of humans, those in power had to argue that Native Americans and Africans were less than human. This dehumanization of Native and black populations laid the groundwork for the formation of racial categories that persist today.[85]

Understanding the evolution of slavery in the United States is essential to conceptualizations of blackness that have increasing influence worldwide. Although the institution of slavery has existed for millennia all over the world, the seventeenth century was the first time slavery became synonymous with blackness. In the American colonies, while legal statutes allowed the enslavement of various types of people, for instance, prisoners of war and people convicted of crimes, racial connotations related to slavery began to form.[86] Racial ideologies in the eighteenth century further linked blackness to servitude, and even blacks who were free had restricted rights due to racial categorization.[87] Meanwhile, nineteenth-century pseudoscience attempted to prove the inferiority of blacks. The stereotypes associated with blackness are very much a part of present-day understandings of race and influence everything from racial bias in policing to negative media representation to the misconception that associates blackness with inferior linguistic norms.[88]

However, the construction of blackness is more complex than simply emerging as the binary opposite of whiteness. Conflict often exists among those who identify as black, particularly between African immigrants and African Americans. Complications arise partially because of a clash between old and new diasporas. Prevailing stereotypes depict African Americans as lazy and Africans as backward. My work foregrounds the role of language in creating and maintaining distinctions. For instance, I show how the perception of African accents can mark people as foreign and therefore eliminate their claim on blackness as theorized in the American context. Similarly, I highlight how francophone Africans are situated lower on the immigrant hierarchy than anglophone Africans. The vignettes throughout this book accentuate the messiness attached to notions of diaspora.[89]

## From Transnational Blackness
## to Transnational Multilingual Subjectivity

In addition to providing a linguistic analysis of racial formation in specific national contexts, *Senegal Abroad* uses a sociolinguistic perspective to intervene in important conversations about blackness beyond national borders. Current debates about transnational blackness attempt to frame it either as a homogenous construct to emphasize the similarities of the black experience throughout the world or as a multifaceted construct to underscore how different spaces forge different understandings of blackness. I argue that only through both perspectives can we more fully analyze blackness. While I show how different sites with their specific histories produce varying understandings of belonging and difference especially as it pertains to blackness, I also demonstrate how my informants' understandings of blackness evolve as they migrate, as they discuss their experiences with others throughout the diaspora, and as they engage with cultural production throughout the world.

Manning Marable and Vanessa Agard-Jones's edited volume *Transnational Blackness* and Thomas Fouquet and Rémy Bazenguissa-Ganga's special issue on blackness in *Politique africaine* lay down important frameworks on how to theorize transnational blackness. Marable introduces the edited volume as a space to present examples of "blackness beyond boundaries as praxis" where the problems and experiences that face black communities are interrogated in a larger transnational context.[90] Similarly, Fouquet in *Politique africaine* argues that the term "blackness" allows for a way to conceptualize and represent Africa both inside and outside the African continent. He stresses that multiple perspectives—analyzing blackness in and across different geographical, temporal, and social contexts—offer insight into all the ways that people understand racial formation.[91]

*Politique africaine: Blackness*, in providing a critical lens in its examination of blackness, not only uncovers different approaches to analyzing blackness but also draws attention to the problematic nature of the term. For instance, in her essay on how African, Afro-American, and Afro-European photographers depict representations of the black body, Sarah Fila-Bakabadio contends that only though an afro-cosmopolitan perspective can we understand how artists portray the diversity of the African world. She argues that the term "blackness" stems from a specific sociohistorical situation in the United States that should not necessarily be applied to black populations in other contexts because it implies a monolithic depiction of blackness that in her estimation does not exist.[92] She further warns that a focus on "race" effaces the specificity of individual experiences. For their part, Jemima Pierre and Camille Niauffre (same volume) counter this critique, noting that because of a long process of racialization due to an international historical reality (seen through racial slavery in the Americas and colonial racism in its various forms throughout Africa), continental Africans and black communities across the globe participate in the construction of a transnational blackness and are aware of their positioning both locally and globally as black.[93] The primary premise of Pierre's research, articulated in detail in *The Predicament of Blackness*, is that "a modern, postcolonial space is invariably a racialized one."[94]

While Pierre puts forth a homogenizing notion of blackness that contrasts with Fila-Bakabadio's more variegated perspective, my research lies somewhere between the two. *Senegal Abroad* shows how blackness is indeed an overarching phenomenon created through global racialization, but it manifests itself differently depending on the context.[95] In focusing on linguistic issues in multiple sites and what they can tell us about racial identity formation, I explore how Senegalese migrants understand blackness in multiple diasporic sites, how they make connections between their experiences and the experiences of others in different global sites, and how language is a tool to convey these conceptualizations of blackness. For instance, as we saw with the opening vignette, Ndiaga's multilingual rendition of *The Color Purple* uses the African American experience to explain his own struggles with being black in Italy.

In addition to deconstructing transnational blackness, this book explores Senegalese identity as a transnational construct. The demographics of Senegal spill out beyond its borders. The various ethnic groups and national languages associated with Senegal are represented in neighboring countries—a consequence of European colonization of the continent that had little regard for already-present ethnic and linguistic divisions. The ways in which Senegalese position themselves in the francophone world show that they are constantly looking outward.

I have coined the term "global Senegality" to refer to a set of main character traits that my informants have repeatedly identified as central to the identity and practices of Senegalese migrants as they travel through the world. According to the multiple voices uncovered in my work, being mobile, speaking multiple languages, and practicing hospitality (especially of the linguistic variety) are the most important aspects of being Senegalese in diaspora. While these three concepts might not necessarily seem connected on the surface, they relate to one another in various ways. Language ability engenders mobility and vice versa. The more languages one knows, the easier one can communicate in foreign spaces. At the same time, being immersed in foreign-language environments facilitates language learning. As for hospitality, one of the easiest ways to make people feel welcome is to be able to talk with them in their own language.[96] As Ousseynou, a taxi driver in New York City, explained, when he receives clients who do not speak English, he loves to find a common language so that he can enhance their experience. One of his greatest joys is to see their surprise when he can speak their language.

Importantly, these three traits transcend boundaries. The very act of being mobile suggests the constant crossing of national borders. The desire for multilingualism means the dismantling of language barriers, and the yearning to provide hospitality signals the opening of the home space to others, one of the most intimate of boundaries. In fact, it is this home space that moves us past the confines of nationhood. Whereas the boundaries of a nation, according to

Benedict Anderson, are imagined as limited and sovereign, the concept of home in relation to nation is a counter-space where belonging becomes multiplied and global.[97] In other words, the imagined Senegalese community is global instead of simply tied to a nation-state. For many of the people I interviewed, while they look back to Senegal longingly, it is not the geographic space that makes them Senegalese; rather it is the cultivation of a global Senegalese identity based on mobility, multilingualism, and hospitality. They imagine their community both from within the nation of Senegal and throughout the world.[98]

It is through exemplifying global Senegality that the Senegalese I interviewed achieve success. They see mobility, multilingualism, and hospitality as markers of what Pierre Bourdieu has called symbolic capital—"the acquisition of a reputation for competence and an image of respectability and honourability."[99] While a person possesses different types of capital (e.g., economic, social, cultural), the recognition and legitimation of these forms of capital transform them into symbolic capital. Senegalese in the diaspora or those who aspire to travel build symbolic capital by crossing borders and languages because they position themselves in a long-standing narrative of Senegalese mobility and multilingualism.

They also acquire what Claire Kramsch and Anne Whiteside describe as symbolic competence, which allows them to use these languages playfully and creatively and go beyond what monolingual speakers of French, or Italian, or English are able to do with each language.[100] These people, whom Kramsch describes as multilingual subjects, enjoy the power that comes with being able to manipulate languages. Furthermore, through this multilingual subjectivity, they construct "imagined identities that are every bit as real as those imposed by society."[101] While host societies map certain racialized and linguistic images on migrants, those in my study are able to push back on these narrow definitions by providing their own conceptualizations of who they are and what matters to them.

The multilingual repertoires that Senegalese utilize both in Senegal and abroad also convey how people control not just languages but also the space between languages. According to Ofelia García, the notion of translanguaging, which includes and goes beyond code-switching, highlights speakers' abilities to access a variety of linguistic features "in order to maximize communicative potential" and "to make sense of their multilingual worlds."[102] In my earlier description of linguistic complexity in Senegal, I mentioned how people using Urban Wolof could be speaking a language or code-switching between two languages. Making this distinction would presuppose that individual languages exist.[103] However, translanguaging, in which the "trans" draws attention not to individual languages but to the liminal space between languages, allows us to focus on movement and the behavior of language in the wake of globalization.[104] Just as global Senegality calls into question the restrictive Andersonian notion of Senegalese as a national construct and transnational blackness envisions racial formation that transcends temporal and geographic boundaries, translanguaging emphasizes the copious resources that multilingual speakers have and the possibilities these resources afford them.[105]

The theorization of symbolic competence, multilingual subjectivity, and translanguaging thus serves to privilege multilingual speakers instead of relegating them to the margins.[106] Similarly, these sociolinguistic concepts and others like them also underscore the role of mobility.[107] By applying these concepts to current trends in migration studies that have begun to look at the centrality of borders as opposed to their marginality,[108] I demonstrate the ways in which transnational multilingual Senegalese move through multiple languages and geographic contexts, which in turn contribute to a global multilingual identity formation. More specifically, the Senegalese in my study often use multiple languages in creative ways and understand how their mobility aids in accomplishing this goal. Therefore, while Senegalese in all three sites are aware of the marginalized positions they occupy, especially with regard to blackness, they use language agency to conceptualize and negotiate the many facets of their complex identities as well as harness the social power that multilingualism bestows.

## *TERANGA* THROUGH THE SHARING OF STORIES: METHODOLOGICAL CONSIDERATIONS

Anyone who has been to Senegal is well aware of what Senegalese call *teranga*. Translated from Wolof as "hospitality," it seems to be a way of life and a trait that many Senegalese in the diaspora consider intrinsic to global Senegality. But it is not only about opening homes or sharing food; it is also about sharing stories and wanting to hear others' stories. When I set out to interview the Senegalese communities in Paris, Rome, and New York City, I knew that my having lived in Senegal and having learned some Wolof would open doors for me; however, I was also aware that some would be hesitant, particularly undocumented migrants. That hesitancy was one reason why I never asked people for their citizenship status. While it would have offered yet another way to explore legitimacy and the ability to claim the right to speak, out of respect and concern for their well-being I opted not to include it in the demographic data I collected.[109] I was amazed, however, that once people were convinced I was not a threat, even those who were in a precarious position because of citizenship status were open to sharing their experiences with me, vividly describing their worlds and letting me witness their journeys.

I encountered people in a variety of ways and participated in a wide range of interactions. Some people agreed to interviews, which averaged an hour. Others became principal informants, with whom I spent time on a regular basis and engaged in various activities. In France, I visited one particular family every couple of weeks, taking notes on language use in the home space.[110] The parents, Duudu and Nafi, were in their early fifties and had been living in France for almost twenty years; some of their children had been born in Senegal and others in France. We enjoyed conversing over home-cooked Senegalese meals. Other principal informants included thirty-one-year-old Lucie from Marseille, who invited me to various gatherings with her friends; twenty-eight-year-old Sébastien, who organized a dinner with both French and Senegalese friends; and thirty-one-year-old Senegalese rapper Abdu, who had been in France for the last few years. Abdu allowed me to sit in on rehearsals with his multinational band, attend his concerts, and meet with him on several occasions. He gave me access to all his music and lyrics, and I took notes at all his events with a view to understanding how he used language to engage his audiences.

In order to find people to interview, I used several different approaches. To meet students, I joined university listservs, which opened the door to events and conferences. To access a different demographic, I hung around public spaces in Paris like Gare du Nord, Barbès-Rochechouart, and Sacré-Coeur to start conversations with people, particularly vendors. I ate at Senegalese restaurants and interviewed staff and patrons. I attended Wolof- and French-language classes. I also found my way to several conferences and meetings, such as one sponsored by an association of Senegalese students from the Grandes Écoles, one by a Senegalese business association, one exploring life in the *foyers* (communal residences for migrant workers) both past and present, and one on the teaching of French to migrants. My goal was to chronicle language use in a variety of settings through a cross section of the different types of Senegalese migrants and people of Senegalese descent found in Paris.

I used similar methods in Rome.[111] My principal site for meeting potential informants and conducting interviews and natural recordings were locales where Senegalese gathered for meals. The central train station of Rome, Roma Termini, was another valuable site for meeting Senegalese migrants, particularly men, because of the high concentration of street vendors. I also followed the large artist community of singers, dancers, and musicians by attending classes and performances. Many from this group were particularly mobile, touring Italy and other parts of Europe. One principal informant was thirty-three-year-old Idi, a dancer, who invited me to what the Senegalese locals referred to as the secret Senegalese restaurant and introduced me to the regular patrons. We would often meet at the restaurant to talk over a meal, and I would record conversations we had with his friends and acquaintances. He also took me to the homes of his friends so that I could interview people in their home environments. There was also forty-two-year-old Ibou, a businessman who was in constant contact with a variety of people and willing to let me observe these interactions. Another principal informant was the aforementioned thirty-six-year-old Ndiaga, whose job was to distribute pamphlets for different companies. We met on various occasions in different settings, and I was able to track his ideas and opinions about certain issues throughout the three-month period. In addition to the interviews and conversations with Senegalese, I shadowed an Italian teacher's elementary language class for migrants and sat in on her *classe media*.[112] I also interviewed an immigration lawyer, a sociologist who helped explain certain phenomena unique to Italy, and the instructor of the language class I shadowed.

In New York City, I focused my fieldwork principally in Harlem's Little Senegal and, to a lesser extent, the Flatbush area of Brooklyn, Parkchester in the Bronx, and Corona in Queens. I ate at various Senegalese restaurants throughout the city, spent quite a bit of time in Harlem's Malcolm Shabazz Market, visited a Senegalese cultural association, and hung out near Columbus Circle, where many Senegalese cycle-rickshaw drivers would try to convince tourists to take tours of Central Park. Among my interviewees, Madina, Omar, and Julien became principal informants. Madina, a twenty-seven-year-old woman who had spent the last fifteen years of her life in the United States, ran a summer program that brings students to Senegal in order to learn about their heritage. Omar was a thirty-one-year-old man working on his master's degree who had been living in the United States for three years. He enjoyed taking me to places such as his local laundromat so that I could talk with other Senegalese in the area. Julien, a thirty-four-year-old man from Casamance, had been living in the United States for a year. He had a master's of science degree but was currently working at Rite-Aid. Because of him, I was able to spend many a Sunday with members of the Senegalese Catholic Association, who would invite me for meals after their church services. In fact, all three of these informants introduced me to many other members of the community, let me record various interactions, and were instrumental in getting me access to a variety of people and environments.[113]

Because my informants in Paris, Rome, and New York came from different educational, socioeconomic, linguistic, ethnic, and religious backgrounds as well as migrant pathways, they offered a range of perspectives. They provided invaluable insights by describing their experiences and generating their own theories about how they existed in the world. In fact, some of the informants positioned themselves as ethnographers, linguists, and historians in the ways in which they told their stories. They advanced theories by scholars and academics, often filling in the gaps. Throughout these pages, I show the reflexive nature of Senegalese in the diaspora and how their stories contribute to our understanding of African migration and language use.

## STRUCTURE OF THE BOOK

This book analyzes a series of vignettes collected from more than eighty people who identify as Senegalese in the diaspora. At the end of every interview, I asked if there was anything they wanted to add to the discussion. An overwhelming number thanked me for wanting to listen to their stories—narratives that they have often shared with their friends or their communities as they try to make sense of where they fit locally, nationally, and internationally but that have never reached a broader public. The aim of this book is to center their experiences in their own words as they reflect on life, language, movement, belonging, nationality, citizenship, and blackness.

Chapter 1 investigates language acquisition and use by examining how the people in my study understand their relationships to French, Italian, English, Wolof, and other Senegalese national languages. Focusing on notions of investment and language ownership,[114] I show how Senegalese develop attitudes from their personal experiences with the languages and the communities that speak them as well as through a historically situated cultural perception. Attitudes about the French language are the most complex because they are very much tied to a colonial past and a postcolonial present. Meanwhile, for most of my interviewees, Italian does not exist in the Senegalese cultural imaginary; it is simply a language they learn if they migrate to Italy but one that is useful because it strengthens their multilingual repertoire and contains symbolic value. Concerning English, regardless of whether they are in Dakar, Paris, Rome, or New York, people are motivated to learn it because of its global importance. However, some of the interviewees in New York realize that the English they learn through schooling does not necessarily prepare them for the English-language reality they encounter in New York, particularly in Harlem. The chapter then ends with a reflection on how Senegalese national languages in general and Wolof in particular allow them to connect with others throughout the Senegalese diaspora. I interrogate the claim by one of my interviewees that one must speak Wolof to be Senegalese, looking at the ways in which this statement creates a sense of belonging for some and exclusion for others.

While chapter 1 establishes a linguistic comparison across the three urban geographical zones, chapter 2 explores the various ways that those in my study strive for cultural legitimacy and national belonging while confronting linguistic and racial barriers in each individual site. In particular, I focus on the desire for inclusion that emerges from historical, social, and linguistic factors that Senegalese migrants evince. Of the informants in all three sites, those in Paris draw most on the cultural and linguistic connection between Senegal and France and are the most frustrated when they find themselves excluded from French society. They realize that their racial identities often overshadow their language abilities. The informants in Rome also detail the exclusion they face in Italy as racialized beings, showing how they use language to convey marginalization. However, these interviewees express less desire to be included in society than those in Paris do, and therefore the effects of this exclusion have less impact. Meanwhile, the New York City respondents reveal how power dynamics play out in the diaspora, where informants' linguistic repertoires serve to mark difference more than shared blackness serves to mark sameness. Failed expectations underscore the desire that many have in creating black solidarity and the difficulty of blackness transcending linguistic differentiation.

Chapter 3 focuses on how the state and individual subjects in the three research sites address integration. What are the different models of integration, and what can the experiences of the interviewees tell us about the effectiveness of these models? How do the ideologies and actions of both individual Senegalese and the receiving countries affect the success of integration? How does the tendency to look beyond national borders influence the ability to integrate? Through this transnational perspective, many of the interviewees in all three research sites do not simply discuss life in their respective adopted countries; they also share their experiences living and traveling throughout the world as well as how these countries exist in the Senegalese cultural imaginary. My research reveals how transnational actors reflect on notions of social and national belonging through multiple overlapping language ideologies. Furthermore, there is a long tradition of Afro-Atlantic dialogue in which the interviewees participate as they offer comparative analyses of racial and national identity formation in the United States, France, Italy, and Senegal.

Chapter 4 looks more closely at the complex ways in which language and access to multiple languages create and maintain certain identities while establishing and enhancing others. It is here that I delve deeply into the figure of the multilingual traveler, why this archetype is so alluring to people in my study, and how it allows scholars to go beyond dominant narratives about migrants and their reasons for and difficulties in migrating. The people I interviewed suggest that the convergence of multilingualism and mobility is a way of life, championing it both for its practical value and for the joy it brings. The data show an overwhelming sense of pleasure and prestige with regard to multilingualism and mobility. In addition, my analyses reveal the performative aspect of code-switching and its contribution to identity formation. I therefore argue that many Senegalese relish the symbolic capital that being multilingual and mobile bestows on them. They express this capital through symbolic competence, which they use to their advantage even when occupying marginalized positions in society.

These collective chapters show how language is a medium through which Senegalese identity is navigated in the diaspora. On the one hand, I investigate how ideologies of race travel. On the other hand, through an exploration of multilingualism, especially encapsulated in the figure of the multilingual traveler, I argue that there is more to both mobility and language learning/use than simple utilitarian purposes. I demonstrate that while the people in my study express complicated and fraught relationships with the languages they speak and the places they inhabit, many of them also find joy and pleasure in both language and travel. Most of the work on transnationalism depicts African migrants succumbing to economic temptations as their sole reason for migrating and creates a depressing picture of their existence in host countries. While I do not minimize these motivations and difficulties, I go beyond political economy and also concentrate on the pride, passion, and happiness that the people in my research achieve through their reflections on language. Their stories blur the lines between utility and pleasure, allowing for a more nuanced understanding of why and how Senegalese move.

# I

# WHAT'S LANGUAGE GOT TO DO WITH IT?

## Language Attitudes and Identity Formation

$\text{O}$ne Saturday afternoon, I stepped out of the metro station at Villejuif Louis Aragon, having taken the seven line as far south as it goes. I had never been to this part of Paris. The buildings were muted grays and browns. They did not tower over people like the housing projects in the *banlieue*, but the streets were wider than what one would expect in the central Parisian neighborhoods. I followed the directions I had jotted down when talking with Ouria over the phone and came to the door of a five-story walk-up. Ouria buzzed me in and met me at her apartment door.

She had insisted that I come at lunchtime after hearing how much I love Senegalese food. She prepared my favorite dish, chicken with *yassa* sauce. Her teenage children were out running errands, she told me, so there would actually be some peace and quiet for our interview. Ouria was in her mid-forties and worked at a daycare center. She moved to Paris twenty-five years ago to join her husband, who had arrived five years prior. It had been a tough transition for her, even after such a lengthy stay, so she visited Senegal as often as possible. Language was one of the reasons why she missed Senegal. Having grown up in a wolofophone family, she found her French limited when she arrived in France. After twenty-five years in France, she still felt that she had not mastered the French language. Between sips of *bissap* (hibiscus juice, the de facto national drink of Senegal), Ouria expressed her frustration with having people correct her: "Ils essaient de me corriger. Je dis que je suis africaine. Laissez-moi tran-quille. Je ne suis pas française. . . . Je suis africaine. C'est pas ma langue. Je suis africaine." (They try to correct me. I say I'm African. Leave me alone. I'm not French. . . . I'm African. It's not my language. I am African.)[1] Ouria never took formal language classes in France, but her job required her to speak French on a regular basis. However, with a defeatist tone, she dismissed any sense of need to speak perfect French. Her words suggested that she should be excused for her language ability on the basis of her Africanness. Speaking French and being African were mutually exclusive in her mind.

As Ouria wondered aloud why the people she encountered placed such an emphasis on her learning perfect French, I reflected on what it meant to invest in learning a language. Defining investment as "the socially and historically constructed relationship of learners to the target language and their sometimes ambivalent desire to learn and practice it," Bonny Norton argues that "an in-vestment in the target language is also an investment in a learner's own social identity, which changes across time and space."[2] While learners understand the need to learn another language, there may be competing forces that nullify any drive to accomplish this goal.

Ouria and the other people I interviewed provide a sense of how various people of Senegalese origin now living elsewhere in the world make sense of their own language learning and use and what sort of connections they make to other aspects of their identity. Therefore, this chapter explores the relation-ships that people in my study have with the languages they speak to shed light on speakers' attitudes and ideologies. In looking at the data from Paris, Rome, and New York City, I wanted to know what motivated people to learn and use particular languages and how they invested in these languages. What notions of ownership did they convey with regard to these languages? How much was dictated by personal experience and by historical and social factors? I looked specifically at French, English, Italian, and Wolof. Since most of the interviewees had opinions about these languages regardless of where they currently lived, I have organized the chapter by language as opposed to by specific research site. The following chapters will then look at how these language attitudes along with understandings about racial, national, transnational, postcolonial, and migrant identities play out in the specific contexts of Paris, Rome, and New York City. This chapter offers our first insights into what it means for Senegalese abroad to speak and be heard.

## POSTCOLONIAL LANGUAGE OWNERSHIP: THE SPECIAL CASE OF FRENCH

While Senegalese develop language ideologies from personal experiences with the languages and the communities that speak them, they also formulate their ideologies through a historically situated cultural perception. Compared to English and Italian, the relationship between French and the people I interviewed was the most fraught because Senegalese must navigate the direct legacy of French colonialism and empire, dealing with the baggage attached to this language. Interviewees from all three sites demonstrated ambivalence toward French, which they saw as a language that was losing international appeal but still useful. Paradoxically, French was a language that some saw as harmful to Senegalese identity but at the same time closely tied to that identity.

When I was a student in Dakar, I was struck by opposing language ideologies. On the one hand, people would convince me of how central French was in Senegal; on the other hand, I was seeing the everyday predominance of Wolof in most public settings. My interviews showed conflicting opinions not just in Senegal but in the diaspora as well. Some people spoke about the insignificance of French. Even though French is the sixth most widely spoken language in the world with over 220 million speakers and representation on five continents and the official language of twenty-nine countries,[3] Boubacar, a businessman in his forties, who was born in Dakar but had spent the last twenty years off and on in Paris, highlighted how French paled in comparison to English at the global level: "Mais l'anglais, c'est mieux parce que dans le monde entier on parle anglais. Le français, c'est ici. Dès que tu sors de France c'est fini, hein?" (But English is better because the whole world speaks English. French is here. When you leave France, it's over, no?) He had conducted business in neighboring Belgium and Switzerland, both francophone countries, yet he said that most of the time he would communicate in English. Meanwhile, Diop, a fifty-one-year-old journalist from the town of Louga in northwestern Senegal, who currently lived in New York City, explained that while French was still important in Senegal because of its official-language status, its global status was waning. Because Senegalese in the diaspora often think about where they fit globally more than within national borders, the global status of language is an utmost concern. Tying the French language to France's economic importance, he contended, "France was one of the five most powerful countries and today it is on the eighth place or ninth in terms of economy, in terms of population." He went on to suggest that France and the French language would never have the global reach they once had.

However, for many, French was still highly important for communication in Senegalese spaces. The following example shows just how embedded the French language is in the Senegalese diaspora, as two people who wanted to express themselves in Wolof through writing were forced to use French to communicate. Lucie, a thirty-one-year-old teacher from Marseille who lived in Paris with her mother and siblings and who only spoke a little Wolof, related the following experience she had with her family in Senegal: "Ma mère, quand elle écrit à sa mère, ça doit être en wolof parce que ma grand-mère ne parle que wolof. Mais ma mère ne sait pas écrire donc elle nous dicte ce qu'on doit écrire en français. Mon oncle au Sénégal va lire la lettre mais il va retraduire la lettre en wolof. En fait, deux personnes qui s'expriment en wolof doivent passer par le français. C'est parce que le français est tellement présent au Sénégal que c'est la passerelle en fait." (When my mother writes to her mother, it must be in Wolof because my grandmother only speaks Wolof. But my mother doesn't know how to write so she dictates to us what to write in French. My uncle in Senegal reads the letter but retranslates it into Wolof. In fact, two people who speak Wolof must go through French. This is because French is so present in Senegal that it is actually the bridge.)

This scene has played out many times: translating from oral Wolof to written French back to oral Wolof is a classic scene in Senegalese cultural production. It appears in a couple of Sembène's films, for example.[4] Because of historical factors, French is the language of mediation, and Lucie furthered this narrative of French as a tool of communication that is heavily entrenched in Senegal and in the diaspora.[5]

Meanwhile, Moussa, a fifty-eight-year-old man from Dakar, who had spent the last thirteen years in New York, enjoyed speaking French in New York. In explaining his preference, he noted, "La France c'est comme le grand-père du Sénégal. [laughs] . . . On apprend le français à l'école. Si tu es en France, tu vas le comprendre. Si tu es à Abidjan, c'est le français la langue internationale. Si tu es à Togo, c'est le français la langue internationale." (France is like the grandfather of Senegal. [laughs] . . . French is learned in school. If you are in France, you'll understand it. If you are in Abidjan, French is the international language. If you are in Togo, French is the international language.) Countering Boubacar and Diop, Moussa saw French as very useful in the international arena and as a method of communication with people in neighboring francophone African countries.[6] He was even able to speak it with the francophone communities in New York. More importantly, he touched on the postcolonial relationship by calling France the grandfather of Senegal and French the national language.[7] The fact that Moussa used a familial metaphor and laughed at France's paternal presence in the region suggests a relatively positive understanding of France's involvement in the linguistic reality of Senegal.

There were others, however, who exhibited ambivalence concerning the postcolonial bond between France and Senegal. For example, in New York Madina shared the following: "I think in Senegal, they respect French even more than their native tongue. Because since we were colonized by the French, they feel that . . . being successful and having money and gaining some sort of respect means you have to speak—it's like imperative for you to speak—French.

Because it makes you feel, it makes them feel like they are more educated than they are. Better well off."

The use of deictic pronouns conveys this sense of ambivalence surrounding the French language. Madina switched between "you" and "they" in a complicated display of perspective. She distanced herself in some cases and included herself in others. For instance, she used "they" to talk about respect for French and its role in obtaining success, suggesting that she herself did not feel similar to those in Senegal who thought French deserved more respect than other languages. However, she switched to "we" to talk about France's colonial control over Senegal, indicating that she also inherited this colonial relationship. In addition, she employed the passive voice to talk about this colonization, limiting the agency of Senegalese and of herself. Concerning the imperative to speak French, she emphasized the imposition of French by using the second-person "you." It was functioning as a command that she was obligated to obey. However, when she explained how it was supposed to make one feel, she began with the second person and then corrected herself by switching to the third person. The use of the third person in "it makes them feel like they are more educated than they are" allowed her to create distance between herself and those who bought into this hierarchy.

Meanwhile, others unequivocally denounced the French language and its postcolonial implications. When asked what languages he knew how to write, Karafa, a man in his fifties who had resided in France, primarily Paris, for around thirty years, offered this scathing indictment: "Le Sénégal était sous domination pendant cinq siècles. On nous a imposé ce qu'il faut faire, ce qu'il faut pas faire. On n'a pas eu cette capacité de pouvoir faire ce qui doit être fait pour ce pays en matière de langue. Tout doit être fait à travers la langue française au détriment de la langue wolof. . . . Maintenant je commence un peu à écrire le wolof." (Senegal was under domination for five centuries. We were told what to do, what not to do. We did not have that ability to do what needed to be done for this country with regard to language. Everything must be done through the French language at the expense of Wolof. . . . Now I am just starting to write in Wolof.)

For Karafa, French served as a tool but only because it was imposed on him to the detriment of Wolof, which could have been as useful as French. Arguably, the arrival of French impeded the ability of Wolof to develop into a widespread written language. His word choice was far from neutral. Words such as *domination* and *imposer* highlighted the power dynamic between the two countries, while the word *détriment* showed the consequences of such power relations. The postcolonial legacy not only influenced investment in the French language; it also called into question language ownership. Just as in the opening vignette, where we saw Ouria proclaim that as an African, French was not her language, Karafa implied that although he was fluent in French, if he had his way, he would use Wolof. The fact that he was now learning to write Wolof indicated the importance he placed on making Wolof a bigger part of his life.

### Rethinking Center and Periphery through the French Language

Reflections on this long history of domination demonstrate the complexity of the relationship between France and Senegal. On the one hand, there remains resentment toward France's continuing dominance in Senegal and arrogance toward Africans, such as the well-publicized reaction to Sarkozy's speech at UCAD in 2007. On the other hand, as Moussa hinted, some people are proud of Senegal's privileged position within French colonization. The historical centrality of Senegal to the French colonial project in Africa, and the consequential development of "prestige" (i.e. white-coded) French in colonized spaces, leads us to rethink the postcolonial analytic frame of center versus periphery in more nuanced terms. When we add linguistic performance to that frame, we see how some Senegalese claim a relationship to "good" French, which centers them as prestige speakers among other formerly colonized subjects, thus revealing the artificial nature of linguistic norms and their relation to processes of racialization. In what follows, Senegalese subjects reflect on their complicated historical and linguistic relation to French as both a legacy of colonial oppression and, precisely because of the structural inequalities resulting from colonialism, as a vehicle to social advancement. In other words, speaking an ideal "classic French" is not an objective indicator of linguistic value but a performance that aligns the speaker with whiteness, whatever the speaker's race.

Although France had considerable colonial territory in French West Africa, Senegal's singular status as the administrative center of West African colonization has present-day implications for how Senegalese understand their place in the colonial narrative.[8] Nyambi, a restaurateur from Dakar, who was in his fifties and who had spent half his life in France, argued: "Je pense que le Sénégal et la France sont très liés dans des évènements très difficiles. Pendant la guerre, pendant la guerre mondiale même il y avait des Sénégalais dans l'armée française. . . . Donc les Sénégalais se retrouvent en France, par l'histoire et puis par la culture. Parce qu'on est très français, les Sénégalais." (I think Senegal and France are closely linked through very difficult events. During the war, even during the world war there were Senegalese in the French army. . . . So the Senegalese find themselves in France, because of history and then culture. Because we are very French, the Senegalese.) Nyambi described Senegalese as very French, as the two countries are bound by a shared history. This link is the main reason why so many Senegalese are in France, drawn to this country not only by historical events but also by a cultural connection. Nyambi suggested a sense of pride in having such an intricate relationship with France, which included having fought in the French army and historically having access to French nationality.

Nyambi went on to say that "au Sénégal on parle le vrai français, ce français littéraire. Bon, on avait un président académicien, Léopold Sédar Senghor donc nous, on était dans cette culture du français, du beau français, du classique, voilà." (In Senegal we speak real French, this literary French. Well, we had a president that was part of the French Academy, Léopold Sédar Senghor, so we were part of this French culture, this beautiful, classic, French, you see.) It is telling that, to date, all Senegalese presidents have studied in France, and so far every single one has moved there after the end of his term. However, Senghor stands out as the first African elected as a member of the prestigious Académie Française. Senghor's politics in the 1960s and 1970s, including Negritude as a mandatory official ideology, were extremely pro-France and pro-French language, so much so that Sembène criticized Senghor for being a pawn of the French.[9]

This historical relationship, which champions French language and culture, contributes to how some Senegalese describe the French spoken in Senegal in comparison with the varieties of the language spoken in other francophone nations. For instance, I witnessed an intriguing conversation between Yasmina and Hakim, a married couple I interviewed in Paris. Yasmina was born in Paris, while Hakim, born in Dakar, had moved to Paris two years earlier. In the interview, they brought to the surface latent attitudes about Senegalese French and its position atop a hierarchy of francophone African varieties. Discussion of this topic began during my questioning about accents. In referring to Ivory Coast, Yasmina contended, "Ils mangent quelques mots ou bien ils ne respectent pas la conjugaison. Mais nous, je pense que, quand on parle, on parle vraiment français parce qu'on respecte la conjugaison, les articles, tout." (They eat their words or they do not respect conjugations. But we, I think, when we speak, we really speak French because we respect conjugations, articles, everything.) Yasmina's word choice was particularly telling of her perspective when she equated missing words as a lack of respect, suggesting a negative opinion of the other varieties of French. Hakim then substantiated this hierarchy with an ethnocentric argument that "dans toute l'Afrique de l'Ouest, il n'y a que les

Sénégalais qui parlent bien le français" (In West Africa, only the Senegalese speak French well).

Fascinated by where the discussion was heading, I asked them to explain:

H:    Bon, c'est vrai que toute l'Afrique de l'Ouest a été colonisée par les Français mais nous avons la chance d'avoir cet accent-là, cet accent un peu différent des autres pays. . . . Il y a le fait qu'on a eu des écrivains, comme Léopold Sédar Senghor qui était président de la République du Sénégal et était poète aussi. Ça a contribué à la culture du français, à la maîtrise du français. Il y a aussi le deuxième président, Abdou Diouf, qui vit maintenant en France. C'est vrai qu'il n'était pas poète mais il parlait très très bien le français. Il a fait ses études en France. C'est la raison qui fait que nous les Sénégalais, nous parlons mieux le français que dans les autres pays de l'Afrique de l'Ouest.

Y:    Il y a aussi que peut-être les Français ont colonisé d'autres pays mais qu'ils étaient plus basés au Sénégal.

H:    Voilà, ça aussi. Il y avait vraiment la base au Sénégal.

Y:    Entre Gorée et Saint-Louis.

H:    Si tu entends les Ivoiriens parler, on sait que c'est un Ivoirien. Les Ivoiriens ne prononcent pas le *R*. *R*, ils ont du mal à le prononcer. Les autres pays aussi comme le Congo, parfois, ils mettent pas l'article. Par exemple, pour dire "je veux," parfois ils ne conjuguent pas. Parfois ils parlent comme Tarzan. Tarzan, quand il parle, il conjugue pas. Il dit "vouloir partir," "moi, avoir faim" voilà.

[H:   Well, it's true that all of West Africa was colonized by the French, but we are lucky to have this accent, which is different from the other countries. . . . There is the fact that we had writers such as Léopold Sédar Senghor, who was president of the Republic of Senegal and a poet, too. It has contributed to French culture, to mastering French. There is also the second president, Abdou Diouf, who now lives in France. True, he was not a poet, but he spoke very, very good French. He was educated in France. This is the reason that we Senegalese speak French better than other countries in West Africa.

Y:    There's also perhaps the fact that while the French colonized other countries, they were based in Senegal.

H:    Well, that too. The base really was in Senegal.

Y:    Between Gorée and Saint-Louis.

H:   If we hear Ivorians speak, we know that it is an Ivorian. Ivorians
     do not pronounce the *R*. *R*, they have trouble pronouncing. Other
     countries such as the Congo, sometimes they don't put the article.
     For example, to say, "I want," sometimes they do not conjugate.
     Sometimes they speak like Tarzan. Tarzan, when he speaks, he
     doesn't conjugate. He says "want leave," "me hungry," like that.]

Hakim couched his explanation in a historical framework. He presented
a shared historical existence, one under colonization, but argued that by luck,
a different accent evolved in Senegal compared to the rest of francophone
Africa.[10] He attributed the positive nature of this French variety to the impact
that the forefathers of the Senegalese Republic had on the creation of the state—
a state that values the French language. Hakim mentioned how both former
presidents Senghor and Diouf studied in France, which he equated with a
certain pride in the language, and which in turn led him to conclude that the
Senegalese speak French better than citizens of any other country in francophone Africa. Yasmina then added a key detail to Hakim's historical perspective by highlighting Senegal's important status under the colonial empire.

Hakim moved from a historical perspective to layman's linguistic evidence,
detailing Ivorians' supposed inability to pronounce the French uvular *R* and
their disregard for conjugations. What struck me, though, was not the evidence
he provided but the way he presented his case, relating their speech to the
speech of Tarzan.[11] Frantz Fanon diagnosed an "inferiority complex" among
the colonized that persists in the postcolonial context: part of the colonial
strategy was to psychologically force the colonizers' subjects into submission
by establishing as obvious their inferiority in matters of language and culture.[12] Fanon wrote specifically of how Martinicans who went to France would
do anything to acquire the French uvular *R* because mastering the standard
French language meant becoming civilized, becoming white—or at least putting on a "white mask" over "black skin," to quote his famous title. Hakim's
depiction of Ivorians speaking like Tarzan was a reproduction of racist colonial
stereotypes. In this case, Senegalese played the role of whites and other Africans
played the role of blacks.[13] The conversation then ended with the joint conclusion that Ivorians spoke French as if it were one of their languages, apparently
making a distinction with Senegalese French, which was mainly reserved for
the domains of administration and education. This limited domain of French
also suggested a class distinction in which only Senegalese of a certain class had
access to French.

Nyambi, however, showed how comparisons were made not just with West
Africa but also with mainland France: "Quand on est venu en France c'est

tout-à-fait différent. Ma première difficulté, moi, j'avais du mal à comprendre les gens." (When we came to France it was entirely different. My first difficulty, I had trouble understanding people.) He told of his difficulty understanding French in France, hinting that the way French people spoke on the street was inferior to his own variety. Nyambi's experience is interesting because it is usually the "native speaker" who has difficulty understanding the foreigner when speaking the official language. Some other informants echoed Nyambi's sentiment, describing how the so-called *Français de souche*—that is, white native speakers—had told them that they (the Senegalese) spoke better than the "real" French people.[14] For example, after lauding the French-language educational system in Senegal, Hakim explained, "Quand nous venons en France, nous n'avons vraiment pas de problème. La preuve est qu'il y a des étudiants, des élèves [sénégalais], qui viennent continuer leurs études ici [en France]. Et ils réussissent beaucoup mieux que les Français qui sont élevés ici." (When we come to France, we really have no problem. The proof is that there are students, Senegalese students, who come to continue their studies here. And they are much more successful than the French who are raised here in France.) For highly educated Senegalese people, mastery and use of a more formal register of French confer linguistic power.

The discussion of where Senegalese French fits in comparison with other African varieties of French and even with the varieties of French spoken in France marks an obvious valorization and hierarchization. The discourse of these interviewees lends itself to a classic postcolonial center versus periphery analysis. While the center traditionally refers to the economically advanced communities of the West in opposition to the economically peripheral countries of the "developing" world, Senegal can be seen as occupying a center position in relation to the rest of francophone Africa based on the different attitudes expressed by several informants from the Senegalese diaspora. As seen earlier, several informants mentioned how many of the forefathers of the republic, most notably Senghor, lived and studied in France. They have immortalized Senghor as the harbinger of a new era that has continued to be steeped in *cette culture du français, du beau français* (this culture of French, of beautiful French), giving Senegal a special status in relation to other countries with similar colonial histories. Many informants also demonstrated the close ties that education in Senegal has to that in France, even fifty years after independence.

More surprising, however, is how some Senegalese speakers see themselves as occupying a center position in contrast to the peripheral one of white, native French speakers.[15] According to the definition put forth by Suresh Canagarajah, Senegal cannot be a representation of the center because of its subordinate position as a formerly colonized space.[16] However, as we saw with Hakim's quote, evidence in my data suggests that many university-educated Senegalese who have continued their studies in France see their variety of standard French as being as good as or even better than the original "owners" of the French language. What do these perceptions mean in defining and understanding center status? I argue that immigrants' understandings of language use and abilities in a postcolonial context should be taken into account by theorists who explore present day notions of center versus periphery. For these theorists, it might be worthwhile to have a less restrictive definition of what it means to be a member of the center or the periphery as well as to investigate how the center versus periphery model maps onto different situations. To further develop the center versus periphery argument, a relationship between the former colonizer and the colonized is not the only dichotomy worth discussing. Senegal can be seen as occupying a center position in the francophone African context because of its historically central position, that is, its perceived cultural proximity to France. After decolonization, the vestiges of this positioning remained in the psyche of some Senegalese, with Senegal becoming a kind of new center.[17]

However, the West not only represents a geographic location but also implies racial and class components. While members of the center are usually assumed to be white Europeans, if we limit our consideration of center versus periphery to francophone Africa, the racial component is rearticulated. One could read Hakim as essentially arguing that Senegalese are closer to "whiteness," real or imagined, than Ivorians, Congolese, or other Africans. The Senegal-as-center paradigm is thus a reproduction of colonial racism. The only point at which it reverses colonial assumptions is when Senegalese speakers put themselves higher than French speakers from France on the linguistic hierarchy of prestige; however, the preservation of the linguistic hierarchy itself still depends on colonialist and racist premises, as Fanon articulated. It is important to also address the class element, in which the elites of Senegal occupy center status over the rest of Senegal and over the elites and masses alike in neighboring francophone countries. Taking into account class and education helps explain why Ouria, someone who did not finish high school, was uncomfortable speaking French—an experience that was very different than that of Nyambi, Yasmina, and Hakim. The relationship that present-day, highly educated Senegalese have with the French language echoes how elites during the colonial era could amass cultural capital through a colonial education and travel to France.[18] Importantly, though, this class issue disguises the latent racist question of who is better at emulating whiteness. Therefore, while it is understandable for a person to strive to acquire the language variety that will confer the most symbolic capital, it is important not to ignore how different varieties of French become hierarchized through the racial and class expectations associated with these varieties.[19]

## LEARNING ITALIAN
### DESPITE ITS GLOBAL INSIGNIFICANCE

While the previous section looked at French, a language that is highly influential to the Senegalese cultural imaginary, this section explores Italian, which occupies the opposite end of the spectrum with regard to the same imaginary even though they are closely related languages. Very few people I interviewed had any interest in or exposure to Italian while living in Senegal. Furthermore, the vast majority of the people interviewed who had thoughts about the Italian language were currently living in Rome.[20] While those in my study often framed the French language in a global context, many tended to discuss the Italian language as something that was primarily confined to Italy. Moreover, with regard to French they conceptualized dialect hierarchies that spanned France and francophone Africa, while with regard to Italian, they reflected more on regional variation throughout Italy.

During interviews in Rome about their desires in learning Italian, many Senegalese commented that Italian's lack of global prominence provided little incentive for them to learn the language. At first, it seemed that this lack of motivation would negatively affect Italian-language acquisition; however, it was countered by other factors, most notably, a sense that multilingualism was a good thing, so learning as many languages as possible should be the goal. Therefore, some interviewees saw learning Italian as simply adding one more language to a linguistic repertoire. The multilingualism celebrated in Senegal persists when Senegalese immigrants migrate to Italy: native languages continue to be spoken and new languages acquired.

Many of my interviewees relied on French to learn Italian since they both are Romance languages and share many similarities. For instance, Alfa, a thirty-nine-year-old man from Dakar with a high school diploma and some college experience, argued that as a French speaker, learning Italian was quite straightforward: "Se hai studiato abbastanza francese, parlare italiano non è difficile. Prendere un dizionario, guardare per esempio il significato di tutto, guardare la televisione, parlare con la gente. Nel giro di un mese, quasi parlavo italiano." (If you have studied enough French, speaking Italian is not difficult. Take a dictionary, look up the meaning of everything, watch television, talk to people. Within a month, I nearly spoke Italian.) With a solid educational background in French, Alfa simply immersed himself in Italian-language contexts and used a dictionary to aid him in making connections between French and Italian.

However, not everyone could rely as heavily on French, and French literacy in particular, as Alfa did. Ndiaga was similar in age to Alfa, but having attended only a few years of primary school, Ndiaga had a much more limited educational background. He found learning Italian quite difficult at first because spoken French and spoken Italian often sound nothing alike. Ndiaga animatedly shared an experience from right after his arrival in Italy when he went in search of eggs at the local store because he was sick of eating pasta every night:[21] "Il problema è che io non so come si dice 'uovo' in italiano. [*laughs*] Ho cercato di fargli capire. Ho cercato di parlare anche in francese '*des oeufs*' ma loro non capiscono. 'Io voglio comprare *des oeufs*.' '*Je veux acheter des œufs*.' . . . Un altro giorno . . . volevo acqua. Ma non sapevo come si dice acqua in italiano. . . . Se tu mi dici, "dammi un po' *d'eau*" non capisco.[22] Loro non capiscono." (The problem is that I do not know how to say *egg* in Italian. [*laughs*] I tried to make them understand. I tried to speak in French "des oeufs," but they didn't understand. "I want to buy *eggs. I want to buy eggs.*" . . . Another day . . . I wanted water. But I didn't know how to say water in Italian. . . . If you tell me, "give me *d'eau*," I don't understand. They don't understand.)

While his tactic was to rely on French, a method the interviewees have used widely, *œufs* (eggs) would probably be one of the least likely to be understood by fellow Romance speakers because it has been reduced to a simple vowel sound: /ø/.[23] He confronted the same difficulty when asking for *eau* (water), another simple vowel sound in French: /o/. Again, his inability to explain what he wanted through cognates left him empty-handed. He was laughing while telling this story, but ten years earlier, an episode like this signified frustration and helplessness.

However, many interviewees have other languages to help in their quest to learn Italian in addition to French. For instance, Ibou showed how some people rely on Senegalese national languages to facilitate their learning of Italian: "Le lingue nazionali africane, o wolof, o pulaar, sono molto simili all'italiano. . . . Wolof, pulaar sono scritti con l'alfabeto latino e spesso si leggono come l'italiano. Si leggono come si scrivono." (African national languages, such as Wolof or Pulaar, are very similar to Italian. . . . Wolof, Pulaar are written with the Latin alphabet and often read as Italian is. They are read as they are written.)[24] Meanwhile, Biondo, a thirty-four-year-old artist from Dakar who was given the nickname Biondo because of the blond locs he wore when he first arrived in Italy, credited the multilingual setting in Senegal for helping him pick up Italian without trying: "Siamo abituati a parlare tante lingue . . . in mezzo alla strada. Io non ho mai studiato l'italiano e lo scrivo perfettamente." (We are accustomed to speaking many languages . . . on the street. I have never studied Italian, and I write it perfectly.) Coming from a country where only the official language is taught in schools while all other languages are learned in the home sphere or on the street, Senegalese are socialized to learn multiple languages in a variety of settings.

A more detailed analysis of multilingual usage in my study is presented in chapter 4, but the general consensus among my Rome informants was that if people decided to move to a foreign country, they should learn the language. Others argued that Italian was worth learning because it opened doors to job opportunities and made daily life in Italy much easier. At the same time, almost all the informants saw Italian as extremely limited and useful only in Italy. Since most of them assumed that they would live in Italy for a short time, they argued that Italian would have little use for them after they returned to Senegal or moved on to another country.

Nevertheless, my interviewees did not consider only practical reasons for learning Italian; they were influenced by a variety of other factors, some of which actually hindered their desire to learn Italian. The following conversation with Ablaay, a forty-year-old man from Casamance in southern Senegal, underlines the multiple desires that can influence a linguistic being. When I asked him what languages he would want his children to learn, he went out of his way to indicate all languages *except* Italian. This was a rather surprising statement for someone who had been living in Italy for five years, who did not know when he would return to Senegal, and who described Italian as a language he could speak fluently:

> M:    Se tu hai bambini, quale lingua vuoi che parlino?
> A:    Voglio che parlino tutte [le lingue] essetto l'italiano.[25]
> M:    Eccetto l'italiano?
> A:    L'italiano si parla solo qua. La lingua internazionale, se parli, si può lavorare. L'italiano è una lingua che solo si parla in questo paese. E poi, sai che il Black non può trovare il lavoro che vuole qua. Perché quelle persone che vedi lavorare qua, tutte quelle che sono venute qua hanno cambiato professione.

> [M:    If you have children, what language do you want them to speak?
> A:    I want them to speak all languages except Italian.
> M:    Except Italian?
> A:    Italian is only spoken here. The international language, if you speak it, you can work. Italian is a language that is spoken only in this country. And then, you know a black person cannot find the job he wants here. Because those people you see working here, all those who have come here have changed profession.]

While this quote shows how the Italian language's lack of global prominence influences opinions of it, more telling is the connection between language and the ability to work. In arguing that his ability to work in Italy was severely stifled not for linguistic reasons but for racial ones, Ablaay demonstrated how experiences regarding his skin color weakened the instrumental motivation to learn Italian. However, his contradictory feelings and desires illustrate the complexity and dynamism of investment because although he claimed he would not want his children to speak Italian, he himself showed pride in being able to speak it fluently.

Those I interviewed not only gave insight into desires concerning learning standard Italian; many also had a good deal to say about Italian dialects. From a practical standpoint, it would make sense to focus on learning standard Italian, especially because many of the interviewees had lived in different parts of Italy as they sought job opportunities. However, many of them could also speak at least a little of whatever regional dialect they encountered.[26] For instance, Anta was a twenty-six-year-old dancer from Dakar who had been living in Rome for five years. Her sister, Ngoné, had joined her in Rome two years ago. As members of a dance troupe that traveled around different parts of Italy, they described using standard Italian as a language of mediation when they were on the road. When I asked them if they spoke any other Italian varieties, Anta replied:

> A:    Forse romano, un po' perché abitiamo a Roma. Quando vado io nelle altre città per fare spettacolo, quando parlo con loro, loro dicono "eh, tu, tu sei romana." [*laughs*] . . .
> M:   Preferisci l'italiano standard o l'italiano romano?
> A:    L'italiano standard è meglio, così. Puoi parlare con tutti. È la lingua giusta.
>
> [A:    Perhaps Romanesco, a little, because we live in Rome. When I go to other cities for shows, when I talk to them they say, "Huh, you, you're Roman." [*laughs*] . . .
> M:   Do you prefer standard Italian or Romanesco?
> A:    Standard Italian is better. You can talk to everyone. It is the correct language.]

The adjective *giusta* (correct) and the inclusive nature of *puoi parlare con tutti* (you can talk to everyone) validated standard Italian.[27] However, although they preferred standard Italian for practical purposes, the way that Anta laughed when people in other towns would call her Roman suggested a certain attachment to this regional identity that the dialect afforded her. She took on aspects of the local culture, which she essentially adopted and which adopted her.

Keita, a thirty-three-year-old musician from Dakar, expressively exhibited the difference between standard Italian and the Roman dialect, Romanesco, when he said, "'Cosa stai a fa'?' cerco di dirti in italiano, 'Che cosa stai facendo'?" ("What are you doing?" I try to say in Italian, "What are you doing?") The preposition *a* with a truncated infinitive is a replacement for the present progressive—a phenomenon found in Romanesco.[28] Keita recognized the differences and achieved a high enough level of competence in both varieties to be able to use them in their respective contexts. In fact, it was not unusual for the interviewees and others in the Senegalese community to make these distinctions. When I asked if they spoke standard Italian, Romanesco, or other varieties, most people answered that they mainly spoke in standard Italian although they would often approximate their speech to the variety of their interlocutor. For instance, Alfa, who had spent even more time in Italy than Keita, treated the varieties in this way: "Anche gli Italiani, non è che loro parlano l'italiano al cento per cento perfetto. . . . Io cerco di parlare l'italiano perfettamente. Però se sei a Roma e tu parli con una persona romana, subito tu parli romano." (Even Italians, it's not as if they speak 100 percent perfect Italian. . . . I try to speak Italian perfectly. But if you're in Rome and you talk with a Roman, suddenly you'll speak Romanesco.) Just as in Senegal, where people switch between languages to accommodate the multilingual diversity there, many of the Senegalese I interviewed in Rome accommodate the rich dialectal range when traveling throughout Italy by picking up a few words from other regions.

## VALUING ENGLISH(ES)

English has a much more prominent position than Italian in the Senegalese cultural imaginary. At the same time, the attitudes appeared less complex than those concerning French. The prestige of English relative to French might seem surprising given its colonial implications—English was also a colonial language, evidenced most strongly by the fact that the Gambia, which bisects Senegal, is an English-speaking country and former British colony. However, English in the Senegalese imaginary is not viewed through the same postcolonial lens as French most likely because it was not the colonizing language of Senegal.[29] I received barely any negative opinions about the English language, which provoked little disdain from a postcolonial perspective and garnered respect because of its global influence. While the rhetoric in some countries, such as France, decries the imposition of English as a globalizing force, in Senegal and its diaspora, it is welcomed with relatively little pushback. In all three sites, most of the interviewees described English as a useful, fun, sought-after language. However, further scrutiny reveals how the construct of English becomes nuanced as we look at the various types of Englishes to which many Senegalese are exposed.

The case of English in Paris is interesting because the position of English in the Senegalese cultural imaginary clashes with its position in the French cultural imaginary. Many interviewees juxtaposed their desire to learn English with the indifference or contempt that they saw many French people have toward English. For instance, I interviewed Nafi, a woman in her fifties from Fouta in northern Senegal who had been living in Paris for the last eighteen years. Although she lacked English-language skills, she loved the language: "Il n'y a pas beaucoup de Français qui savent parler anglais. Moi, j'aime bien l'anglais." (There are not a lot of French people who know how to speak English. I like English.) Latif, a twenty-seven-year-old master's student from southeastern Senegal who was continuing his studies in Paris, picked up on this strained relationship to English in France as well: "Ici, il faut parler français. Néanmoins dans le milieu intellectuel, je crois que les gens ont compris qu'il faut nécessairement utiliser l'anglais. . . . Dans la mentalité française, les gens ont tendance maintenant à utiliser l'anglais parce que l'anglais s'est imposé comme langue mondiale." (Here, you must speak French. Nevertheless in the intellectual milieu I believe that people have understood that it is necessary to use English. . . . In the French mentality, people have the tendency now to use English because English has been imposed as a world language.) While Latif demonstrated a fairly positive view of English, he conveyed the negativity toward English in France through the verb *s'imposer* (impose). Much scholarship describes the view of the English language as a menace both to the French language and to French national identity.[30]

In Rome, people I interviewed reacted less to surrounding cultural perceptions of English and more to the role that English played in the world or in one's life.[31] For instance, Keita explained how he ranked his European languages: "Le lingue servono. Soprattutto l'inglese. Voi siete fortunati perché con l'inglese, si comunica dappertutto. Dovunque vai in Africa. L'italiano, solo qua. Il francese, un po,' sì." (Languages are useful. Above all, English. You [English speakers] are lucky because with English, you can communicate anywhere. Wherever you go in Africa. Italian, only here. French, a little, yes.) He made sure to stress the significance of all languages but foregrounded the importance of English for its global reach. Furthermore, even though he was from francophone Africa, he talked about English as the language that allowed people to travel throughout Africa. He was taking a more continental perspective while also indicating the increased importance for English, even in non-anglophone spaces.

This interest in English in non-anglophone spaces sheds light on hierarchies of prestige. In Paris and Rome, the global prowess of English adds to its prestige factor, but as Diop mentioned, it is the fall of French as the quintessential global language that puts the current hierarchy into more relief. In addition, the postcolonial friction produced by French's legacy situates French below English but above Italian for many people. While this complex postcolonial relationship simultaneously enhances and devalues French's prestige, there are historical factors that also complicate people's relationship to English. In other words, although in my data the English language does not induce the same type of friction that French does, not all Englishes are treated equally, evidenced by attitudes about Gambian English. A colleague of mine who has spent much time in Senegal often suggests to his friends that they go to the Gambia if they want to learn English since it is much closer and easier to visit. The reaction is almost unanimously negative. There is little interest in going to the Gambia or learning Gambian English. Perhaps they do not see the people of the Gambia, an African country, as rightful owners of the English language, subconsciously replicating racist restrictions on language legitimacy. Perhaps the pushback stems from the fact that English is a colonial language there, whereas English in other contexts can be viewed as a globalizing language. Or perhaps far-off destinations such as the United States and Britain just seem more interesting than traveling to a neighboring country.[32]

In the New York context, most of the people I interviewed were motivated to learn English, either in order to align themselves with speakers in their immediate environment or because of its global prominence. What stood out in these interviews, however, was that the English they expected to speak or learned to speak often varied from the English they encountered once in New York. Of those interviewees born in Senegal, the younger generation, particularly the more educated, began to learn English formally while still in Senegal. However, there are disparities between the type of English learned in formal settings in Senegal and the types of English-language environments to which they have access postmigration. According to my interviewees, the Senegalese learn British English in school.[33] For instance, Charlotte, a forty-five-year-old woman from Casamance who had spent almost half her life in New York, realized early on that her English foundation only somewhat prepared her for the linguistic situation in the United States: "When I got here the first thing I noticed was you guys were speaking different English. I learned British English. This wasn't what I learned [*laughs*]." Similarly, Daphne, the native-English-speaking white American wife of principal informant Omar, noticed the evolution of her husband's English: "It was much more British. Much more by the book. He didn't really know any slang. And as our relationship progressed, he added more slang. Once he got here, his English changed a whole lot. . . . I think his English is very good now." In highlighting both the British features as well as the academic nature of his English when noting it was "more by the book," she seemed to conflate a British dialect and a formal register. While it is unclear exactly to which aspects of his English she was referring, the fact that she equated the addition of slang to a more authentic American English conveyed a value judgment about the evolution of his English. To her, Omar had been successfully socialized into American English.

Furthermore, Daphne hinted at the importance of language setting when learning a foreign or second language. In her eyes, good English was not necessarily textbook English, a view shared by many others. For instance, Idrissa, a thirty-one-year-old man from Casamance, provided detail about his evolution during two years in New York from someone who strove to speak "perfect" standard English to someone who now placed communication above all else:

> Yeah. I mean sometimes I got problems because my English is a little bit from school. In school they say to you, "This is the rule. This is the grammar. You have to respect this. You have to do this." But when I come here, many people learn the English from the street. So they don't respect those rules. . . . Sometimes when I heard people say, "I'm gonna do this." I said, "Come on, man, why do you say, 'I'm gonna do this?' You have to say, [*slowly and pronounced*] 'I am going to do this.'" They say, "I wanna." I say, "Why do you say, 'I wanna?' I want to. Come on, man . . ." They said, "We don't have time for that. Life is time. You have to speak quickly. There's no importance about this. What is important is the communication. If you make yourself understand, that's it." So now I understand that this is the most important thing, communication.

While these examples hint at a spectrum of English registers that one must learn to navigate, some of the informants in New York realized that the type of English to which they were most often exposed was not Standard English, whether American or British. Due to the demographics of the neighborhoods that most Senegalese communities inhabit, neighborhoods that tend to be low income and less white, the people with whom they most often communicate are less likely to use academic English or even Standard American English (SAE).[34] Julien, a friend of Idrissa from the same region of Senegal, related his experience with grammatical forms he had never seen in English class back in Senegal: "You ain't know. . . . She ain't scared. Something like that, that's new for me. I never know that kind of sentence." Through interactions with his friends, he received a different type of language education: "They teach me sometimes. I say, 'Please, I don't understand what you mean. Go slowly. Or go word by word.' 'You're African, man. You don't understand nothing. Go go go.' [*laughs*] . . . They told me that they've never been in school. They told me that they don't know the academical language. They told me, 'You been learning English back home, but when you speak we don't understand you. . . . You should go to hell with your academical English.' [*laughs*] It's funny. It's great."

Julien appeared amused by this disconnect between the English he learned in a Senegalese school setting and the English he would use when conversing with friends in New York City. Although the British English he spoke would be seen as more prestigious in some contexts, in his case, it marked him as a non-native speaker and an African and therefore not someone who belonged in that community. He realized that if he wanted to create a connection between himself and his friend group, he would have to adapt.

While some of the examples reflect a more informal register of English, for instance, "gonna" and "wanna," others show dialectal variation, in particular, the use of African American Vernacular English (AAVE). "You ain't know" and "she ain't scared" are prime examples. Although AAVE is not the only English dialect to use "ain't" for "am not" or "isn't," using "ain't" to replace "didn't" such as with "you ain't know" is a distinctive feature of AAVE.[35] Indeed, through conversations that I witnessed with Julien as he talked with friends on the phone, I realized that he had picked up AAVE forms. And his reflections on this language use in interviews with me demonstrated a desire to fit in and be accepted into an AAVE-speaking community even if he described this speech as non-"academical" English.[36] Chapter 4 will look more closely at nonstandard English and its relation to identity formation by showing that not only does the immediate environment influence attitudes about English, but American cultural production in general and African American cultural production in particular also inform the Senegalese cultural imaginary.

Meanwhile, Omar took a different approach. Instead of making a concerted effort to speak in a way similar to the speech of those around him, he simply recognized the difference. Attributing the linguistic difference to a different subset of American culture, Omar mused: "When I first got to this country, the problem *que j'avais* [that I had], I couldn't understand what people were saying. But then I realized it was African American culture. You have to respect that, the way they speak."[37] Omar—who was currently living in Harlem, in a historically lower-income and black neighborhood, but who was studying at Columbia University, a predominantly white, middle- to upper-class Ivy League institution—was aware of how he straddled two different English-language settings on a daily basis.

Furthermore, Omar was cognizant of how his choice to continue using predominantly SAE directly influenced how others saw him. He realized the divide he maintained with the younger generation in Harlem: "Immediately they know. You don't speak like them. You're speaking correct English. You don't cut out words. You don't use slang. You just speak the way it's supposed to be spoken." Omar was very explicit throughout his interviews about his desire to speak "correct" English. He had strong notions about acceptable English, evidenced by phrases such as "the way it's supposed to be spoken." While he made concessions and no longer insisted on using more noticeable British features, he maintained a high register of SAE the majority of the time. In doing so, he conveyed how he positioned himself with regard to class and social register.

Omar would take great pleasure when those around him complimented his English-language use. For instance, he noted, "Some people love it. They respect you for that. Especially older women here. When you speak they're like, 'Oh, this little guy here, this young man here, he's intelligent. You're from Africa, right?'" Omar imitated the older women in his neighborhood by raising the pitch of his voice and using the diminutives that they have used to refer to him, such as "this little guy here." What is particularly fascinating is that his SAE use marked him as African in these instances, creating a distinction between African immigrants and African Americans. Furthermore, in this example we see a positive association between Africanness and language usage that stands in opposition to Idrissa's and Julien's experiences with people closer to their age, where the use of SAE creates barriers. In a way, this is a version of colorism where the respect and compliments Omar received for speaking SAE aligned him with a variety of the language associated more readily with white speakers. This example mimics the phenomenon we witnessed with regard to Senegalese French and its relationship to center status and to the emulation of whiteness in a postcolonial context.

## SENEGALESE NATIONAL LANGUAGES IN DIASPORA

Up to this point, this chapter has focused primarily on Senegalese informants' attitudes about and experiences with European languages (French, Italian, English). However, African languages are also central to identity formation in the Senegalese cultural imaginary. This section looks at the maintenance and/or transformation of ideologies tied to Senegalese national languages, delving more deeply into how these languages connected my interviewees to their immediate communities and to a larger Senegalese diaspora.

Since more than 80 percent of the population of Senegal speaks Wolof, it is unsurprising that many Senegalese in the diaspora also speak it. However, before we consider Wolof-language use and attitudes attached to it, it is important to acknowledge that Wolof as the de facto language of Senegal is somewhat contested. While I did not find the same wariness of and occasional contempt for Wolof that Fiona McLaughlin did in her research on Pulaar-speakers in Senegal, some of my interviewees definitely privileged other Senegalese languages over Wolof.[38]

For instance, in Paris I interviewed Faatu, a twenty-eight-year-old Parisian native whose parents were from Casamance.[39] When I asked her about speaking Senegalese languages, she stressed the importance of Jola: "Pour moi la priorité est de connaître parfaitement le diola avant d'apprendre le wolof. Le wolof, c'est secondaire." (For me the priority is to perfectly know Jola before learning Wolof. Wolof is secondary.) She went on to explain that while she did not deny the importance of Wolof from a pragmatic standpoint, her emphasis was on the cultural aspect: "L'importance pour moi c'est surtout de garder les racines. Je suis née ici, donc je n'ai pas la même culture que celle de mes parents. En fait c'est pour garder tout ce qui est culturel. . . . C'est très important d'apprendre la langue maternelle." (It is important for me to keep my roots above all. I was born here so I don't have the same culture as my parents. In fact, it is to keep everything that is cultural. . . . It is very important to learn your mother tongue.) As a French person of Senegalese descent, she recognized that she was different from her parents culturally. Learning her mother tongue has helped bridge that cultural divide.

Having moved to Paris from Saint-Louis the previous year, Latif had a different profile than Faatu did, but he also emphasized his attachment to a national language other than Wolof: "Je désire que la langue pulaar soit comme l'anglais, une langue internationale. Pourquoi pas? Ça affirme la fierté. Donc je choisis et je préfère parler ma langue parce que si je perds ma langue, je perds la valeur culturelle qui peut passer les informations culturelles de ma race, mon pays." (I wish that Pulaar were like English, an international language. Why not? It affirms my pride. Therefore, I choose and I prefer to speak my language because if I lose my language, I lose the cultural value that can pass along the cultural information of my race, my country.)

He identified as ethnically Fulani and highlighted his pride in knowing Pulaar, which he marked as *his* language, effectively staking ownership. He also mentioned that if it were seen as an international language, it would garner even more respect.[40] Equating language with culture, he argued that if he were to lose his ability to speak his language, it would threaten the loss not only of cultural values tied to his country but also of those connected to his race. The next chapter examines racial construction regarding blackness, but I note here that most of the people I interviewed were also quick to distinguish ethnic differences among the Senegalese. Being Fulani or Wolof or any of the other numerous ethnic groups was as important as being Senegalese, and one of the best ways to display these ethnic differences was through language.

Nonetheless, many of the interviewees, regardless of their ethnic affiliation, spoke Wolof more than other Senegalese languages for pragmatic reasons. For instance, Ndiaga, introduced earlier, was from Matam, a Pulaar-speaking region in northeastern Senegal. His family moved to Dakar around the time of his birth, so he spent most of his life in the Wolof-speaking capital. When I asked him whether he preferred to speak Wolof or Pulaar, he answered with Wolof: "Perché per esempio sono nato tra gli wolof. Capisco tutto quello che dicono. Pulaar, ci sono certe parole che non capisco bene." (Because for example I was born among the Wolof. I understand everything they say. For Pulaar, there are certain words that I do not understand well.) Ndiaga's preference is a prime example of the effects that internal migration has on language in Senegal. While Pulaar was his mother tongue, Wolof was the language of the capital and the language he knew best.

In New York City, Mariama, a twenty-six-year-old woman who was born in Oakland and has traveled to Dakar occasionally, shared a similar scenario. While she had always thought her family was from Dakar, she had recently learned that they were actually from Podor, the northernmost town in Senegal, bordering Mauritania: "They only spoke Pulaar. It wasn't until they moved from Podor to find work in Dakar that they had to then learn Wolof, to be able to navigate and to find work and things of that sort. . . . When I understood that, I understood why my father was like, 'Oh you need to learn Pulaar.' But then they speak Wolof more than they speak Pulaar. Some of the time they'll speak Pulaar but most of the time they'll speak Wolof. So it's difficult." This anecdote reiterates both the strong history of migration within Senegal, where Dakar is the main hub, as well as the national primacy of Wolof. Even though Mariama's father insisted that she learn Pulaar, she needed to reconcile this cultural bond with the fact that Wolof was the dominant language, even among members of her family. For many, Wolof was the pragmatic choice.

Whether considering Wolof in Senegal or in the diaspora, most interviewees agreed that Wolof is a practical language to learn. It permits communication with the vast majority of people in Senegal as well as in neighboring countries. It also permits communication with most Senegalese people all over the world. However, even with Wolof-language dominance, Senegal has yet to make Wolof an official language. Keeping French as the sole official language indicates the prestige that French still has in francophone Africa as well as the hesitancy to raise one national language above all others in this multilingual country. How-ever, this multilingual and hierarchical situation in Senegal is rearticulated and nuanced as Senegalese go abroad.

In parts of the diaspora, speaking Wolof has become synonymous with Senegalese identity. Nowhere is the connection between Senegalese identity and Wolof more evident than in New York City. Harlem's Little Senegal has become a sort of Wolof-language enclave where one is expected to communi-cate in Wolof. Diallo, a twenty-three-year-old woman born and raised in Har-lem, painted the following picture of the community: "When I go to 116th, that's when I talk to people in Wolof. Or when I go to Senegal, I speak in Wolof. . . . Most Senegalese, most Africans, live on 116th. So you're just going there assuming that they speak Wolof regardless of what they're wearing."[41] For Diallo, both Senegal and Harlem were sites of Wolof exchange, which she viewed in similar ways. There was also a conflation of Senegalese and Africans. Diallo spoke to all Africans in Wolof regardless of whether she knew their ori-gins, perhaps expecting that they would be able to communicate with her be-cause the setting dictated it. Just as Wolof is the lingua franca in Senegal for various ethnic groups to communicate, Wolof has also established itself as a lingua franca in Little Senegal.[42]

As Diallo described the linguistic situation of Little Senegal, her friend Aminata, who was born and raised in Dakar but had been in living in New York for five years, joined the discussion. Together they created the image of Little Senegal as an extension of Senegal, a place where food and other com-modities were traded freely and whose reputation reached back to Senegal itself:

> Yes, it's really normal when you're in 116th and you hear people talk in Wolof. Like they say, it's Little Senegal. It's like you're in Senegal. So it doesn't surprise you when you're walking and talking in Wolof or you hear some Senegalese person. It would be different if I were, if I was let's just say in Times Square or like or, like, you know, Central Park and I just hear some Senegalese people. Of course I would turn around and look, who's saying that? So it's different. So when you're in Little Senegal, 116th, you know. . . . Harlem there is like the only, everybody comes there. If you want Senegalese food, everybody knows you come to 116th. Like the whole avenue is full of Senegalese food, Senegalese people, Senegalese stores . . . everything. Like whatever you need that is from Senegal, whenever you want to like talk to or ask a question about something that has to do with Senegal, you always have to go to 116th. It's like the main site. Even people in Senegal, they heard about 116th.[43]

The heart of Little Senegal, 116th Street, is the place for all things Senegalese. Hearing Wolof, along with smelling the food and buying typical Senegalese products, offers proof. In other parts of New York, hearing Wolof is an exceptional experience. In Little Senegal, not hearing it is exceptional.

But what happens when someone fails to live up to this implicit social contract? While many of my American-born interviewees could speak Wolof, some of them could not, and others spoke a variety that was deemed inferior, encountering disappointment from members of the Senegalese community in New York. For instance, twenty-four-year-old Bronx native Ndiaye—a friend of Diallo, Aminata, and Madina, and one of the leaders of the organization that took youth to Senegal to learn about their heritage—related the following:

> I feel like a lot of Senegalese judge me before even knowing who I am. Like the elders in the community because automatically they're like, "Oh she's an American. She doesn't speak our language." . . . It's funny because when I do speak Wolof, they're like, "Oh, but you sound like you're from the Gambia, instead of Senegal." Because in the Gambia they speak, they were colonized by the British, so they speak Wolof and English. Senegal, the French colonized us, so we have French and Wolof. . . . Now, I'm comfortable with who I am. I really feel like my parents did a wonderful job with all that they could to teach me and my sisters our cultures and traditions. Our language.

For Ndiaye, it was not her inability to speak Wolof but her variety of Wolof that allowed others, particularly an older Senegalese generation, to challenge her claim on a Senegalese identity. In voicing the elders when saying, "She doesn't speak our language," she used the deictic marker "our." At this moment, she was not included in the "our," as it was obvious that the elders were excluding Ndiaye from any claim on Wolof. However, Ndiaye was not ready to relinquish her claim because later, in the same turn of talk, she included herself when saying "our language" to refer to Wolof.

Surprisingly, a European historical influence has ramifications for a contemporary hybrid identity thousands of miles away. Because of the historical legacy of colonialism, a Senegalese identity attached to Wolof is marked by French, even in the United States, a non-French setting. In other words, the elders who admonished Ndiaye were championing a Senegalese identity that emerged in opposition to both Gambian and American identities, which were born out of colonial and migratory histories respectively, and for which English-language use marked difference. This realization thus nuances multiple linguistic hierarchies. In looking at varieties of English, while American English may often garner more respect than Gambian English, in this case, both varieties are problematic in the ways they affect Wolof. Meanwhile, with regard to European languages, although English may have more prestige than French in both Senegal and the diaspora because of its global prowess and lack of association with French colonialism, in the context of speaking Wolof in New York City, French language confers prestige, particularly for the older generation.[44]

Similar to Ndiaye's difficulties in claiming ownership of a Senegalese identity when interacting with some older members of the Senegalese community in America, Mariama (MM) also recognized the correlation between the ability to speak Wolof and being Senegalese:

> MM: I feel judgment in not being able to speak Wolof. Some people will be very vocal. They will be like, "How are you Senegalese?" Well you're not Senegalese when you don't speak the Wol—the language.
> M: But there are many languages in Senegal.
> MM: Yes. It is true. It is true. But Wolof. You have to be able to speak Wolof. That makes you Senegalese. And um, it creates an issue with me because I'm not then going to turn around and say I'm not Senegalese. I can't deny my heritage because I don't speak the language, you know?

She foregrounded the conflict between her inner self and her outer environment because while she did not want to deny her heritage because of her language skills, those around her were suggesting she was less than Senegalese. Mariama's words were quite thought provoking when she said, "You have to be able to speak Wolof. That makes you Senegalese." She did not mince words when talking about Senegalese identity. For her, Little Senegal socializes one to believe that in order to really be Senegalese, Wolof is mandatory.

Little Senegal represents the quintessential example of a space where this conflation of speaking Wolof and identifying as Senegalese exists. The following anecdote involving Samba, Madina's thirty-one-year-old half brother, who was born and raised in North Carolina, demonstrates a connection between identity formation in Senegal and Little Senegal. In showing his support of Madina's organization, he agreed to speak at her fund-raiser in Harlem in a location that held many events for the Senegalese community. In ending his speech to a predominantly Senegalese audience, he apologized for not speaking in Wolof. I asked him later why he felt the need to do so:

> Well I could see the, like, my message wasn't fully received. . . . It could be that I was dressed in nontraditional clothes. Nothing that represented

the culture. Then it is like, just like, very limited Wolof that I speak. That is, I think at that fund-raiser, that was a no-no. . . . And also the young woman, I think her name is [redacted], she didn't speak as much Wolof and was like, like brought to tears because she couldn't express herself. It was an expectation that you know something, just a little bit, you know because you are representing, if you go to Senegal and are teaching English, but we also want them to retain a part of their culture. The African part is what we're preaching. That wasn't represented in my speech, which was solely in English. So those things become very very complex, especially when we are traveling to Senegal with my sister. I mean she is constantly explaining, "No no no, him not knowing Wolof is not a representation of how much he loves his Africanness. You know, but it's just that he hasn't learned it fully yet." [*laughs*] I felt like I had to apologize because of the tension in the room. When I started speaking, they were thinking: "OK, you're Senegalese, what is up? What's the deal, brotherman?" You know?

Ruminating on why his message was not well received, he argued that nothing he did tied him to Senegalese culture. While he mentioned his Western dress as being problematic, he dwelled on the linguistic issue. Samba believed that the crowd questioned his authenticity and his desire to identify as Senegalese primarily because of his linguistic failures. He endured similar criticism in Senegal, suggesting that Wolof was a requirement to Senegalese identity in both Senegal and Little Senegal.

Little Senegal has also left its mark through what it can offer consumers. For instance, strong transnational trade networks have allowed many Senegalese to control the goods that flow through the Malcolm Shabazz Harlem Market.[45] Likewise, over the years entrepreneurs and restaurateurs have opened shops and restaurants catering to nostalgic Senegalese people in particular and West Africans in general. Diallo and Aminata's description of 116th Street depicted this. Even though rapidly gentrifying Harlem has made it difficult for many immigrants and long-term residents to live in Harlem—many are now opting for cheaper neighborhoods in Queens, the Bronx, and Brooklyn—the heart of the Senegalese community is still Little Senegal. Julien, for instance, was living in Queens because of the lower rents but came to Harlem any chance he could for Little Senegal's vibrant culture.[46]

I found no place quite like New York's Little Senegal during my time in Rome, arguably because Senegalese migration is so recent. While cities in northern Italy have established Senegalese communities,[47] Rome is too new a destination. Nevertheless, I could expect to find Senegalese selling their wares outside Roma Termini, the central train station. I heard predominantly Wolof spoken there, making it a dependable spot for me to recruit people for my research. However, even though I could safely bet that they would be there every day, there were no permanent structures representing a Senegalese space. They picked up their merchandise every evening and returned the following day. In addition to the markets, most of the public Senegalese spaces in Rome were music or dance classes catering to an Italian audience. The one place I could bet on hearing Wolof was the makeshift, secret Senegalese restaurant, known only to the Senegalese community and its confidants. I will analyze this space in detail in chapter 4 because while Wolof is the primary language spoken there, the space is most fascinating for its multilingualism.

With the long history of migration from Senegal to France, one might expect a demarcated Senegalese space in Paris, comparable to New York's Little Senegal, but none exists. The longer history of African and Arab migration to France seems to have had the opposite effect, integrating some Senegalese people into French society, which, in turn, downplays Senegalese cultural markers. This phenomenon would also be consistent with French assimilation efforts, which beseech migrants to champion French societal ideals at the expense of cultural differences. Another factor may be that the designation Senegalese is too narrow for Parisian neighborhoods. For instance, the Goutte-d'Or neighborhood by the Château Rouge and Barbès-Rochechoart metro stations in Paris's Eighteenth Arrondissement has been dubbed Little Africa.[48] As the name suggests, a mixture of people from many different North African and sub-Saharan African countries reside there, reflecting the vast expanse of France's former colonial holdings as well as the geographic proximity of France and Africa. The markets serve as a central meeting place for Africans living all over Paris and the suburbs. Senegalese constitute just one demographic that shares this space. When I asked my interviewees about Senegalese gatherings, I learned there was no specific, well-known space. Many of them tended to go to friends' homes, which could be anywhere throughout the city and suburbs.

While Paris does not have a thriving, specifically Senegalese space like New York or a place where one commonly expects to hear Wolof, my research offers a different but equally fascinating perspective on the role of Wolof in Senegalese identity formation. More specifically, the Paris data highlight a shift in how self-described native French speakers tap into a Wolof-speaking tradition that did not really exist for them while in Senegal. For instance, Sébastien, originally from Dakar but who had spent the last eight years studying and working in Paris, explained his uneasiness with growing up in a French-speaking household in Senegal: "Pendant longtemps je n'ai pas aimé parler d'autres langues. Je parle wolof mais je ne parle pas très très bien. Je n'aime pas avoir de trop longues conversations en wolof avec les gens que je ne connais pas bien. En fait, le fait de vivre en France a renforcé mon wolof parce que quand je rencontre des gens du Sénégal, je parle systématiquement en wolof. Même avec ma famille, je parle plus en wolof depuis que je suis venu en France. Ça renforce un lien culturel." (For a long time I did not like to speak other languages. I speak Wolof, but I do not speak very well. I do not like having conversations that are too long in Wolof with people I do not know well. In fact, living in France reinforced my Wolof because when I meet people from Senegal, I always speak Wolof. Even with my family, I speak more in Wolof since coming to France. It reinforces a cultural link.)

This excerpt calls attention to those people who do not possess a strong competence in one of the national languages, particularly Wolof. How does the inability to speak Wolof fluently or in an unmarked way influence a speaker's own self-identification? Sébastien described himself as a French speaker first and foremost, but as I will expound later in chapter 2, the ability to speak French perfectly in France does not necessarily grant access to a French identity, even if one has French citizenship, as many of my Parisian informants do.[49] One is almost imprisoned in a linguistic no-man's-land, not belonging to any group. In addition, Sébastien also indicated how investment in a language could change when the environment changes. He was uncomfortable speaking Wolof when living in Senegal because of perceived repercussions for his linguistic inadequacy. However, being away from home and all the things that signify home turned Wolof into a cultural link for him. Wolof transformed from an alienating factor to a connective force that brought him closer to his former life.

Sébastien was not alone in noticing an improvement in the ability to speak a Senegalese national language after moving to France. Salif, a Dakar native and currently a business student in Paris, considered Wolof his mother tongue but lacked fluency and was thus more comfortable speaking French. Upon moving to Paris, he made a concerted effort to reconnect with his culture:

> Mais en venant en France j'entends beaucoup plus le wolof. C'est marrant. Le fait de t'éloigner de ta culture, de chez toi, c'est un souci. Je t'explique. La musique sénégalaise s'appelle le mbalax. Au début, quand j'étais au Sénégal, tu mets une chanson mbalax, arrête, j'ai envie d'écouter du R&B, j'ai envie d'écouter du rap, 50 Cent et tout. Dès que j'arrive en France, mes premiers mois, j'étais vraiment très très content d'écouter Youssou N'Dour. Ça me rapproche de chez moi. Je sens cette nostalgie. En France quand tu vois un Sénégalais, c'est automatiquement le wolof qu'on parle. Par rapport aux autres qui habitent en Côte d'Ivoire, au Cameroun, eux, ils parlent beaucoup beaucoup beaucoup de langues chez eux. Au Cameroun disons 150–200 langues, je dois vérifier.

Pour eux, c'est assez difficile de trouver quelqu'un qui parle leur langue. Chez nous, presque tout le monde parle le wolof. On se voit, automatiquement on le parle. C'est un truc qui nous rapproche. Tu te sens vraiment très proche de la personne. C'est un échange vraiment assez particulier. Il y a des choses que tu n'arrives pas à traduire en français.

[But by coming to France I hear much more Wolof. It's funny. Going away from your culture, your house, it's a concern. I'll explain. There's a type of Senegalese music called mbalax. At first, when I was in Senegal, if you put on a mbalax song, stop, I want to listen to R&B, I want to listen to rap, 50 Cent and all. As soon as I arrived in France, my first month, I was really very happy to listen to Youssou N'Dour. It brings me closer to home. I feel this nostalgia. In France when you see a Senegalese person you automatically speak Wolof. Compared to those living in Ivory Coast, Cameroon, they speak many many many languages at home. In Cameroon something like 150–200 languages, I have to check. For them, it is quite difficult to find someone who speaks their language. With us, almost everyone speaks Wolof. You see each other and automatically speak it. This is something that brings us together. You really feel very close to the person. It's a really rather special exchange. There are things you cannot translate into French.]

This excerpt is particularly telling because when talking about the need to speak Wolof, Salif framed this need in relation to culture. While he preferred to listen to black American music in Senegal, the process of coping with the distance from his home country created a new connection with the music from Senegal, especially *mbalax*, a popular form of music that is usually sung in Wolof. Therefore, while *mbalax* represented a link to his Senegalese culture, it also connected him with a Senegalese language that he was hesitant to use when he lived in Senegal.

Salif then made an interesting comparison between Senegalese migrants and those from other West African countries in France. He noted that because the vast majority of people in Senegal speak Wolof, there is an instant connection with a Senegalese person when one is out of the country. While people from a predominantly monolingual country such as the United States might take this ability for granted when they meet Americans abroad, in countries whose residents speak a variety of languages and whose borders were arbitrarily imposed through colonization, being able to speak the language of a fellow countryman is not guaranteed. Salif's references to Ivory Coast and Cameroon remind us of this point.

Salif also mirrored Sébastien in his relationship with French and Wolof, finding French to be an easier language for him to speak. He told of how his Senegalese friends would often make fun of him when he spoke Wolof: "Ils se moquent de moi en disant, 'Mais tu as grandi au Sénégal?' Ils disent, 'Est-ce que ta maman t'a parlé wolof?' Et puis, ils me le traduisent en français. J'en profite pour apprendre notre langue." (They make fun of me by saying, "But you grew up in Senegal?" They say, "Did your mom speak to you in Wolof?" And then they translate it into French for me. I take the opportunity to learn our language.) Although Sébastien and Salif found themselves in similar situations, Salif seemed less bothered by his superior competence in French in comparison to Wolof. This may be because he did not feel alone in his predicament. His words captured a sense of brotherhood when referring to Wolof as *notre langue* (our language), using a deictic marker that signaled his connection to Wolof in relation to others like him. When I asked him if he was bothered by his friends laughing at his Wolof, he thoughtfully replied: "C'est vrai quand on se moque de toi, tu as tendance à dire je ne peux pas être assez sénégalais [*laughs*] mais . . . personne n'a une connaissance très très complète, surtout nous les jeunes" (It's true when they laugh at you, you tend to say I'm not Senegalese enough [*laughs*] but . . . no one has complete knowledge, especially we young people). Salif's response suggested that using French when speaking Wolof did not affect his identity as a Senegalese person. However, it is worth reflecting on the type of Wolof in question. Dakar Wolof is heterogeneous, in which each person uses a combination of French and Wolof in a dynamic manner.[50] Many speakers are aware of the great extent to which French influences their Wolof. Salif demonstrated how while he failed to know certain words or phrases in Wolof, in some other instances he was the Wolof expert. The youth in Dakar have grown to expect this, making this dynamic hybrid their language. For Salif, it was only natural that he sometimes failed to recall words when speaking Wolof because French was the primary language in many of his linguistic domains.

## CONCLUDING THOUGHTS

Through a sociolinguistic lens, this chapter has investigated the complicated nature of language acquisition and use. Focusing my attention on notions of motivation, investment, and language ownership, I have looked at the complex ways that people in my study understood and engaged with the languages in their linguistic repertoires as well as the societies and communities in which these languages were spoken.

In the case of French, those in my study navigated the direct legacy of French colonialism and empire, leading to ambivalent attitudes about the French language among the global Senegalese community. Assumptions about the French language related to how it was conceptualized in Senegal or in a collective Senegalese mind-set. Because French carried the historical weight of its ties to colonization, an inferiority complex with regard to language choice, acquisition, and use emerged, most evidently in Ouria's exasperation with learning French and Karafa's disapproval of the dominance of French in the linguistic landscape of Senegal. Surprisingly, however, some of the people I interviewed managed to position themselves in a way that defied this perceived inferiority, turning it on its head. Through different strategies, such as evoking a colonial history in their favor or providing evidence of why their language skills were superior to even some French speakers from France, they refused to accept a devaluing of their language abilities, on the one hand, but played into colonial stereotypes, on the other.

With regard to Senegalese attitudes about Italian, the people I interviewed in Rome viewed it as a national language with very little clout on the global stage and as a language that was essentially absent from the Senegalese cultural imaginary. However, most of them happily accepted the task of learning Italian and claimed that the multilingual context to which they were accustomed in Senegal created both the linguistic background and the motivation to learn another language such as Italian. In fact, the interviewees in Rome displayed a level of competence that often surprised native Italian speakers. This phenomenon along with a general lack of ownership claims on Italian meant that the majority of my informants had positive opinions about Italian. Reflections on regional dialects alongside standard Italian were also important because they indicated how the emphasis that Italians placed on regional sociolinguistic variety influenced Senegalese migrants' conceptualizations of Italian.

Meanwhile, because of its importance on the global stage, English was starting to overtake French as the most sought-after language in Senegal. It was also almost universally respected, although specific contexts helped to nuance these attitudes. In Paris, some of the interviewees picked up on French attitudes toward the globalizing threat of English and compared their more accepting views to these. In Rome, the interviewees reflected what I also saw during my time as a student in Dakar: English was vital for a community that spent a lot of time looking beyond its borders. New York, as a predominantly native-English-speaking space, showed what happened when people were confronted with real-life English-speaking situations as opposed to the English-language classroom. Whether it was the discrepancies between British English and American English or between Standard English and nonstandard varieties, people in my study recognized their need to adapt in order to communicate effectively or to invest in particular social identities.

Finally, Senegalese national languages connected people to their cultural and familial roots. While some people championed languages other than

Wolof, such as Pulaar, Jola, and Sereer, most people saw Wolof as the most pragmatic option for communicating within Senegal and the diaspora. Wolof was also conceptualized as a primary marker of Senegalese identity, especially when one was abroad, although its very nature shifted depending on the particular city as well as the global and/or postcolonial situation. In New York, Little Senegal was the quintessential Wolof-speaking enclave, where people who identified as Senegalese but who did not speak Wolof—or the correct variety of Wolof—were chastised for this transgression. A feeling prevailed that one could truly be Senegalese only if one could speak Wolof, a harsh reality for second-generation Americans of Senegalese origin. In Paris, this expectation did not quite exist in those terms for French people of Senegalese descent, perhaps because the city has no exact equivalent to Little Senegal or perhaps because proving French-language competence was a more pressing goal. At the same time, some native French speakers who grew up in Dakar found that Wolof created a cultural connection to Senegal that they did not experience when living in Senegal. Finally, while those I interviewed in Rome spoke predominantly Wolof, they did not convey this conflation between speaking Wolof and being Senegalese. Speaking Wolof was treated as a given, and much more emphasis was placed on multilingualism instead, tapping into the notion of global Senegality.

The following chapters look more closely at how these language ideologies influence understandings of belonging and access to legitimacy for members of the Senegalese communities in Paris, Rome, and New York. How do identity markers such as linguistic competence, race, ethnicity, nationality, citizenship, and various cultural factors interact with national discourses in each site? How is the notion of blackness formed and understood both in white-majority settings and among black-majority subgroups? What sort of hybrid identities emerge as the people in my study make sense of their place in the host site as well as in Senegal? In answering these questions, the next chapter in particular investigates how language attitudes at both a personal and a societal level influence feelings of belonging as well as identity formation, particularly a racialized identity rooted in the construction and negotiation of blackness.

# 2

## Speaking while Black

## The Quest for Legitimacy in Exclusionary Spaces

On a dreary Paris morning in December 2009, I attended a teaching conference hosted by l'Association pour l'enseignement et la formation des travailleurs immigrés et leurs familles (AEFTI; Association for the Teaching and Training of Immigrant Workers and Their Families). As I sunk into one of the cushioned folding chairs that lined the back wall of the large lecture hall, I noted how overwhelmingly white and female the audience was, which was often the case in spaces dedicated to providing services for migrants in Paris. Most of the one hundred or so attendees were wearing dark, monochrome pantsuits and listening intently as the panel was being introduced. They took notes with the same intensity they had used when socializing and milling about the room just moments earlier. However, the energy of the room started to stagnate as Michel Aubouin, from the Direction de l'accueil, de l'intégration et de la citoyenneté (DAIC; Office for Reception, Integration, and Citizenship), began giving his remarks. The audience was visibly uncomfortable with the way he framed his speech. Bemoaning the fact that only a small percentage of immigrants attended French-language classes, he argued that learning the official language was essential to being granted French citizenship. After Aubouin finished his speech, Véronique Laurens from CIMADE (Comité inter-mouvements auprès des évacués; Inter-Movement Committee for Evacuees), a nongovernmental agency that helps asylum seekers, refugees, and immigrants, stood up and countered Aubouin's claims, contending that requiring immigrants to prove they had a certain competence in French for obtaining citizenship was not only exclusionary but might actually impede language acquisition. If France were to turn its back on people and deny citizenship because of language, she argued, it would be a violation of human rights. As the vast majority of the audience began to applaud, her comment recaptured some of the energy that was present earlier.

Article 21-24 of the current French civil code states that in order to pass the citizenship test an immigrant must have sufficient knowledge of the language, history, and culture of French society: "Nul ne peut être naturalisé s'il ne justifie de son assimilation à la communauté française, notamment par une connaissance suffisante, selon sa condition, de la langue, de l'histoire, de la culture et de la société française" (Nobody may be naturalized unless he proves his assimilation into the French community, and notably by a sufficient knowledge, according to his condition, of the language, history, culture, and society of France).[1] The law demonstrates a direct connection between societal assimilation and linguistic and cultural competence.[2] However, requiring immigrants to prove their level of linguistic competence is controversial. Echoing Laurens's fear that the law is exclusionary, James Archibald argues that "la France met elle aussi un accent très important sur la langue dans l'évaluation des candidats à la naturalisation dont un pourcentage non négligeable se voit refuser la nationalité française pour des raisons de défaut d'assimilation linguistique" (France puts such a major emphasis on language in the evaluation of applicants for naturalization that a significant percentage is denied French citizenship due to lack of linguistic assimilation).[3]

This policy, which highlights the relationship between language and citizenship, suggests that once one can speak French, one will be an integrated member of society, accepted by the greater French community. However, French speakers, even those who are native speakers, often tell a different story. Interrogating the concept of the native speaker elucidates the disconnect between linguistic policy and the reality faced by these French speakers who are positioned as societal outsiders. There is a certain gatekeeping mechanism involved with native speakership in which those belonging to the in-group have the power to confirm or deny legitimacy.[4] Access to native-speaker status is contingent on various identity markers, which must match the image of a legitimate speaker, an image constructed from notions of legitimacy based on not just

linguistic but also racial factors.[5] Questioning someone's linguistic competence
may be not so much about the way the person uses language as about who
is using the language and that person's perceived right to this language. In
other words, focusing on linguistic competence is a way to avoid being politically incorrect in places where commentary on other identity markers is socially
unacceptable.[6]

The questionable link between linguistic competence and acceptance in
French society is contested in such French-language cultural production as
Fatou Diome's *La préférence nationale*, a collection of short stories about the Senegalese narrator's experiences in France. The narrator often homes in on how
the people she encounters use language to discriminate or express racial animus.
For example, when the owner of a bakery in Alsace refuses to employ the narrator because of her inability to speak Alsatian dialect, the narrator muses to herself, "Je croyais que tous les Français parlaient le français au moins aussi bien
que ceux qu'ils avaient colonisés. Et voilà que j'étais linguistiquement plus française qu'un compatriote de Victor Hugo." (I thought that all French people
spoke French at least as well as those they had colonized. But here I was linguistically more French than a compatriot of Victor Hugo.) The owner then chides
her in a French marked with Alsatian features: "Mais pourquoi fous n'allez
donc pas trafailler chez fous?" (But why don't you go back to where you come
from to work?)[7] The narrator follows the owner's "go back to where you come
from" insult with an interior monologue: "Ce *vous* n'était point celui de la poli-
tesse, puisqu'il m'avait précédemment tutoyée. C'était un sac; oui, un sac
poubelle où il mettait tous les étrangers qu'il aurait aimé jeter dans le Rhin.
Cela me donna le droit et le devoir d'être impolie." (That use of the formal *you*
was not one of politeness, since he had previously used the informal *you*. It was
a bag; yes, a garbage bag where he put all the foreigners he would have liked to
throw in the Rhine. It gave me the right and the duty to be impolite.) Following
this linguistic analysis, the narrator launches a silent diatribe, voicing to the
reader all the things she would like to say to the owner.[8]

The way Diome animates the African migrant experience in France resonates with the stories my interviewees shared. For instance, the supremacy that
the narrator expresses about being linguistically more French than the Alsatian
baker is similar to Nyambi's discussion about his French being better than that
of white native speakers in France in chapter 1. In addition, Diome's focus on
the informal *tu* and formal *vous* in conversations where power dynamics are
front and center emphasizes the implications of language use in specific contexts
that my informants have learned to decode as well. And the narrator's unspoken
insults directed at the bakery owner, which fill three pages of the book, are eerily
similar to how my informants frequently do not speak up when enduring racial

or discriminatory remarks but carry this pain with them throughout life, often in silence. As the analysis of my interview data will show, regardless of the informants' legal status, an overwhelming majority expressed an inability to feel completely included or integrated in French society, even if they considered their language skills to be excellent. For many, linguistic ability was inextricably linked to and often overshadowed by other identity markers, most notably race. The vignettes that follow capture the elusive nature of linguistic legitimacy in a racialized world.

## "D'être noir en France, c'est ça": Native Speakers and Broken Promises

Lucie, noticing that I was a new face in the intermediate Wolof language class, sat next to me and introduced herself. She was a vivacious woman with one of those smiles that had its own gravitational pull. A natural-born interviewer, she asked why I was in the class, and with her interest piqued, she continued with a series of follow-up questions about the research I was conducting. Lucie was one of four Frenchwomen of Senegalese descent who made up about half of the intermediate class. The class met weekly in the second-floor meeting room of a tiny office building in Château Rouge.

As we continued our conversation in whispers during lulls in the class session and then in more depth on the sidewalk right outside the building, I asked if I could conduct a formal interview with her. A couple of weeks later, we met at her apartment in one of the southern neighborhoods on the outskirts of Paris, where she lived with her mother and younger siblings. Lucie had an abundance of energy throughout the interview. Her profession as a teacher shone through because she had a way of explaining things that was both very clear and full of enthusiasm. She was also incredibly inquisitive, so the interview sounded more like a philosophical conversation between two friends. However, as she related an incident that happened while she was a teaching intern in Montpellier, her whole demeanor changed. The happiness that had been in her voice throughout the discussion promptly dissipated. She closed her eyes and slowed her speech to recount a traumatic experience with a mother at a parent-teacher conference:

> J'expliquais à une mère que sa fille a fait du bon travail mais elle avait quelques petites fautes d'orthographe, et dans ma formulation je ne sais plus ce que j'ai dit mais j'ai dû faire une faute que j'ai corrigée après et la maman m'a dit "c'est gênant de la part d'un professeur qui a du mal à s'exprimer." . . . Et après il y avait des attaques, des attaques, des attaques. Donc elle a mis en question toutes mes méthodes. . . . J'ai

analysé plusieurs fois cette faute-là—donc je pense que si je n'avais pas fait cette faute de langage elle n'aurait pas eu l'opportunité de me parler comme ça. . . . La fin est arrivée et je suis sortie, allée pleurer dans les toilettes. C'était trop fort. Je me suis sentie attaquée. Quand je suis sortie des toilettes j'ai vu mon collègue qui m'a dit "Ça va? Tu vas bien? J'ai vu comme madame t'a traitée. C'est pas bien." Je lui ai dit "Mais d'être noir en France, c'est ça."

[I was explaining to a mother that her daughter had done a good job but she had a few spelling mistakes, and I don't know what I said but I must have made a mistake, which I corrected, but the mother told me "a teacher who has difficulty speaking is embarrassing." . . . And then began the attacks. She challenged all my methods. . . . And I think if I had not made this language mistake, she would not have had the opportunity to talk to me like that. . . . The end came and I went to the bathroom to cry. It was too much. I felt attacked. When I came out of the bathroom, I saw my colleague who asked me, "Are you okay? I saw how she treated you. This is not good." I told him, "This is what it means to be black in France."]

Lucie showed how her language mistake was a pretext for the woman to denigrate her, to demonstrate her annoyance with having someone like Lucie as her child's teacher. Because of life experience and a shared experience with others like her, she assumed the attack was racially motivated, something that came with the territory of being black in France.[9]

Although Lucie was a native speaker of French, in this moment—and as I would soon learn in many moments of her life—her claim on native-speakerness was illegitimate in the eyes of many French people because her racial identity superseded her actual language abilities. According to Lucie, she was marked as an Other partially because of her race: "On n'est pas un citoyen comme les autres. Quand tu es noir, tu n'es pas un Français comme les autres. Le Français de base, il est blanc. Il n'est pas noir." (We are not citizens like the others. When you are black, you are not French like the others. Your typical French person is white. He's not black.) Lucie suggested that in the mind-set of many people in French society, by virtue of being black she could not be French; therefore, she could not be a native speaker of standard French. The fact that Lucie was French born, grew up in the French educational system, had no discernible foreign accent, and spoke French as her only mother tongue proved that the issues of native-speakerness and language ownership go much deeper than the ability to speak the official language.[10] Native Frenchness presupposes whiteness. Therefore, while Lucie was a native speaker of the French language, she was often positioned as not being so because of her overriding racial identity.

The story of Jean-Paul, a thirty-two-year-old Senegalese man who had spent the last eleven years in France, further complicates the notion of competence when he reflected on his language ability and notions of acceptance. In the following example, he told of the time that he was talking to a French colleague who remarked that Jean-Paul spoke as if he were reading a dictionary:

> J:  I remember a French colleague, when I say French, I'm thinking of a white person, born of parents both born here for two or three generations, who asked me once why I was thinking that much and expressing myself as if I was reading a dictionary. At that point I wasn't speaking in a formal way. It was just the way I was used to speaking with people.
>
> M:  How did that make you feel when he made that comment?
>
> J:  Two things. I was thinking warning warning warning, if you want to integrate, and when I say integrate I mean when you are in a certain context you have to be at the level of the people but you can still show your differences as I don't want to be at the level of the masses. I still keep my proficiency, and I'm not going to be like uneducated people just so they can feel better. But in the same way, I was extremely shocked and surprised.[11]

Jean-Paul gave a description of a French person that was more than just a legal definition. He equated French with whiteness. He also indicated that the person's family must have spent a few generations in France to ensure authenticity. He was essentially describing a *Français de souche*, a "real" French person—someone who was white. Second, Jean-Paul referred to a certain register of French that he did not consider formal but that was not something used by "the masses." What is particularly interesting is his response to having his style of speaking scrutinized. He took the critique as a warning sign—evidence that he was not successfully integrating or "blending in."

Looking at Lucie and Jean-Paul's experiences together reveals a lot about the nature of linguistic competence. The parent who verbally attacked Lucie positioned her as an incompetent speaker based on one mistake in her speech. In wrestling with her grammatical mistake, Lucie suggested that people who are marked as Others must be vigilant to never commit an error. They are held to a higher standard—an impossible standard. Meanwhile, Jean-Paul was labeled as incompetent in the eyes of his colleague because although he had great command of the language, his choice of diction sounded either pretentious or stilted. Neither of them had acceptable French according to their critics. However, judging by how both Lucie and Jean-Paul related their respective stories, they perceived this unacceptability as not just about language ability but also about race. In other words, they both felt the need to transcend a label of the Other that is based on their race, but in different ways. Lucie needed to speak in a way that overcame a racist expectation of incompetence, while Jean-Paul needed to sound more authentically French in order to overcome the *Français de souche* expectation of whiteness.[12] Jean-Paul's racial definition of *Français de souche* and Lucie's lament that "d'être noir en France, c'est ça" (this is what it means to be black in France) highlighted their perceptions of French expectations with regard to race and language and provided insight into why people who are marked as Others feel that finding acceptance in society can be so difficult that it is impossible.

### "Le problème c'est pas l'accent mais d'où vient cet accent": Accent's Silent Barriers

I met Sandrine in the beginner Wolof class. Unlike the intermediate class, which had an even number of white French people and black French people of Senegalese descent, the beginner class was filled mainly with white French-women married to Senegalese men. Sandrine was one of those women. Soft-spoken but with a lot to say, she readily volunteered her Senegalese husband for an interview with me.

A week later, we met in a bustling coffee shop in the Marais. Sandrine gave me a kiss on each cheek before introducing me to her husband, Ngirin, a thirty-eight-year-old Senegalese man from Touba in central Senegal who had spent the last seven years of his life in Paris and who seemed very intrigued by my research. Sandrine wanted to listen to our conversation. Thinking that her experience would offer invaluable insight, I let her know that she was welcome to chime in as well. She proved to be a great asset because of her ability to get Ngirin to elaborate his answers. As the discussion moved toward the topic of accent, Sandrine forced Ngirin to recall his various experiences with his French accent in Paris:

> S: Une fois, dans un entretien pour un emploi, ils ont dit que son accent pose un problème.
> M: Comment est-ce que tu t'es senti?
> N: [*laughs*] J'étais pas du tout content. [*laughs*]
> S: Le mot accent, tout le monde a un accent. Pour un Marseillais, ça ne poserait pas un problème. Mais pour un accent africain, là tu dis, ça pose un problème.

M: Parlez-moi plus de ça. C'est intéressant, parce qu'il semble que c'est pas parce qu'il a un accent mais d'où vient cet accent—

N: Oui, exactement, c'est bien ce que tu as dit là.

M: Quelles sont vos opinions sur ça?

S: Je pense que la personne qui dit ça ne se considère pas comme raciste, alors que c'est raciste. La personne qui le dit ne se rend pas compte qu'il est raciste.

M: Tu as mis le mot "raciste." Il faut expliquer un peu.

N: Le problème c'est pas l'accent mais d'où vient cet accent parce que ça se voit ici. Tu as des anglophones. Les anglophones américains, ça c'est chic, c'est sexy. L'accent anglophone si tu viens du Ghana, c'est dur. Il parle l'anglais comme l'autre, c'est juste que sa zone géographique est différente. Pour moi, il y a plus de racisme dedans mais ils ne vont pas l'accepter. . . . Il y a plein d'Américains, Anglais, Irlandais qui viennent, s'installent en France qui ne comprennent pas un mot de français. Ils veulent pas parler français. . . . Autre chose. Combien de fois j'ai vu les gens qui entendent bien ce que je dis, je suis sûr qu'ils comprennent mais—mon accent pose un énorme problème. . . . C'est juste un prétexte. C'est faux.

[S: Once, in an interview for a job, they said that his accent is a problem.

M: How did you feel?

N: [*laughs*] I was not at all happy. [*laughs*]

S: The word "accent," everyone has an accent. A person from Marseille, it wouldn't pose a problem. But an African accent is problematic.

M: Tell me more about that. It's interesting, because it seems that this is not because he has an accent but because of where this accent comes from—

N: Yes, exactly, you've said that well.

M: What are your views on that?

S: I think the person who says it does not consider it racist, but it is racist. The person who says this does not realize that he is racist.

M: You used the word "racist." Explain a little.

N: The problem is not the accent but where the accent is from, because you see that often here. American Anglophones are chic, sexy. The English accent from Ghana, that's hard. He speaks English like the other, but the geographical area is different. For

me, there's racism there, but they are not going to admit it. . . .
There are plenty of Americans, English, Irish, who come, settle in
France, who do not understand a word of French. They do not
want to speak French. . . . Another thing. How many times have I
seen people who understand what I say, I'm sure they understand,
but apparently my accent causes a huge problem. . . . It's just an
excuse. It's false.]

In this excerpt, Ngirin produced evidence of how people have dubiously claimed
not to understand him.[13] Both Sandrine and Ngirin attributed interlocutors'
inability to understand Ngirin not to accent per se but to a racialized accent.
They argued that only some types of accents were scrutinized in French society,
and these were the accents that corresponded with marginalized groups.[14]

According to Ngirin and Sandrine, people from the United States, England,
and Ireland moved to France and often refused to learn the language but were
seldom criticized for failing to learn French or for speaking with a foreign accent.
Meanwhile, English-speakers from Ghana, who shared a common language
with those from the United States, England, and Ireland, were held to a different standard. Ngirin and Sandrine contended that the difference in these
experiences was due to racism.[15] French society was not threatened by the
presence of Americans or British people on an individual level (there was an
implication of whiteness in this geographic designation); therefore, no effort
was made to single them out as different or as people who did not belong.[16]

Sandrine also juxtaposed the accent from Marseilles and an African accent,
arguing that only the latter posed problems. She and Ngirin both argued that
the treatment he received was much worse compared to a (presumed) *Français
de souche* from Marseilles, illustrating a phenomenon similar to the interaction
between the Alsatian baker and the protagonist in Diome's *La préférence nationale*.
However, Lucie's experience suggests that the stigma associated with regional
accents could be problematic as well. Lucie, who came from Marseille, reflected on how she also had to contend with negative attitudes about her Mar-
seillais accent when she began teaching near Paris: "Je dirais qu'à Paris, il faut
essayer de pas parler avec un accent parce qu'à Paris, c'est la capitale et quand
on remarque que tu as un accent, il y a le côté parisien supérieur aux provinces.
Donc tu es inférieur aux Parisiens. Souvent parmi mes collègues au lycée, il y a
quelques-uns qui cachent leur accent. Moi, j'ai essayé au début parce que je ne
voulais pas que mes élèves sachent que je viens du sud." (I would say that in
Paris, you should try not to talk with an accent because Paris is the capital and
when someone notices that you have an accent, there is the Parisian side that is
superior to the provinces. So you're inferior to Parisians. Often some of my

colleagues in high school hide their accent. I tried at first because I did not want my students to know I'm from the south.) She highlighted how Paris's position as the capital bestowed certain superiority on the speakers of Parisian dialect. She admitted to wanting to hide her regional accent, putting into relief the importance that Paris garnered as a metropolitan city in a highly centralized nation-state.[17] However, unlike her accent from Marseilles, which she was able to adapt after years of living in Paris, she could not hide her skin color, which she identified as the real marker of difference in her case.

These perspectives offer a point of reentry into the center versus periphery argument. Suresh Canagarajah has argued that while there is a noticeable difference in accent, vocabulary, and discourse conventions among countries that represent the center (e.g., Britain and countries that developed through settler colonialism such as the United States, Canada, New Zealand, and Australia), these different varieties are all considered prestigious because of political, historical, cultural, and economic reasons. Meanwhile, the periphery is labeled as subordinate more for these same reasons than for linguistic reasons. However, within France the periphery is no longer restricted to speakers of French who were born in former colonies. The notion of periphery extends to marginalized communities throughout France, of which many members were born in mainland France and have French nationality.[18]

In Lucie's case, she faced marginalization because she came from a region that did not have the same cachet as Paris, which was not only the capital of France but also the cultural capital of the Western world. Any rhetoric concerning the importance of the French language in France was doubly heightened in Paris—the gold standard. However, the phenomena of center and periphery also relate to how perceptions of race and nationhood serve to marginalize. In other words, even though Lucie was French, she did not feel she belonged in France. On paper she possessed citizenship, but cultural citizenship eluded her because of the importance of race in constructing national identity.[19]

## ROME: EXPANDING ITALIANITÀ

In 2013 Cécile Kyenge, an Italian citizen of Congolese origin, became Italy's first black minister when she accepted Enrico Letta's appointment as minister of integration in his coalition government. She was one of a few highly visible black Italians, joining others—such as footballer Mario Balotelli, a member of the Italian national team—as a symbol of the changing image of Italian identity. Sports and politics constitute two areas that are heavily linked to national identity formation, and Kyenge has recognized their parts in generating discussion on what it means to be Italian: "Balotelli and I are both opening new paths in our fields . . . and anyone who does that will face huge difficulties."[20] These trailblazers have been met by a vocal group of white Italians who are unable to reconcile being black with being Italian. From soccer fans harassing Balotelli by chanting "a Negro cannot be Italian" to members of parliament such as Roberto Calderoli calling Kyenge an orangutan and right-wing supporters throwing bananas at her, the place of African immigrants and black Italians has been called into question on the national stage.[21]

Debates about race in Italy should not just emerge from racist or discriminatory incidents but should be analyzed against the backdrop of the long-term racial formation of a country. Italians have long assumed that being white is a normative aspect of being Italian, effectively othering anyone who is not identified as white.[22] Some have argued that this racial formation has not encountered resistance because there have never been enough black voices to question it. However, since current demographic changes are increasing the number of people who identify as black, adding to both visibility and audibility, the strength that comes from numbers facilitates discussions about one's place in society.[23]

In addition, just as in France, although it is often assumed that linguistic competence transcends blackness, skin color clearly imposes restrictions on black Italians' claim to Italianness even when they possess Italian language abilities. In emphasizing how linguistic competence does not guarantee societal acceptance in Italy, Christina Lombardi-Diop and Caterina Romeo argue that "*Italianità* seems unattainable for black Italians precisely because national belonging is generally understood in terms of specific traits (both cultural and biological) that cannot be simply acquired by a perfect mastery of the language and the Italian way of life."[24]

Regardless, just as we saw in French-language cultural production, a growing body of black Italian cultural production uses the Italian language to challenge the racially restrictive nature of contemporary Italian identity. For instance, Pap Khouma, an Italian writer of Senegalese descent, depicts the lives of African immigrants in Italy through his novels, such as *Io, venditore di elefanti* (*I Was an Elephant Salesman*). He has also articulated his own alienation in Italy when he writes about encounters he has had with police officers or border control in newspapers such as *La Repubblica*: "'Tu possiedi il passaporto italiano ma non sei italiano.' Oppure, con un sorriso: 'Tu non hai la nazionalità italiana come noi, hai solo la cittadinanza italiana perché sei extracomunitario.'" ("You possess an Italian passport, but you're not Italian." Or, with a smile: "You do not have Italian nationality like we do; you only have Italian citizenship because you are non-EU.")[25] The deictic marker *come noi* ensures that Khouma's brand of Italianness, one based on citizenship and not nationality, is illegitimate in the eyes of the dominant group. Therefore, Khouma and those like him are placed outside an invisible barrier, regardless of citizenship status.

Many argue that these insults come from fringe groups, in particular, xeno-phobic political movements such as Forza Nuova and the Lega Nord. Kyenge herself has been quick to point out that children in Italy are less likely to see the world in terms of race than their parents' generation.[26] However, to argue that Italian racism comes from the margins ignores the everyday lived experiences of the people whom racism targets.[27] In particular, black Italians and African migrants struggle as much with everyday racism as with acts of overt discrimi-nation. The Senegalese community in Rome, just like African communities throughout Italy, conceptualizes and understands identity formation as for-eigners and as linguistic, racial, and ethnic minorities. The analysis of the fol-lowing excerpts support Khouma's depiction of a reduced Italianness in which race and skin color constitute identity markers that contribute to the establish-ment and maintenance of boundaries for many Senegalese immigrants in Rome and minimize any chance of them ever really being accepted as part of Italian society.

### "Je suis *nero*, je suis *brutto*, *ma* je suis *vivo*": Conceptualizing Blackness in Rome

I had my first meeting with Ndiaga on a bench in Parco delle Valli, near my apartment in Rome. As I waited for him to arrive, I watched old Italian men engaging in their daily routine. Two or three abreast, hands clasped behind their slightly hunched backs, they would meander through the park, chatting about soccer and politics, consistently stopping to flash their brilliant smiles when young women would jog by. A timid voice snapped me from my people watching. I looked up to see a man of medium build. He was dressed in jeans and an overcoat, holding a sack of posters and what looked like a squeegee. In Italian, he introduced himself as Ndiaga and sat down next to me in response to my welcoming gesture. He seemed nervous at first. The only thing our mutual friend had told him was that I was an American looking at language practices of Senegalese in Rome. He didn't know how much help he could be, but he did speak a language, several of them to be exact, and thought that would be a good start.

We began chatting as if we had known each other for years. There was an instant connection, and the interview hardly felt like an interview at all. Ndiaga ended up becoming not just a friend but also a principal informant. We would meet on a regular basis to chat informally, visiting his favorite parks and monu-ments around Rome so that he could show me Rome through his eyes, as he liked to put it. Through these encounters, I also got to share with him the direc-tions my research was taking and hear his thoughts on my analyses. He involved himself heavily in my research because he said my questions struck at the heart of his immigrant experience. He often reflected on our first interview and continued to explore those questions from time to time. When he experienced something related to our conversations, the next time we met he would excitedly provide follow-up details and vibrant anecdotes. He also introduced me to his friends and convinced them to speak with me.

Two months into my friendship with Ndiaga, I met with him and Professore, his forty-year-old Senegalese friend, in a park. Professore was not very forthcoming at first, still skeptical about why I would want to interview him, but with Ndiaga's gentle urging, he opened up a bit. The conversation was a linguistic rollercoaster. The three of us switched between French, Italian, and English throughout, and the use of code-switching conveyed a complex sense of identity:[28]

> P:    La demande, c'était?
> M:    Tes pensées sur l'Italie?
> P:    **Vabbèh**—
> N:    —Tu as, tu as [*trails off*]
> P:    Les—
> N:    Tu as vu, vu le film <u>Co, Col, Color</u> *Viola*.
> M:    Non. <u>Oh, The Color Purple.</u>
> N:    <u>Color</u> *Viola*.
> M:    <u>The Color</u>, oui.
> N:    Tu [l'as vu?
> P:          [<u>Color Purple.</u>
> M:    Oui. Oui. C'est, [c'est fort.
> N:                        [Je suis noir—je suis *nero*, je suis *brutto*, *ma*, je suis *vivo*!
> M:    *Esatto.*
> N:    *È bellissimo.*
>
> [P:    The question, it was?
> M:    Your thoughts about Italy.
> P:    **OK**—
> N:    —Have you, have you [*trails off*]
> P:    The—
> N:    Have you seen, seen the film <u>Co, Col, Color</u> *Purple*?
> M:    No. <u>Oh, The Color Purple.</u>
> N:    <u>Color</u> *Purple*.
> M:    <u>The Color</u>, Yes.
> N:    You [saw it?
> P:          [<u>Color Purple.</u>

M:    Yes. Yes. It's, [it's powerful.
N:                          [I am black—I am *black*, I am *ugly*, *but*, I am *alive!*
M:    *Exactly.*
N:    *It is beautiful.*]

Professore demonstrated difficulty in broaching the subject of his thoughts on living in Italy. He asked me for clarification, effectively stalling. He then paused after saying, *vabbèh*,[29] allowing Ndiaga to interject. His hesitation signified an attempt to find the right words for what he wanted to say. It also granted Ndiaga the opportunity to steer the conversation toward race, a topic that allowed the two of them to construct together a racialized narrative in which they cut each other off, spoke over each other, and repeated each other, such as when Professore echoed Ndiaga's "Color Viola" with "Color Purple."

Ndiaga quoted a line from this iconic film where the abused and battered Celie responded to Albert's taunt: "I'm poor, black, I might even be ugly, but dear God, I'm here! I'm here!"[30] Although Ndiaga had seen the movie in Italian, he began the quote in French, the language currently spoken, yet he inserted Italian for the adjectives. He switched mid-utterance when correcting himself from "je suis noir" to "je suis *nero*." He then continued this pattern with *brutto* and *vivo*. It may be the case that the "I am" remained in French because after Wolof, French was the language in which he could best express himself, thus the language that most closely reflected his identity. Or it might be that he said the adjectives in Italian simply because he saw the movie in Italian or because those were the adjectives that he perceived Italians would use to describe him.

However, the exploration of the social motivations through metaphorical code-switching allows for a more compelling reading of what was happening.[31] Unlike situational code-switching, where the interlocutor or context drives the language choice, metaphorical code-switching conjures what Penelope Gardner-Chloros has called the metaphorical world of a language.[32] From an open-ended question such as "what are your thoughts about Italy?" Ndiaga directed the conversation toward the topic of race through his language choice. By switching to Italian for the operative words *nero*, *brutto*, and *vivo*, Ndiaga foregrounded his exclusion. There was a linguistic divide between his French-speaking identity "I am" and his Italian adjectives to which society had reduced him. In other words, the divide indicated his positionality as an outsider in his current social environment. Furthermore, by voicing a black female character in a story centered on gendered and racial strife, Ndiaga aligned himself with the marginalization that pervaded the film and the book. The quoted words evoked struggle as well as defiance in the face of this struggle, and the creative multilingual usage that Ndiaga employed further reinforced his racialized position as a black man in an Italian society that conceived itself as white. Paradoxically, he also signaled his stake in *italianità*: living in Italy and learning Italian opened the door to an Italian identity that he partially embodied by using Italian for the operative words.

For Ndiaga and Professore, one of the prerequisites for existing in an Italian space was the need to construct their blackness. While Ndiaga was quite straightforward with his racial theorization, Professore sometimes conveyed his racialized experience not through what he said but through what he did not say:[33]

> P:   En Afrique ça va être différent parce que là on ne parle pas
>       de, euh, *blacks*. Non. Tu as vu? Mais bon. Je sais que tu, tu dois
>       comprendre un peu ce que je suis en train de dire.
> M:   Oui. Bien sûr.
> P:   Voilà. Je ne veux pas trop rentrer dans les détails.
>
> [P:   In Africa that is going to be different because there one doesn't
>       talk about, uhh, *blacks*. No. Understand? But anyway I know that
>       you, you must understand a bit of what I am saying.
> M:   Yes. Of course.
> P:   There you go. I don't really want to go into detail.]

It is important to remember that while the questions in the interview guide did not specifically broach the topic of race unless prompted by the informant, it was discussed in the majority of the interviews. Professore's formulation of race was similar to what Ibrahim told of his own experiences of becoming black once he had moved to Canada because his social environment there signaled him as black.[34]

Also noteworthy is the fact that the European understanding of race and ethnicity with regard to Senegalese immigrants may vary greatly from the Senegalese perspective. A European might assign the classification of black or African or more specifically Senegalese. A Senegalese immigrant in Europe might also accept these very same terms in describing himself or herself. However, most of my Senegalese informants were also quick to distinguish their own ethnic differences from those of other Senegalese in the framework of the various multiethnic societies found all over the African continent. Being Wolof or Fulani or any of the other numerous ethnic groups was as important as being Senegalese, and often more important than being black until they arrived in majority white spaces.

Professore implied that he was constructed as black when he left Africa for Europe, and he has had difficulty accepting this heightened awareness of his black identity. He has arguably been affected by the social processes of racism based on the way he refused to discuss the matter in detail. Additionally, he chose to use "black" instead of *noir* after some hesitation. There are various possible reasons for why Professore used the English word to refer to blackness. For instance, talking about a racial feature in a foreign language can lessen the impact of the word.[35] Using descriptive terms concerning race in a foreign language serves to elude taboo words. In fact, twenty-seven-year-old Ajuma explained that this was a common phenomenon in France: "Ils disent, 'ah, tu es le seul *black*.' Ils ne peuvent pas utiliser le mot 'noir' parce que le mot 'noir' est tabou." (They say, "Ah, you are the only *black*." They can't use the word "black" because the word "black" is taboo.) By using a word borrowed from English, Professore could avoid the connotations attached to the French word.

Another possible explanation is that the use of the word "black" signals the African diaspora. In describing how young blacks have often embraced a racial identity forged from American models in response to being labeled as immigrants in France, Tyler Stovall contends that the English word "black" represents "both a certain investment in the concept of African diaspora, and a challenge to the French idea of the nation, color-blind in theory, racially coded in practice."[36] The manner in which Professore included me in the conversation gives credence to such conjecture. His body language indicated his implicit understanding of me, the interviewer, as a fellow black person. I did not pursue the subject because Professore preferred not to go into detail. Rather, he simply led me to believe that he assumed that because of who I was (an African American), I would understand. When I verified his assumption, his *voilà* ended the discussion: there was no need to say more. Thus, by including me directly in this discussion of race, he created the boundary of us versus them in which I become part of the "us." The racial identity that he assigned to me (and that I accepted) separated us from the identity that he has given to Italian people. Therefore, this decision to use "black" instead of *noir* allowed him to simultaneously distance himself from the connotations associated with the word in French, contest French republican discourse, make a connection between me and a black consciousness that emerged from the United States,[37] and convey an affinity to a global conceptualization of blackness. Similarly, the fact that Ndiaga quoted an African American novel through a movie showed the reach and importance of diasporic cultural production in articulating blackness throughout the world.[38]

While it is impossible to know all the specific incidents that shaped Professore's perception prior to our encounter, the data from other informants shed light on the types of racially charged experiences in Italy. For instance, Abi, a thirty-one-year-old dancer, has had a difficult time during her stay there. In a retelling of an experience, Abi's language use made manifest the us/them schism:[39]

> Moi, un jour, où j'ai prends le bus, et je rentre et je fais, j'ai le v̲i̲ quatre Italiens. Mais les enfants. Mais, elles m'ont fait quelque chose. Ça me mal jusqu'à aujourd'hui. Je ne pas oublier ça. . . . "Regarde le *nero*, là, là le *ner*::." Quand je parle au téléphone ils criaient "oua oua oua oua oua." J'obligeais de dire, je le dis "mais si te plaît." On dit "Ici c'est italien. C'est chez nous. Vous êtes des *ner*::." *Mamma mia*, ça me blesse. Ça me mal. Ça me mal.

> [Me, one day, where I have catch the bus and I return and I do, I have s̲a̲w̲ four Italians. But children. But they did something to me. That bad me until today. I no forget that. . . . "Look at the *black*, there, there the *black*::." When I speak on the phone, they yelled, "Wawawawawa." I obliged to say, I say him "but please." They say, "This is Italian. This is our home. You are *blacks*::." *Oh my*, that hurts me. That bad me. That bad me.]

Through the blatant signaling of her color, *nero*, the youths positioned her as the Other by highlighting her dark skin, a trait that contrasted with their view of Italian society. This word had a tremendous effect on Abi as it was the only content word in this excerpt that was in Italian. (I will treat *mamma mia* as a discourse marker separately.) *Nero* was directed at her in a discriminatory manner, and she, in turn, kept it in its original form. By revoicing it in Italian, Abi conveyed the original hatred behind the word and its effect on her. She also emphasized the word through repetition and through elongation of the *R* sound.[40] In choosing to voice a key word in Italian, Abi conveyed the word's power.

Judith Butler has explored the injurious nature of language: "To be called a name is one of the first forms of linguistic injury that one learns."[41] It is only fitting then that Abi would internalize this word with its specific connotation in Italian, even though she had limited command of the Italian language. While the word *nero*, in reference to a person, is not necessarily an insult in Italian, its connotation varies from a descriptive marker to a derogatory comment depending on context.[42] Judging from Abi's retelling, the use of *nero* in this case was highly offensive.

Abi was fully aware of this linguistic injury.[43] Her skin color was what separated her, excluded her, and it was this appellation that stayed etched in her mind, resurfacing in its Italian form in a discussion that was predominantly in

French. While the simple act of labeling by skin color was not necessarily injurious by itself, because people use skin color as an excuse to exclude others economically and socially, a simple word becomes injurious.

This episode harkens back to the experience of Fara, the protagonist in Ousmane Socé's novel *Mirages de Paris*, who left his village in Senegal to take part in the 1931 Colonial Exposition. In an incident on the Paris metro, a child points at Fara, drawing attention to his blackness as he remarks how Fara's hair looks like mustaches. He is then amazed when Fara's black skin does not rub off on him.[44] While this could be read as an innocent child encountering difference, several pages later, Socé underscores how this is just one episode in a series of debilitating othering in which Fara is exposed "aux plaisanteries grotesques des 'sans éducation,' aux quolibets des innocents bambins à qui les livres d'images, le cinéma et les récits fantasques enseignaient qu'un Noir était un guignol vivant" (to grotesque jokes of the "uneducated," to the jeers of innocent children whose picture books, movies, and fantastic tales taught them that black people were living puppets).[45]

While this literary example focuses on the physical features that enable othering, Abi's skin color was not the only part of her identity that the youths attacked. Upon hearing her speaking in Wolof, they imitated her with "wawawawawa" to the point that she could not concentrate on her phone call. They had reasoned that since Italy was their home, it was necessarily italophone. Those who taunted her were further positioning her as Other by drawing attention to her language. They created a boundary in which only those who spoke Italian could enter. Furthermore, as hurtful as the racial insult was, it was the linguistic insult that she enunciated as the more injurious act. The attack on her mother tongue and her continued lack of acceptance in Italian society wounded her. *Mamma mia* was an exclamation that several of the informants had picked up, and it was often used to express emotion. While Abi seldom employed Italian words throughout the interview, in this instant this phrase best described her injury. Abi felt like a linguistic and racial outsider in Italy and expressed this sentiment through different discourse strategies, painting a bleak and disheartening picture.

## New York City: Negotiating Blackness

### "Like all African Americans, of course": Becoming Black in White Spaces

Diop met me right outside one of the Senegalese restaurants in Harlem. Noting it would be quieter at his home, he asked if I would accompany him a half block down the street to where he lived. Upon entering his apartment, spacious by Manhattan standards, he offered me a seat in his living room and set a Coke on the table in front of me. His wife stopped in briefly to greet me but quickly retreated to the bedroom. As a journalist, Diop reached a primarily Senegalese audience through newspaper and radio. He noted that he had his finger on the pulse of the Senegalese community both locally and globally. As I asked him about his experiences as a multilingual speaker, this question about language morphed into a discussion about race:

> M:   Do you ever feel you've ever been treated differently the way you speak English?
>
> D:   Based on the race? Oh yes. Like all African Americans, of course. Based on the race, YES. Not based on my nationality . . . that's what's interesting with the U.S. When you are new here you don't even realize much of it, because you are not just used to it, being treated any which way because of your skin. . . . Because of where you come from the goods are black, the bads are black, the poors are black, the rich are black, the beautifuls are black, the uglies are black, so you don't think of your skin color unless you spend time here. . . . But while you live here for years you realize not only you're living it yourself, but your friends, African Americans and other minorities, are telling you about their experiences. You become aware of that.

It is significant that Diop took no time in directing an open-ended question about language toward race, demonstrating the centrality of race in these types of discussions. Furthermore, he portrayed a shared experience in a matter-of-fact way in the line "Like all African Americans of course," which suggested that it was unsurprising that blacks would face discrimination or judgment. Referring to himself as African American, he erased the cleavages often depicted between Africans and African Americans. Mirroring discussions of blackness in Paris and Rome as well as illustrating Ibrahim's racialized articulation of the social imaginary, Diop acknowledged how coming to a non-black-majority setting triggered an increased awareness of blackness.[46] His own experiences and learning about the experiences of others had led Diop to understand blackness and his own racial formation.

Interviewees encountered their blackness in various ways. For instance, when I asked Fatoumata, a thirty-one-year-old native of Dakar who has spent almost half her life in the United States, if she had ever been treated differently based on any reason other than language, she responded, "Yeah, I've been followed around in stores. [*laughs*] So yeah." When I asked why this was the case, she reasoned, "Because, um, I'm [*pauses*] black. Yeah. Not looking like they want me to look." Fatoumata's laugh appeared to be an uncomfortable one, one that I read as a defense mechanism to avoid being weighed down by the negative experience. This discomfort continued when she paused before describing herself as black, understanding that her blackness was undesirable in this situation.

However, while there were examples of institutional racism in commercial and corporate spaces as well as hurtful, racist incidents involving white people, what set the New York City data apart from the other two sites was the limited interaction that most of my informants had with members of the white community. When I asked Mariama who her friends were and the types of people with whom she interacted on a daily basis, she went through different racial and ethnic groups. Concerning whites, she remarked: "With Anglo-Americans, I don't really have that much experience. Maybe just corporate. And in that instance I always felt like I had to protect myself. I always felt like they always had an air of superiority. Or maybe I gave them that air of superiority." Interaction with white America was primarily relegated to the corporate work environment, and even then she would keep her distance because of a perceived superiority complex. By her own admission, she was unsure whether this "air of superiority" she attributed to her white colleagues was imagined or real. Regardless, there was a distance between her and her colleagues tied to notions of hierarchy. Mariama also discussed friendships with white Americans: "Um, never really felt comfortable but I had friends that were white. But I always felt like I would always be different. I could never get comfortable that our friendship was secure." Her discomfort regarding difference made it hard for her to have a true friendship, evident in the insecurity she displayed.

Julien also related his interactions with different communities:

> J:   White Americans, I don't have a lot of contact with them because I don't know most of them, living in Washington Heights. Most of the neighborhood is Spanish or black. That's why I don't have. Sometimes at the workplace, but at the workplace you got to be professional and that's it.
>
> M:   Do you have any white friends?
>
> J:   White friends? Just one. But he's from Russia. He's not from here.

Indeed, most of the people interviewed lived primarily in neighborhoods of color and did not have regular interactions with whites. When they did, these people tended to be recent immigrants with whom they could connect through the shared immigrant experience. Even those who were studying in higher education settings indicated this divide. For instance, when I asked thirty-three-year-old Ablaye, who had spent thirteen years in the United States, where the majority of his friends were from, he replied:

A:   I would say 90 percent are immigrants. But other friends will be like in school.
M:   Why do you think 90 percent of your friends have an immigrant background?
A:   I think the type of schools that I go to. . . . If I went to Columbia instead of going to City College.

I expected socioeconomic and racial backgrounds to influence the access that some of my informants had to certain settings; however, even the people in my study who were in college, which is traditionally a predominantly white space, had limited access to white-majority environments, thus highlighting the pervasive, racially segregated reality of America. Almost across the board, when I asked interviewees who their friends were or who were the people with whom they interacted most, the response was first and foremost other Senegalese, followed by other immigrant communities, followed by communities of color in general, which mainly include African American and Latinx populations. However, while many of them discussed limited access to white communities, there was still a robust exploration of blackness in the data. And just as in Paris and Rome, linguistic identity was a crucial marker in the formulation of blackness. The following section focuses on the nuances of blackness and how ideas of blackness are constantly being rearticulated through language and other identity markers, even in black-majority settings.

### "It doesn't make you black; it makes you African": Exploring Africanness in Black America

It was a hot day in the middle of July as the young women brought out plastic folding tables and chairs from the Brooklyn brownstone where Madina's mother lived and set them up on the sidewalk of a quiet tree-lined street only a block off a very noisy Flatbush Avenue. Madina, continuing her fund-raising efforts, had recruited help from her friends and fellow members of the non-profit she had founded. She hoped that this effort, along with the event at the Senegalese Community Center in Harlem, would raise enough money to send all the Senegalese American youth participants to Senegal that summer.[47] As they gingerly unfolded batik blankets and laid them on the table, a spattering of jewelry emerged. The women had gotten their mothers to donate any jewelry they could spare. Ndiaye displayed traditional Senegalese *boubous* along the

fence, as another member of Madina's nonprofit, Diallo, tended to her preco-
cious younger brother, who was befriending everyone who walked by. For seven
hours, I interviewed the different members, all women in their early to mid-
twenties, all Senegalese Americans who impressed on me the need for them
to know their roots and to give others around them that opportunity as well.
As night fell, they asked me to join them for a meal of scrambled eggs, turkey
sausage, brie, and French bread. It was Ramadan, and since I was so wrapped
up in their fascinating and co-constructed narratives of growing up between
two worlds, I only then realized that I had inadvertently fasted all day with
them. As we waited for our meal, each woman shared her food wish list: if she
could break her fast with anything, what would it be? Obi, a Nigerian American
friend helping with the fund-raiser, chimed in: "You're not an official African
American until you know deviled eggs and mac and cheese." We all licked our
lips in agreement and anticipation.

This notion of an "official African American" resonated in many conversations among members of the Senegalese community in New York. The interaction that many in my study had with black communities in New York City led
to interesting formulations about race and blackness that entailed a continuous
construction and reconstruction of a hyphenated identity. Here, being African
but not necessarily black in the American context complicated notions of what
blackness is. Because of a different history, cultural norms, and language use,
many of my informants were unable to fit into the established black community
in New York City and even remarked how that community sometimes called
into question their blackness.

While there have been many documented cases of antagonism between
Africans and African Americans,[48] this othering still came as a shock to many
of the informants who imagined, perhaps naïvely, that African Americans would
welcome them with open arms due to a sense of diasporic connection. For instance, when I asked Julien about his thoughts on living in the United States,
his first response was one of disappointment:

M:   What disappointed you the most?
J:   Uh, first time the black people.
M:   How so?
J:   Because I was thinking that they loved African people. Africa,
     too. But sometimes I see they don't. They don't, some of them,
     don't love and they treat us like monkeys. Things like that. That
     disappoints me.
M:   So what have people said to you?
J:   Something like, "Monkey-ass, go back home."

Julien expected a common bond held together by notions of a black diaspora but encountered competing images that nullified any racial similarities.[49] There was an obvious equating of Africans to animals, unsurprising when one thinks about the images with which Western media bombard us. When the focus is not on hunger, disease, and poverty, the images are of safaris, often the only "positive" takeaway about Africa. Even Disney's sole animated film to take place in sub-Saharan Africa, *The Lion King*, uses only animals as characters.[50] Animalia as insult was a common theme among my informants' discussions of interactions with the black community.

Meanwhile, Idrissa ruminated on the often-strained diasporic link between Africans and African Americans after relaying a negative interaction he had with a friend:

> And the other thing is the fact that they reject us. . . . One day we were joking and one black American said to my friend, "You monkey-ass, you got to go back home." "How can you call this guy a monkey-ass? . . . He's black, you're black. The only difference is that they bring you here and impose you to live here. But your roots are in Africa. You don't belong to this country. That's why they call you African American. They use two pejorative words. African, American. You can't be two at the same time. You just can be one." . . . That's what Du Bois was trying to say about double consciousness, when you are between the two. You are trying to go one way, these people are saying, "No you don't belong to this place. You have to go back." And you try to go back and people are saying, "No, you are not from here." And you are in the middle. You can't be with this one, and you can't be with that one.

While Idrissa acknowledged that this hurtful comment was made in a joking context, the way he related the story showed that the joke fell flat. He could not fathom why someone of African descent would speak about being African in a derogatory manner. He signaled the struggle of African Americans, who, according to W. E. B. Du Bois, wrestle with two warring selves, the African self and the American self, neither of which truly belongs anywhere.[51]

It is important to reflect on the knowledge production of many of the people I interviewed throughout the three sites. Many consciously theorized their own positions in their immediate communities and society at large by building on a large body of academic and literary/filmic work. Idrissa, who was well versed in Du Bois, used this knowledge to shed light on why some African Americans champion this sort of negative rhetoric concerning Africanness. Similarly to Ndiaga, whose evocation of *The Color Purple* relied on a rich cultural production to make sense of the world, Idrissa indicated how the ideas of an African American at the turn of the twentieth century provided explanations for his experiences as an African immigrant in the American context in the twenty-first.

Their relegation to the margins was in part because of the immigrant stigma. Their classed identity as immigrant signaled their otherness even when other identity markers such as race/skin color should create some sort of in-group connection. As Julien succinctly put it, "They see you like African, like immigrant." Mariama illustrated the difficulties of the immigrant label when she recounted her struggles growing up in America and being marked as other:

> I would hate to believe that people can be racist against their own people but it was definitely that. And it kind of baffles me because the same people who were saying these things look just like me. I mean, same skin color. I mean almost to a T. . . . They knew I was West African. You know. They knew that my name wasn't common. Maybe I had an accent. I can't remember if I did but I probably did. Um, yeah. They just knew. You're different, you know. It doesn't make you black. It makes you African. Therefore, I guess they feel validated in making fun of me. Though I look just like them.

The way she conveyed the experience suggests that those who excluded her did not see her as black, complicating simple definitions of racism. Judging by the way she structured her anecdote, namely, leading with the topic of skin color, Mariama appeared to expect this outward trait to be the main criterion for access to blackness and ultimately to acceptance. However, Mariama's blackness was being read not in those particular racialized terms among her black peers but through other forms of difference related to language, accent, and geography—identity traits that marked her specifically as foreign and that set her apart from her classmates. In this case, African and black were mutually exclusive identities in which African embodied the out-group, relegated to the margins.[52]

Because of this rejection, Mariama decided to seek acceptance elsewhere. She became friends with a Puerto Rican girl with whom she had a shared immigrant experience and felt a connection:

> And um, so my, me being close to that community made me feel like I was a part of them and that I could possibly begin to look like them. So, I began to self-hate and wish I was lighter and straighten my hair and try to move away from my African culture. Telling people I was half Puerto Rican. Trying to learn the language, eating the foods. And

> I really wasn't supposed to eat the foods because I was Muslim. But anything just to be a part. Anything just to be a part. Because I felt more accepted. And maybe I wanted to be more accepted because they had lighter skin. And the things I was being beat up about, they were the opposite.

Again, in this racialized exploration of identity, skin color occupied an important position in her theorization of belonging. She recognized the correlation between acceptance and lighter skin, coming face-to-face with the phenomenon of colorism, the product of centuries of identity formation in which lighter skin and more European-looking features have often translated into actual societal benefits.[53]

In fact, several of the people I interviewed, especially the young women, shared experiences of dealing with colorism, where the black community often perpetuated negative critiques of blackness. For instance, twenty-five-year-old Sonia related her childhood experience: "It could be really difficult growing up, especially in Brooklyn, where people judge you. A lot of times you hear, 'You're black and ugly.' . . . So knowing your actual heritage and culture drives you to allow how to deal with these situations." For her, "black" was synonymous with "ugly." Diallo told of a similar experience: "I hated my skin tone. I hated being dark. Like it got to a point I wouldn't even tell people I was African if they didn't ask me. I was skeptical to tell people, 'Yeah, I'm African.' Now, psshh, that's the first thing I say." Surprisingly, while much research has been done on the use of skin lighteners to obtain this symbolic capital, none of my informants mentioned using such products.[54]

However, Mariama employed other tactics to gain acceptance in a context that stigmatized blackness. As a child, Mariama spent most of her energy embracing the culture and the identity markers of her friend. In order to convince people of an invented Puerto Rican heritage, she eschewed her own cultural and religious norms, such as when she, a Muslim, began to eat pork for a while. In much the same way that some African immigrants go beyond national citizenship or linguistic commonalities to create connections with other diasporic structures, Mariama's desire to learn Spanish and connect with the Puerto Rican community in New York City indicated her recognition of the cultural cachet that language embodied in her attempts to learn Spanish.[55] What is particularly fascinating is that even though Spanish, in the U.S. context, is often a stigmatized language associated with immigrants, it commanded more respect than her native language of Wolof during her childhood. This hierarchy could be because Wolof is squarely an African language whereas Spanish is a colonial language whose speakers represent a wide range of ethnic, racial, and geographic identities.

Madina's experience further complicates the relationship between language and belonging and also blurs the lines between immigrant and nonimmigrant, African and African American. Similarly to Mariama, Madina expressed her shock that people who looked like her physically, most notably through skin color, were labeling her as Other. However, Madina noted that those perpetuating this otherness could even be other Africans: "Growing up, it was difficult. I was often called an African booty-scratcher. I was, and it's from people who look just like me. That are from the West Indies; that are within the African diaspora. West Indians, Africans, even Africans would call me booty-scratcher. . . . I guess, you know, they don't identify with who they really are. And I think with children, children can be really cruel. And ignorant at the same time."

Madina recognized an element of communal self-loathing that enabled these people to insult her with derogatory remarks. Denial permitted people who looked like her to not see themselves in the way she saw them. She chalked it up to ignorance. However, her brother Samba understood the situation differently. Highlighting the distinction between anglophone and francophone communities within the African diaspora, he remarked, "The whole time she was here she had difficulties because the children would fight her. They called her African booty-scratcher because she spoke French and other languages." He recognized that her difference derived from her linguistic repertoire. Remarkably, it was her ability to speak French that signified not only difference but Africanness. While prestige is often attached to the French language, this francophone ability coincided with negatively read identity markers, which, in turn, further alienated her. In other words, even people from the West Indies and anglophone Africa, regardless of their citizenship status, were able to position themselves in the in-group because of their English-speaking backgrounds at the expense of French-speaking Africans such as Madina.[56] Unlike the experience Ndiaye recounted in chapter 1 where speaking an English-inflected Wolof incited disdain from the older generation of Senegalese in New York, in Madina's case, it was French that created problems because of its position on the lower end of a colonial language hierarchy. The ways in which different languages are read rely on the context in which they are spoken and the associations that people make with these languages.[57]

## Concluding Thoughts

This chapter has explored the link between racial and linguistic identities and what these identities meant with regard to the people in my study claiming legitimacy and the right to belong in specific geographic contexts. While experiences in each site were fraught with the tensions and often pain of colonial histories as well as linguistic and racial differentiation, these legacies manifested themselves differently depending on the place. Racialized incidents happened in all three sites; however, the effects in Paris and New York were more likely to be enhanced by expectations rooted in historically situated cultural perceptions about language and race.

Upon moving to Rome, many informants were forced to come to terms with identity aspects that had been dormant in Senegal, such as citizenship status and blackness. For instance, in Senegal, a place where ethnic differentiation was important, race was more an abstract concept, not necessarily something dealt with in day-to-day experiences. In Rome, blackness was more central to their identity, and the ways in which interviewees used language conveyed the centrality of blackness in their everyday experiences. In choosing between *noir*, *nero*, and "black," some informants demonstrated how code-switching was a tool to both underscore and minimize feelings of exclusion. Other informants, such as Abi, emphasized the relationship between racial and linguistic exclusion, as seen in her account of the episode on the bus when the children taunted her simultaneously for her skin color and her language use. She was othered for being both a linguistic and a racial outsider. However, as the works of Khouma show, even if a black person is fluent in Italian and has Italian citizenship, his or her claim on *italianità* is tenuous because blackness inherently excludes Italianness.

In Paris, the othering that interviewees experienced seemed more problematic than in Rome because of their greater expectation and desire to be regarded as full-fledged members of society due to overlapping cultural and linguistic histories between Senegal and France. Informants often emphasized claiming the right to speak.[58] Many of them saw linguistic competence as a means of accessing social mobility, buying into the rhetoric in France that foregrounded the link between linguistic assimilation and acceptance. They believed that if they could just prove French linguistic competence, they would be accepted by the larger society. However, linguistic competence was often determined by more than just one's ability to use a language well; one's linguistic competence depended on the ability to prove cultural legitimacy, which extended beyond language to include other identity markers, most notably race. Even when they wore a white mask in the Fanonian sense (i.e., became whiter by mastering the French language), the mask was nothing more than a mask. People in my study lamented that to the *Français de souche*, they were never anything other than black. Furthermore, the inability to talk about race and process the effects of racial marginalization intensified the negative lived experience of race. In other words, the ways in which French discourse stressed linguistic assimilation while silencing discussions on racial differentiation offered nothing more than false hope of actual cultural assimilation. Language, in fact, could not transcend blackness.

Meanwhile, the New York City excerpts problematized the definition of blackness, even in situations where those who identified as black were in the majority. While informants in New York encountered a setting where discussions about race were often front and center because of the primacy of race in American political discourse, for many of them the bigger issue was the way black Americans sometimes othered them more than white Americans did. This othering took the form of linguistic differentiation: the languages they spoke marked them as foreign. The trauma that these informants suffered and the confusion they experienced when people who shared seemingly similar racial traits hurled racialized insults illustrated the messiness attached to understandings of the diaspora. Although for some of them, understandings of the diaspora afforded solidarities, these solidarities were negotiated through context-specific relationships of power. Not only did speaking an African language such as Wolof create distance, but even the ability to speak French, a globally prestigious language, could mark someone as Other and therefore unworthy of belonging. While in Paris many informants expected acceptance through a shared language, in New York this expectation was attached to a shared racial formation. In this case, blackness could not transcend language. Understanding marginalization related to linguistic repertoire is a particularly compelling way of thinking about notions of racial formation in diaspora studies. The following chapter delves more deeply into language and blackness by focusing more intently on the concepts of integration, immigration, and global mobility.

# 3

## NEITHER HERE NOR THERE

## Reflections on National and Transnational Belonging

I met Karafa near the end of my time in Paris. As I sat on the terrace of a bistro in the Fourteenth Arrondissement, he walked up to me. Satisfied that my appearance matched my description in the text message I had sent him, he put his phone in his pocket and introduced himself. I invited him to sit down and ordered a coffee for him. Fifty-something-year-old Karafa (who declined to tell me his exact age) had an imposing presence. He was easily over six feet tall, had a baritone voice that was powerful but not loud, and exuded a defiance-tinged wisdom. During our discussion, he built his arguments on a mountain of evidence such as when he enumerated the reasons for his displeasure with the role of the French language (as we saw in chapter 1 when he described the dominant, imposing, and destructive nature of French). He was also very critical of his thirty-five years of experiences living in France.

Karafa arrived in France to study accounting after graduating high school. As he talked about his career as an accountant, his citizenship status came out: "Je ne suis pas français. Je suis immigré et les immigrés se trouvent dans des situations assez difficiles dans ce pays. Quand il y a une récession, ceux qui sont touchés d'abord sont les immigrés. J'étais un peu victime de ça" (I am not French. I am an immigrant, and immigrants find themselves in difficult situations in this country. When there is a recession, immigrants are affected first. I was somewhat a victim of that). Karafa discussed his employment instability because of his status as an immigrant. Considering his job insecurity, I asked him why he did not apply for citizenship since as a long-term permanent resident from a former colony, he could probably become a citizen relatively easily. With a defiant tone, he remarked that he had never applied for French citizenship because he liked his skin color:

> K:   Non et je n'ai jamais demandé non plus.
> M:   Vous ne pouvez pas ou vous ne voulez pas?
> K:   Je ne veux pas parce que moi j'aime bien la couleur de ma peau.
>
> [K:   No and I never sought it either.
> M:   You can't or you don't want to?
> K:   I don't want to because I like the color of my skin.]

His principles, which were rooted in his identity formation, overrode the practical considerations for applying for citizenship. His reasoning suggested that being French and being black were mutually exclusive; he was perpetuating a racial restriction on Frenchness, using skin color as the main criterion. People such as Karafa, who have been positioned as outsiders, have in turn internalized this positioning. Exclusion was thus a two-way street where race pervaded notions of nationality and citizenship. Karafa, who was a permanent resident but also a Senegalese citizen, had the luxury of refusing French citizenship and/or identity on the basis of skin color. But for those people born in France who knew no other home, a sense of nationality or belonging was even more problematic.

Karafa's stance was still fresh in my mind when I interviewed Lucie the following day. Lucie had just shared the story of the mother in the parent-teacher conference who had berated her for a mistake she made while speaking. For Lucie, the feeling of belonging was contingent on skin color, advancing the argument that language could never be the main factor in proving nationality or in feeling a sense of belonging even if national discourses on integration said otherwise. She expressed resentment or sadness that the *Français de souche* would never see her as being French or as a legitimate French speaker:

> L:   Moi, je vais te dire que pendant toute mon adolescence, je ne
>       me sentais pas française, pas forcément. Les gens me disaient que
>       j'étais sénégalaise. Même pas sénégalaise, africaine. Je suis noire,
>       donc je suis africaine. Je ne peux pas être noire et française. C'est

trop surréaliste. Notre président Sarkozy, quand il est né, son père était encore hongrois. Moi, je suis née de parenté française mais ce que je trouve extraordinaire, lui, il est blanc. Moi, je suis noire.

M: Comment est-ce que tu te sens?

L: Je me sentais rejetée, quoi. Tout le monde me disait que je suis étrangère, donc je le sentais. Mais moi, je ne connaissais pas le Sénégal. Je ne suis pas comme les gens qui se sentent algériens, sénégalais, parce qu'ils ont l'habitude de visiter ces pays. Moi, non. Donc j'étais entre les deux. . . . C'est quand j'allais au Sénégal qu'ils me disaient que je suis française. J'ai un passeport français, je vis en France, je ne parle pas de langues sénégalaises.

[L: Throughout my teenage years, I did not feel French, not really. People told me that I was Senegalese. Not even Senegalese, African. I'm black, so I'm African. I cannot be black and French. It's too surreal. Our president Sarkozy, when he was born, his father was still Hungarian. I am born of French parentage, but what I find extraordinary, he is white. I am black.

M: How do you feel?

L: I felt rejected, you know. Everyone would tell me that I am a foreigner so I felt it. But I did not know Senegal. I am not like people who feel Algerian, or Senegalese, because they are used to visiting these countries. I am not. So I was in between the two. . . . It was when I went to Senegal that they told me I'm French. I have a French passport, I live in France, I do not speak any of the languages of Senegal.]

She brought up the case of then-president Sarkozy to highlight the place that race had in the discussion and conceptualization of nationality. Sarkozy was mentioned a significant number of times in the interviews, with most people finding it unjust that the nationality of someone of Hungarian descent went unquestioned, while someone of Senegalese descent was never acknowledged as French. Lucie's commentary elucidated the particularly difficult and frustrating position that she and others like her occupied. She realized that the identity she tried to appropriate, that of a Senegalese person, was also beyond her reach because her experiences were different from theirs. Lucie's predicament was common for many French of Senegalese origin. She had grown up in the French educational system, an institution that supposedly taught French citizens how to be French. She was even a teacher herself. She spoke what she considered standard French. For all intents and purposes, she was integrated into French society, having done what was expected of her as a French citizen; yet, she did not feel French. People in France did not assume she was French. Instead, people questioned her Frenchness. She was simply African to them.

The experiences of Karafa and Lucie show how the intersection of citizenship status, sociolinguistic legitimacy, and understandings of blackness at a personal and societal level are all part of the complementary and competing factors that contribute to dynamic identity formation. People in all three sites wrestle with societal expectations concerning integration as well as with their positioning in global Senegality. In continuing the discussions from chapter 2, this chapter will thus foreground understandings of belonging on multiple levels by exploring what it means to be a resident in Paris, Rome, or New York, how people I interviewed conceive of the immigrant label, what other identity markers come to the fore, and how identifying as Senegalese influences their interactions with their local environment, with Senegal, and with the Senegalese diaspora.

## INTEGRATION AND A SPACE FOR DIFFERENCE

### "Tu es de quelle origine?"
### Using Code Words to Mark Difference in Paris

I met Faatu at a café in the heart of La Défense near where she worked. This central business district was studded with skyscrapers that contrasted starkly with the low-rise buildings typical of most of the Parisian landscape. In a strange way, these skyscrapers almost mimicked the *banlieue* landscape even though these two landscapes symbolized wholly contrasting sectors of society. We were seated near a window that opened onto the Grande Arche. Faatu agreed to be interviewed during her lunch break. She was wearing a black suit with a fitted white top and stylish shoes. Her braids were so thin they looked like strands of hair, which she pulled back tightly in a ponytail. Her style fit in well with the café's clientele.

She was very forthcoming throughout the interview; therefore, I was surprised with her change in voice and body language when she critiqued the French educational system's handling of the topics of colonization and slavery.

> F: Les Français ont exploité beaucoup de pays d'Afrique. Ils ont volé beaucoup de richesse. L'histoire de l'Afrique est très forte.
>
> M: Dans le système éducatif en France, est-ce qu'on parle du colonis—
>
> F: Non, justement. Dans nos cours, ce qui manque, on ne parle pas de l'histoire de l'esclavage.
>
> M: Non?
>
> F: Non! On ne parle pas de ça en France.

[F:   The French exploited many African countries. They stole a lot of
       wealth. The history of Africa is very strong.
M:   In the education system in France, do they talk about coloniz—
F:    No, actually. In our courses, what's missing, we do not speak of
       the history of slavery.
M:   No?
F:    No! We do not talk about it in France.]

When I asked why she thought it was so hard to talk about colonization and slavery, she looked around, lowered her voice so that it was barely audible, and confided that in her mind, it was out of guilt. While she did not use the word "race," she explained that the way France categorized *maghrébins* or *africains subsahariens* was similar to racial discourse. It was race by another name.[1] Through whispers, Faatu was performing language strategically to convey the silencing power of academic and national discourse regarding France's inability or unwillingness to come to terms with its violent past.[2]

    France participates in what Gloria Wekker dubs "white innocence" through a systematic denial of its colonial past and its position in a postcolonial present,[3] a phenomenon most clearly articulated in recent controversies involving the commemoration of France's involvement in the transatlantic slave trade. On the one hand, Christiane Taubira's 2001 legislation marking slavery and the slave trade as crimes against humanity and the 2005 report by the Comité pour la mémoire de l'esclavage (Committee for the Memory of Slavery) directed by Maryse Condé, which led to an annual commemoration on May 10 (beginning in 2006), represent steps in the right direction with regard to acknowledging France's traumatizing and racialized past. On the other hand, public outcry against these advances and a lack of public spaces such as museums and memorials to process this legacy show that reconciliation has a long way to go.[4] Furthermore, in a place where the state curriculum minimizes the French colonial project, where racial statistics are illegal because of the guilt stemming from the Vichy government's collaboration with Nazi Germany during World War II, and where "true" French identity myopically evolves from Gallic ancestors instead of from centuries of migration into and out of France, French discourse articulates French civilization as synonymous with whiteness.[5] This omission of the past connects to the omission of the present whereby people of color are erased through colorblindness. Faatu's whispers mirror Ajuma's argument about race in France as taboo or Professore opting to substitute "black" for *noir* to avoid committing a sociolinguistic transgression.[6] In this crowded café surrounded by white French people, Faatu did not want anyone to hear her, suggesting that even though in theory everyone was the same, people actually marked her as different.[7] In a similar vein, French discourse avoids talking about race, seeing it as antithetic to the assimilation of a French identity, all the while ignoring the fact that the nation-state's emphasis on a singular French identity presupposes a white identity.

According to Faatu, the French saw her as an immigrant above anything else: "C'est pas comment [les Français] nous classent mais comment ils nous perçoivent, c'est comme si nous étions des immigrés. Ils parlent d'intégration mais l'intégration n'est pas totale." (It's not how the French classify us but how they perceive us, it's like we are immigrants. They speak of integration but integration is not complete.) In other words, the immigrant is positioned in relation to and against the black subject.[8] The repetition of positive self- and negative Other-images in French discourse reinforces stereotypes that cause people to associate societal problems with the non-white Other.[9] Faatu was stuck in a system where she, a Frenchwoman of Senegalese descent, would never fully integrate in France no matter how educated she was or how professional she dressed or, as Lucie and Jean-Paul showed, how well she spoke.[10] As a result, societal discourse provides codes of critique that simultaneously widen the material/cultural reality of belonging while racializing this belonging.

While Faatu hinted that it was her skin color that impeded her from full acceptance into the society in which she was born, others considered religious identity and its effect on integration. For instance, Sébastien argued that the accepted mode of integration in France was assimilation and that people such as himself could not really be assimilated because of religious beliefs:

> Je suis croyant musulman et quand les gens l'apprennent, ils disent "mais je ne savais pas que tu étais encore aussi proche de ta culture d'origine." . . . Je trouve ça drôle, en fait ça me rappelle le modèle d'intégration française et le modèle d'assimilation. . . . Je pense que c'est à l'échec parce que je ne peux jamais assimiler la couleur de peau. Pourquoi les immigrés italiens, polonais, espagnols peuvent être intégrés à la population? C'est parce qu'ils sont tellement assimilables. C'est-à-dire, tu peux franciser ton nom mais tu ne peux pas devenir blanc.

> [I am a practicing Muslim and when people learn that they say, "But I did not know you were still so close to your home culture." . . . I find it funny. Actually it reminds me of the French integration and assimilation model. . . . I think it is failing because I can never assimilate my skin

color. Why can Italian, Polish, Spanish immigrants integrate into the population? It's because they can be assimilated. That is to say, you can Frenchify your name but you cannot become white.]

One can deconstruct this excerpt in terms of how the *Français de souche* viewed him ambiguously. In many ways, this corresponds with Junaid Rana's and Stanley Thangaraj's theorization of how racial exclusion involves various adjudications of culture, phenotype, religion, and science in the production of the Other. Race, as such, emerges not through a single register of the body but through the various discourses and epistemologies that already shape the body.[11] Therefore, the (raced) body as perceived by others is never simply seen but is always perceived through a series of overlapping factors that more or less predetermine how it will be viewed. Sébastien grew up speaking French as his mother tongue in Senegal, and he talked about how people in France would always remark on his lack of accent or other linguistic features that distinguished him as a foreigner (although the fact that people would remark on his language use in the first place indicated the Fanonian expectation of linguistic inferiority tied to blackness). However, when people would learn he was a practicing Muslim, he did not fit into their notion of a Catholic or secular French citizen. Importantly, his religious status seemed less important than his skin color in his assimilation based on the way that he moved effortlessly from talking about religion to skin color. He had much more to say about skin color arguably because it was more a factor in his day-to-day life. It was not obvious that he was Muslim. It was obvious that he was black.[12]

Jean-Paul also reflected on his racial and religious identity and how these markers played into his positioning in society: "It's known that most of the people with a foreign background, and as I say, what I was saying earlier, if you were white and Christian, after one generation you can be seen as a French. . . . Being black and Catholic doesn't change. I know because I'm Catholic. It's not an 'or,' it's an 'and.'" According to many of my informants, if one were to truly assimilate, one would have to completely fit into a normative model of a French person that was linguistically and corporeally indexed as white, male, Christian, and middle class (similar to Audre Lorde's description of the "mythical norm").[13] Unfortunately for those people who want to be accepted in their adopted country, there is no way to successfully imitate this model because people cannot transform skin color and most people do not want to give up religious beliefs and customs. Exclusion thus works through various registers of race, thereby making the ground of belonging always shaky, unpredictable, and treacherous for blacks in France, regardless of their religious affiliation.[14]

These examples depict the multiple ways that everyday discourse communicates an in-group/out-group dichotomy.[15] The use of the designation *d'origine* is yet another way of calling attention to this dichotomy. Nyambi, the restaurateur, conveyed the following experience: "Quand ils parlent des étrangers ils disent tu es d'origine. Ça n'est pas bon. Tu es d'origine sénégalaise ou algérienne ou gabonaise. Il faut qu'ils arrêtent ça. Si tu es français, tu es français. Et ça on dit toujours à la télé. Quand quelqu'un est champion, il est français; quand il a des problèmes, il est d'origine, quoi." (When they speak of foreigners they add the ancestry. That's not good. You are of Senegalese or Gabonese or Algerian descent. They have to stop that. If you are French, you're French. And it is always said on TV. When someone is a champion, he is French; when he has problems, he is of some foreign ancestry.)

Nyambi demonstrated how the label could mark inclusion or exclusion and how the line between the two was fluid and unstable. The nation was happy to include a person if he or she was valuable in some way. If someone was depicted in a negative light, that person was labeled as *d'origine*. This use of language emphasized the ways in which success is highlighted when talking about Frenchness while, on the flip side of the coin, failure marks someone as an immigrant. This phenomenon was particularly evident when comparing the media treatment of the French football teams in 1998 and 2010. When the team won the World Cup in 1998, *France multiculturelle* was celebrated.[16] However, when it lost in the first round of 2010, disgraced and embattled, the multicultural team was demonized for not extolling French values and for not representing France as it should have. The nation questioned its national identity. Discussions about the riots in the *banlieues* throughout the past decade resurfaced, drawing connections between the infighting on the team and the civil unrest by marginalized sectors of the population. "Tu es de quelle origine?" (What is your origin?) is code for "your presence is problematic." And when something such as skin color automatically evokes questions of origin, the "best" French or proof of citizenship is not enough to achieve legitimacy.

Importantly, the positionality of the person who uses the term *d'origine* matters. Faatu proudly identified as "française d'origine africaine, sénégalaise, casamançaise" (French of African origin, Senegalese, from the Casamance region) in much the same way that one would use African American or Black British—as a way to claim some type of identity since she felt that society denied her French identity. And yet for many *Français de souche*, minimizing the French identity is unconscionable. In addition, most often the question of *de quelle origine* does not come from some genuine desire to understand all the markers that contribute to a person's identity. Racial and religious minorities are caught in a catch-22 where the same people who inquire about their countries of origin are the same people who admonish minorities for taking pride in their differences. It is as if using this phrase in its interrogative form as an attempt to categorize the Other is acceptable (e.g., a *Français de souche* asking a person of color "tu es de quelle origine?") but using the phrase as a declarative in order to stake an identity claim is perceived as communitarianism (e.g., "Je suis français noir" [I am black French] or "Je suis français d'origine sénégalaise" [I am French of Senegalese descent]). In other words, only those in positions of power and privilege can use the phrase *de quelle origine*. In declaring a hybrid identity that goes against the homogenizing nature of national discourse, people such as Faatu are challenging the status quo and the power structure that it implies.

With the phrase *de quelle origine* essentially underlining various forms of difference, one wonders about the effectiveness of a colorblind model of society. Since *de quelle origine* in the interrogative sense is almost always asked of people who identify or are identified as nonwhite, it is obvious the being "real" French implies whiteness. Curiously, Senegalese who migrate to France often find themselves lumped into preexisting West African communities that are race based, as opposed to nationality based, dispelling the myth that the French do not conceive of race. In other words, just as Lucie noted that people in France called her not Senegalese but African (*même pas sénégalaise, africaine*), "black African" is a more salient category to white France than Senegalese versus Gabonese, for example. As stated earlier, terms such as *maghrébin* or *africain subsaharien* convey racial connotations that efface the nuances found in each national heritage environment. As for people who are French citizens of Senegalese descent, the *d'origine* moniker follows them wherever they go. Regardless of the lack of racial statistics in France, the race of racialized beings is still flagged on a daily basis. In fact, many informants considered race more problematic in France than in the other sites precisely because of how France conceptualizes race as a nonentity. It was this expectation of equality and the realization of its illusory nature that made a colorblind model sting more than a model where race had a central position in the national discourse.

## "È il mio sogno": Complicating Integration in Rome

I entered a well-maintained courtyard off a busy street in central Rome and was greeted by a friend of a friend, an immigration lawyer who had agreed to answer some of my questions about migration to Italy. She invited me into her sparse but pragmatic office, the wall behind her lined with law books, a window onto the courtyard at my back. She looked frazzled and acknowledged that it had been a tough day, one of many tough days. Ever since Silvio Berlusconi came into power in 2001, her legal work with immigrants had become more difficult. The push for reasonable integration enshrined in the 1998 Immigration Law had given way to a hostile climate framed by discriminatory and racist rhetoric meant to dehumanize and deter immigrants from coming to and staying in Italy.[17] While she described her job as tough, she took great pleasure in helping people through the arduous bureaucracy. She was not worn out yet, she said defiantly.

She patiently answered all my questions. However, when I asked her specifically about her experience with Senegalese people acquiring permanent residency, she requested that I stop the recording and simply take notes. She furrowed her brow, searching for a way to explain her confusion about why this specific demographic had a hard time gaining residency. According to her, the Senegalese community learned the Italian language better than almost any other group (she specifically mentioned migrants from Bangladesh, India, and the Philippines) but was the least likely group to achieve permanent residency status. She confided that they were impossible to work with in the sense that they did not keep appointments. They did not want to work as health-care aides, one of the few jobs available for recent migrants, so they often sought work on the black market. They also failed to do what was necessary to keep the legal process going. She entreated me to brainstorm with her about why this was the case. Based on what I was seeing in my interviews, I proposed that few Senegalese people actually planned to live in Italy forever. Senegalese thought they would be here for a few years, a decade maybe, sending money back to Senegal, with the idea that one day they would either return to Senegal or move to another foreign destination. So perhaps the idea of permanent residency was not as important, especially if they were able to work on the black market and make the money they wanted for their remittances. She paused for a moment, cocked her head to the side, and nodded.

It was obvious that by specifically highlighting the language difficulties of groups that tended to complete the necessary requirements for achieving residency, she assumed that language competence was an important factor in integrating and successfully gaining permanent legal status.[18] For the most part, Senegalese are neither assimilating into nor segregating themselves from the population; rather they participate in what Bruno Riccio describes as a third way of integration.[19] The average Senegalese migrant in Rome does not envision living a lifetime in Italy and therefore does not see investing in language classes as worthwhile, especially because taking classes means time lost that could be spent working. At the same time, there are myriad other incentives to learn the language. On one end of the spectrum, people are motivated by economic reasons such as finding jobs or selling merchandise on the streets, in which case they often learn terminology on the job. On the other end, there

are intrinsic reasons such as those we saw earlier in which people enjoy learning Italian because of its beauty or because they want to be as multilingual as
possible.

There is also something to be said about this constant look outward, away
from Italy, which will be central to chapter 4's discussion of the multilingual
traveler and the propensity for onward mobility. In addition, evidence supports
Riccio's argument that many Senegalese focus their gaze toward their homeland. The concept of home, which is constantly negotiated and changing according to context, helps convey understandings of immigrants' positioning in
the host country.[20] The following excerpt underlines the importance of home
and of positioning as the artist Biondo (B) and his friend (F) discuss a return to
Senegal:[21]

| | |
|---|---|
| M: | Pensate di tornare in Senegal? |
| B: | Oooooh, hai mai visto un senegalese che non vuole tornare? [*laughs*] |
| M: | Sì, esatto. |
| B: | Non esiste proprio. Dovunque sia. Australia, America, Europa. |
| M: | Sempre, casa è casa. |
| B: | Casa. Casa è casa. Basta. *Bëggoo dellu Senegal?* |
| F: | Eh? |
| B: | *Bëggoo dellu Senegal?* |
| F: | Sì, chiaro. |
| B: | Non esiste un senegalese che non vuole tornare a casa. |
| F: | Senegal è il paese più bello del mondo. |

| | |
|---|---|
| [M: | Do you all think about returning to Senegal? |
| B: | Oooooh, have you ever seen a Senegalese who doesn't want to return? [*laughs*] |
| M: | Yes, exactly. |
| B: | It doesn't even exist. Wherever. Australia, America, Europe. |
| M: | Always, home is home. |
| B: | Home. Home is home. That's it. *Don't you want to go back to Senegal?* |
| F: | Eh? |
| B: | *Don't you want to go back to Senegal?* |
| F: | Yes, of course. |
| B: | A Senegalese who doesn't want to return home doesn't exist. |
| F: | Senegal is the most beautiful country in the world.] |

The content of this conversation established a notion of boundaries and of displacement, both geographic and temporal. Through his conceptualization of

home, Biondo erected boundaries. He was physically far away from his home country, Senegal, and this boundary existed not because of what Italy was but because of what it was not. By mentioning other places (Australia, America, Europe), he not only underscored the global reach of Senegalese; he also created a dichotomy that juxtaposed Senegal against the rest of the world.

Going beyond content, an analysis of the actual language use also demonstrates the existence of boundaries. For instance, Biondo used a negative construction in Wolof when he asked his friend about his desire to return to Senegal. Often, negative questions suggest the expectation of an affirmative response.[22] Indeed, Biondo's interrogative received an adamantly affirmative response from his friend, and Biondo reiterated the importance and expectations placed on home by continuing the negative articulation in Italian when remarking that there was no Senegalese who did not want to return home.

Furthermore, while the language of the conversation was Italian, Biondo chose to direct a question in Wolof to his friend. One pragmatic explanation is that Biondo switched to Wolof to indicate a different interlocutor, evidenced by his turning his attention from me, the interviewer, to his Senegalese friend. Switching languages helped signal this change. However, Carol Myers-Scotton's Markedness Model, which details social motivations for code-switching, offers another perspective to explain the switch to Wolof. Myers-Scotton has contended that code-switching can be used in the negotiation of interpersonal relationships and the signaling of group membership.[23] One could argue that Biondo switched languages to create a collective sense by highlighting the linguistic connection between himself and his friend. The Italian language bestowed a particular identity on the country in which he currently lived that contrasted with his identity as a Wolof speaker. By speaking in Wolof, he further emphasized an identity that was not Italian but Senegalese. This decision reinforced the boundary between him and his environment and the link between himself and other Wolof-speaking Senegalese people.

In addition to the conceptualization of boundaries, analyzing multilingual usage such as code-switching also sheds light on notions of home. In multilingual spaces where the languages one speaks among family are often different from the larger social setting, the concept of home and how it relates to languages is central to understanding identity formation and positionality. In Senegal, as a country whose official language is French, local languages such as Wolof or Pulaar are often understood as home languages, and it is the home where people can cultivate particular cultural and ethnic identities. The case of Wolof is complex, however, because in Senegal Wolof may be a home language for some and the lingua franca for others. Biondo, for example, grew up in a Pulaar-speaking family but used Wolof in day-to-day life. However, once a Senegalese person is in the diaspora, regardless of his or her mother tongue, Wolof becomes the language that the person equates with Senegal and, by extension, home (e.g., Sébastien and Salif's increased connection to Wolof while in France because it reminded them of home).

In the above conversation, what I find particularly interesting is that when Biondo code-switched into Wolof, after having ruminated on the idea of home in the statement "Casa è casa," he did not use the Wolof word for home. It may be that the very action of uttering this question in Wolof meant that home was implied in the word Senegal. Penelope Gardner-Chloros, in applying the Markedness Model to the conceptualization of home, proposed that "in any given social circumstances, a particular variety is the expected or 'unmarked'— i.e., the unremarkable—one. So, for example, switching to the local vernacular to talk about home/family is 'unmarked,' whereas switching to the local vernacular in a public speech is a 'marked' choice."[24] Therefore, in this case it was not surprising that Biondo switched languages because he was demonstrating through language how he conceived of and related to a specific environment. In other words, the use of Wolof indexed home so that "home" did not need to be explicitly stated.

In this statement about returning home, Biondo spoke in absolutes as he channeled the voice of a whole people. He, therefore, further accentuated the us/them schism by taking isolated instances and generalizing them. In the next example, Professore (P), in his conversation with his Ndiaga (N) and me (M), used a different tactic to express desire for his homeland. He utilized intertextuality to answer the question of whether he thought he would return to Senegal one day:[25]

P: *C'est mon souhait, quoi.*
N: **Inch'allah.**
P: È il mio sogno. <u>I have a dream.</u> [*smiles*]
M: [*laughs*] <u>OK.</u>
P: <u>That's my dream.</u>

[P: *It's my wish, you know.*
N: **God willing.**
P: It's my dream. <u>I have a dream.</u> . . . . [*smiles*]
M: [*laughs*] <u>OK.</u>
P: <u>That's my dream.</u>]

While the full conversation was in Italian, French, and English, at this point, French had been spoken for a while. In the first turn, Professore spoke in French. After Ndiaga inserted the Wolof/Arabic phrase "God willing," Professore repeated his original thought in Italian. He then evoked Martin Luther King Jr.'s "I Have a Dream" speech. By intertextualizing King's words, Professore infused the conversation with a hint of gravitas under the guise of humor (he smiled when he said it, eliciting a laugh from me). By citing a well-known civil rights leader, Professore aptly conveyed just how much he yearned to return to Senegal and the effects of his sustained absence from his homeland. However, the use of King could also be read as a way to signal the racial work he had to do to create home in hostile terrain—combatting the alienation he felt in a new land and the racial subtext fueling this alienation. In addition, by moving between the indefinite article in "I have a dream" and the personal pronouns *mon*, *mio*, and "my," he showed both the collective desire of Senegalese migrants to return to a space where racial difference was not a central concern and his proprietary claim on this particular dream.[26]

However, not all discussions of identity and belonging among the informants in Italy were negative or suggested a desire to remain unattached to the host county. There were examples where interviewees took a more optimistic approach to their position in society and to possible improvements in the way members of the dominant group viewed them, which in turn allowed them to question the nature of *italianità* and where they fit. For instance, Ibou was able to create a home space in both France and Italy:

> Al livello culturale, strutturale, mentalità, sto molto meglio in Francia perché sono abituato al sistema sociale, culturale, la lingua. Ho amici. In Italia, conosco molto bene l'Italia e vedo la mia dimensione africana più in Italia. Forse io, da Senegalese o Francofono, la dimensione occidentale, in Italia è il mio punto di equilibrio. Nel senso della famiglia, calore umano, l'improvvisazione un po. La nozione del tempo è più vicina all'Africa, anche il sole e il clima. Ho più la mia dimensione africana in Italia.

> [On a cultural, structural, mental level, I'm much better off in France because I am used to the social, cultural system, the language. I have friends. In Italy, I know Italy very well and I see my African side come out more. Maybe I, as Senegalese or French-speaking, the Western side, Italy is my point of balance. In the sense of family, human warmth, improvisation. The notion of time is closer to Africa, even the sun and the climate. Italy fits my African side better.]

Ibou's reasons for feeling more at home in France were related to how accustomed he was to France's social and cultural system and the French language. He had been a French-language instructor in Senegal. However, this command of French and affinity for certain social structures were not enough to sway his overall feeling of comfort in Italy. He saw the values placed on family, the slower pace, and the climate as some of the factors that brought out his African side, factors that were indispensable for him. Many of the informants mentioned similar reasons for feeling a connection with Italy. For Ibou, this connection led to a proactive transformation of Italy as home, in that his Senegalese wife and child lived with him in the suburbs of Rome, and he did not discuss the prospect of returning to Senegal. Ibou represented someone who, regardless of any exclusion perpetuated by the dominant culture, had decided to put down roots and integrate.[27] Ibou was an outlier, however. The conversations with the vast majority of my interviewees reflected the experience of the immigration lawyer with regard to integration.

### "But they never go back": A Little Senegal Abroad in New York City

In chapter 1, Aminata and Diallo described 116th Street in Harlem as a site where you expect to hear Wolof, see people sporting *boubous*, and smell *ceebu jen* (the national dish of Senegal—a delicious take on fish and rice) wafting from the doorway of Senegalese restaurants. The fact that Little Senegal represents a well-established Senegalese enclave is important because it points to the existence of a community space where Senegalese cultural norms can flourish within a larger American context. When I asked the journalist Diop his thoughts about living in the United States, he responded:

> D:  I find it almost as natural as living in Senegal.
> M:  Really? How so?
> D:  Because I don't see anything that reminds me that I don't belong here. What you call in France the *délit de faciès*. Because you are wearing African clothes or Senegalese clothes, no one is stopping you to say where are you from.

It is telling that Diop structured his understanding of belonging by using a negative construction, which led directly into the French expression *délit de faciès*, roughly translated as "racial profiling."[28] He implied that unlike in the United States, in France one should not signal Africanness or do anything that suggests one differs from the sanctioned French identity. To further drive home his point, he added, "There is no particular standard an American needs to look like. That I find very, very helpful for somebody who's foreign born, who comes to the country, who struggles with the language. . . . It's not really a problem for the society." This openness to difference means that languages can coexist and thrive and that those who see the value of multilingualism can be proud to identify as multilingual.[29] This is not to say that African clothing and languages did not exist on the streets of Paris; however, there was a pervasive feeling that New York was more accommodating to these outward displays of cultural difference and to the building of communities where these differences were commonplace.[30]

It was not just those who lived in New York City who noticed this freedom to show difference and live collectively in difference. Interviewees in Paris took note. For instance, Nyambi pointed out, "Aux Etats-Unis ou en Angleterre, il y a le communautarisme, les noirs entre eux, les Arabes entre eux, les Chinois entre eux, et ils sont tellement forts qu'un Noir qui a fait des études, qui est très brillant, il peut être un maire d'un quartier noir, même un chef noir." (In the United States or England, there is communitarianism; blacks among themselves, Arabs among themselves, the Chinese among themselves. And they are so strong that a black who is educated, who is very bright, can be a mayor of a black area, even a black boss.) Nyambi argued that communitarianism created spaces where minorities could thrive and be represented. He compared this set-up to France: "Mais en France c'est plus pervers. Ils disent, pas de communautarisme ici. Nous faisons l'intégration. Mais . . . à la société française, vous voyez la télévision française ici, vous avez l'impression qu'il n'y a pas de Noirs dans ce pays, pas d'Arabes." (But in France it is more perverse. They say, no communitarianism here. We champion integration. But . . . in French society, you watch French television here, you have the impression that there are no black people in this country, no Arabs.) Throughout his argument, he used language to mark bodily erasures from national representations of the self. Communitarianism, where people bound by ethnic or national affiliation live together, poses an affront to assimilation, and attempts to champion communitarianism are often seen as an Anglo-American importation, something inherently un-French.[31] But as Nyambi indicated, assimilation effaced marginalized groups. They did not seem to exist in the national narrative. Prohibiting communitarianism essentially ensured that they were not seen en masse and could be more easily ignored. Furthermore, the discourse in France put the onus on those marked as different to assimilate; however, the experiences of many showed how overriding identity markers made it impossible to be fully accepted into French society.

Just like Nyambi, Diop saw the merits of living in a place such as Little Senegal where he could share the customs and values of those in his immediate environment. Nonetheless, he also presented a cautionary tale with regard to immigration, integration, and home building. According to him, it was great to be proud of who one was, where one came from, and the parts of the person that made him or her unique, but that person still had to see himself or herself as part of the larger society in order to fully feel at home. Failure to do so relegated the host country to a space of transition that never solidified into a home.

Diop reflected on his own arrival to the United States in the 1980s:

> When I come here . . . I tell my relatives, "I want to find a school where I can learn English." They say, "Come on. What do you need that for? You're not coming here to get money and go home?" I say "Guys, you see this country, I need to take the time to speak their language, at least. We're not going home." And they say, "You are crazy. Don't jinx us." The same people, twenty years later, are *garding* the exact same job as when they just come.[32] Because they never think of themselves as part of the society. Never done anything to improve their life here because they are waiting to go home to have a life. And they're not going home.

Currently, he was on a crusade to change this perspective about home. He used his voice as a radio personality to plead with listeners not to send all their earnings to Senegal, just enough to help out their families because there was a need to invest in their local community as well. He could not stress enough the importance of establishing roots in the United States: "Get your roots deep here. And even if you think of going home, try to make a good living here that will help you go back home. But if you are suspending your life, thinking, 'When I go home I'll start living,' you will not go home. You will never go home."

Diop noticed that the reticence of the previous generations to claim the United States as their home was starting to dissipate. This change was particularly noticeable when considered in light of language ideologies. Diop's focus on English-language acquisition demonstrated the primary role that language plays in investing in an identity, in this case an American identity. Whereas others from his generation avoided learning English because it signaled a form of cutting ties with Senegal, he saw it as a way of opening doors. Similarly, the younger people and more recent migrants I interviewed placed learning English as a top priority. Having spent five years in the United States, thirty-year-old Laurent from Casamance explained, "Once you come here, after years, you're going to find out like the best thing to do, when you come here, is to go to school and learn English. Because communication matters. It's the basic skill." He made the argument that even if someone had no plans to stay in the United States, it was important to learn English and adapt because once a person was there, it was hard to ever go back: "Myself or a lot of people like me, once they come here, they don't want nothing from here. They want to live here, make money, and send the money back to Africa. And every day they're going to be like, I'm going back home, but they never go back" [*people laugh*]. The laughter from his friends as we spoke suggested just how true this statement was. Person after person shared stories of how New York was supposed to be a transitory destination, a stop for a couple of years. Most of them realized this was no longer the case. Many people were more likely to move to another foreign destination than to return to Senegal, where job prospects were sparse and the image of the successful migrant reigned supreme.

The competing generational views concerning language acquisition also put in relief how the concept of global Senegality transforms across time and space. While the basic tenets of global Senegality, namely, being mobile, speaking multiple languages, and practicing hospitality have existed for centuries and throughout the diaspora, these ideas are expressed differently depending on the context. The older generation who arrived in New York in the seventies and eighties migrated with the idea that they would return to Senegal in a few years. They did not learn English because they never imagined putting down roots and instead successfully established a space in Harlem where English was not normally necessary. They still respected multiple languages, but their linguistic repertoires consisted mainly of Senegalese national languages and French. They created a space that was a microcosm of postindependence Senegal. At the same time, they emphasized Little Senegal as a wolofophone space, imploring the second generation not only to speak Wolof but to speak a Wolof that was not too anglicized, as we saw with Ndiaye in chapter 1.

The younger generation of Senegalese in New York, either those who were second-generation Americans born in the eighties and nineties or recent arrivals in the United States of a similar age, practiced different types of movement and communication. Many of the young Senegalese migrants engaged in onward mobility, either coming from or heading to countries other than Senegal, happy to see the world and try their luck in various receiving countries. They were much more interested in learning the languages of the countries in which they lived than the previous generation of Senegalese migrants were. The second-generation Americans meanwhile sought out family both in Senegal and in different parts of the diaspora and would often travel for vacation and work. Importantly, they enjoyed the privileges that an American passport afforded. This passport served almost as a talisman, and many of the people I interviewed recognized the symbolic capital it bestowed. In addition, the U.S.-born informants spoke English as a primary language, which, like the passport, conferred a certain American identity and symbolic capital. The recent arrivals foregrounded the importance of learning American English in acquiring cultural cachet. English was not only about integrating into the host society; it also concerned what Bayo Holsey has dubbed as "looking diasporic."[33] While Holsey was referring specifically to the ability of Ghanaians in Ghana to "look good" by donning certain styles of dress and listening to certain types of music, the people in my study also used English as a way to channel a diasporic and racialized aesthetic. Through their interactions with family and friends back in Senegal, they showcased their success in mastering different types of cultural production and language use associated with America in general and African American culture in particular.

## IDENTITY FORMATION IN A GLOBAL CONTEXT

While my informants talked about their experiences of integrating against the backdrop of national discourses and within local settings, they also often reflected on where they fit at a global level. This global perspective was particularly evident in how people in my study compared their experiences to those of other Senegalese across the world or they shared their experiences through references to various types of cultural productions. We have seen glimpses of these comparisons in the previous section. The current section will more explicitly show how my interviewees advance a global consciousness of race and fit into a history of Afro-Atlantic dialogues concerning global racial formation.[34]

With regard to the longue durée of Afro-Atlantic dialogues, Idrissa's evocation of Du Bois in chapter 2 channeled Du Bois's work at the 1921 Pan-African Congress in London, where black leaders across the globe assembled, wrote the *London Resolutions*, and set up the Pan-African Association headquarters in Paris. This dialogue between the Americas, Europe, and Africa culminated in resolutions concerning racial equality and African sovereignty, which Du Bois articulated in the *Manifesto to the League of Nations*. While the message went unheard, the manifesto showed how people who identified as black created a space to voice their concerns about their treatment at a local, national, and global level. Further back in time, Frederick Douglass traveled around England and Ireland for two years, speaking to abolitionists and reflecting on his brief respite from America's brand of racial discrimination. Bringing the American fight for freedom to Britain, where he could converse with abolitionists who worked to end slavery in the British colonies, Douglass signaled this transnational stand against bondage. More recently, Stuart Hall's exploration of hybridity as a Jamaican in Britain and Paul Gilroy's conceptualization of the Black Atlantic have added to the interrogation of what it means to be marginalized while still maintaining some agency in fighting against this marginalization. In the past couple of decades, one of the spaces that has been most active and productive in combating marginalization is the domain of music, particularly hip-hop.[35]

In the francophone context, Fanon's work in the mid-twentieth century, which emerged from experiences in both his native Martinique and his adopted

Algeria, proved that regardless of geography and background, colonized peoples were dealing with very similar issues. These issues continue in the present and are engaged by scholars such as Mbembe who confront neocolonial discourses, exemplified in Sarkozy's condescending speech about Africa, and hip-hop artists in France and Senegal who take to task problematic political speech.[36] The discussions I had with my interviewees show iterations of this transnational dialogue on race and belonging. Adding to previous discussions on transnationalism, I will highlight what language use and discursive strategies can tell us about race and belonging.

### Beyond Paris: "Nous ne sommes plus des immigrés"

I sat near the front of a dark room, trying to blend in even though my jeans and black shirt contrasted sharply with the bright prints and more formal clothing worn by most of the people around me. Rows of folding chairs faced a raised platform where five guest speakers from the Senegalese community in Paris were asking one another in Wolof how they and their family members were doing. Members of the audience were milling about as they waited for the panel, made possible by the Senegalese Business Association in Paris, to begin. The overarching theme of this forum was inclusivity and belonging: where do the Senegalese fit in? The conversation began with the topic of remittances. One of the panelists tried to convey the immensity of annual remittances to Senegal; another panelist wondered if the people who were sending these remittances were ready to go to Senegal to build it up instead of just throwing money at Senegal from afar.[37]

Then, a third panelist stood up and presented a rousing, applause-provoking sermon about the importance of investing in France because this was now their country, too. He argued that it was all well and good to want to give back to Senegal. However, France needed to know they were here, and they needed to act like it was their country. Instead of simply investing money, they needed to invest in education so that they could access every rung of French society:

> J'ai eu la chance de voyager à travers le monde. J'ai fait pas mal de pays. J'ai vécu longtemps aux Etats-Unis. Si vous regardez bien l'histoire américaine dans les années 60 où c'était l'identification "Black Power" et tout, et maintenant ce pays a réussi à mettre à sa tête un Noir. . . . Ça veut dire qu'ils ont travaillé pour pouvoir réussir et se battre pour envoyer leurs enfants aux grandes écoles pour avoir des diplômes. C'est ça. Nous devons investir en nos enfants pour que nos enfants puissent avoir une éducation, pour que nos enfants puissent aller dans les grandes écoles parce que nous ne sommes plus des immigrés. L'immigration est

finie. . . . Nous sommes des Français à part entière. Nous ne sommes pas des Français d'ailleurs mais un peuple d'ici.

[I have had the opportunity to travel all over the world. I've been to many countries. I lived a long time in the United States. If you look at American history in the sixties when there was this identification with Black Power and everything and now this country has managed to have a black president. . . . That means that they worked to be able to get ahead and to fight to send their children to receive diplomas from top universities. That's it. We must invest in our children so that our children can get an education, can go to the top universities because we are not immigrants. Immigration is over. . . . We are wholly French. We are not French from elsewhere but a people from here.]

This panelist mirrored Diop's realization about the importance of seeing the host country as home. In addition to his applause-inducing oratory skills, the panelist seemed to position himself as an ethnographer and historian, conveying a sense of expertise and knowledge in the way he introduced his argument. He forefronted his credentials as a world traveler, as someone who had witnessed similar phenomena in other settings. By doing so, he proved himself as someone who fit the quintessential Senegalese traveler identity. Furthermore, he highlighted the length of time he had spent in the United States, which afforded him an appreciation for the history there and allowed him certain insider knowledge. He evoked the Black Power movement to emphasize the political mobilization on which blacks have relied to stake a claim to American-ness, and he contended that this agency and investment allowed the country to usher in its first black president. While his impassioned speech was well received, the ensuing debate at this forum as well as periodic discussions among Senegalese in Paris showed how this community frequently wrestled with the often-competing desires of belonging in France while maintaining a connection with Senegal. The panelist's mention of the United States also demonstrated the importance placed on understanding how migratory phenomena manifested themselves in other locations.

References to places such as the United States occur frequently in the data from Paris, demonstrating how people were looking outside their immediate communities or national borders for guidance. Being Senegalese in France and being French of Senegalese descent were never limited to the material territory where one stood but relied on a performance of global cosmopolitanism as well.[38] For instance, Lucie cited the United States and England as places where race was no longer linked to nationality to argue that it was only a matter of time before people, regardless of their differences, would be accepted. Conveying a sense of hope, she argued that this inability to be accepted as a nonwhite French person was a generational issue that would one day disappear: "Ça va peut-être se résoudre parce que c'est un problème de génération. Dans dix ans, quinze ans, vingt ans, cinquante ans ça changera parce que quand les Italiens sont arrivés, ils ont connu ce même phénomène. La seule différence c'est la couleur, mais on s'est intégrés aux Etats-Unis, en Angleterre. Pourquoi pas ici?" (It will perhaps be solved because it is a generational problem. In ten years, fifteen years, twenty years, fifty years, it will change because when the Italians arrived, they experienced the same phenomenon. The only difference is the color, but we [people of color] integrated in the United States, England. Why not here?) Because of African American representation in such domains as government, film, and music, many Senegalese assumed that blacks in the United States had integrated. Having a presence meant that discussing race or signaling differences were not necessarily received badly. Although the United States wrestles with racial issues, evidenced in chapter 2, and national discourse often equates Americanness with whiteness, many of the interviewees had a positive view of the United States and the role of race in national identity.[39]

Faatu also looked to the United States in expressing her frustration with how France continued to deny its history in order to deny her racialized presence. In the same conversation where she whispered her critique of France's treatment of race and colonial history, she declared: "Je trouve que par rapport aux Etats-Unis, la France est très en arrière" (I think that compared to the United States, France is behind). If Faatu were to spend time in the United States, she might realize that the same inability to acknowledge and atone for its past also plagues the United States.[40] However, by making it clear that she wanted French society to acknowledge Senegalese and all colonized peoples in its history books and include them in France's historical narrative rather than treat them as some current invader who does not belong, she also recognized the existence of different models for accomplishing these goals that could be useful in the French context.

At the end of the interview after I stopped recording, Faatu leaned toward me and continued to whisper. I moved closer to hear her, listening intently because I knew it was through these whispers that she would convey the thoughts she wished she could scream the loudest. She thanked me profusely for giving her the opportunity to express herself candidly. She lamented that the only time the French talked about racism was when they looked at the American context. It was never discussed as a French problem. In a way, the word "racism" indexes Americanness where this signification of America serves many purposes and has multiple valences. On the one hand, many of the informants argued that America was further along in race relations because it directly addressed race. On the other hand, French discourse labels racism as an American import.[41] For instance, mentioning racism in a French context often signals an American brand of racism and communitarianism that French discourse depicts as foreign. In Faatu's case, although she was uncomfortable with talking about race and racism in the French context in a voice louder than a whisper, she was still able to express her discomfort with a system that claims to be color-blind but still manages to classify and hierarchize.

### Beyond Rome:
### "Ma qua tu vedi per strada la gente che vende i CD"

While in Paris many of the outward-looking discussions focused on the United States, in Rome these conversations often looked toward France. People in my study foregrounded how the prolonged presence of Senegalese immigrants in particular and African immigrants in general meant that France had been forced to think about where nontraditional inhabitants fit in the nation. France's extensive postcolonial network and the fact that it had overseas departments and territories with predominantly black populations also engendered discussions on race and national identity, albeit reluctantly. As for everyday experiences, there was a sense that more options were available for people of color in France, even if many questioned what they saw as discriminatory practices that impeded integration there.

For instance, Karim was a thirty-two-year-old dancer from Kaolack who had lived in Paris for four years before spontaneously moving to Rome after visiting a friend for a week. Now having lived in Rome for three years, Karim was able to provide a comparative perspective: "In Francia se vedi la polizia, vedi polizia *black*. Se vai al municipio, vedi un sindaco *black*. Se vai all'aeroporto, vedi un pilota *black*. Dovunque vai. Qua, non c'è un poliziotto *black*. Non c'è un barman *black*. . . . Ma qua tu vedi per strada la gente che vende i CD." (In France, you see *black* police officers. If you go to the town hall, you see a *black* mayor. If you go to the airport, you see a *black* pilot. Wherever you go. Here, there are no *black* police officers. There are no *black* bartenders. . . . But here you see people selling CDs in the street.)

According to Karim, an implied notion of economic class was part and parcel of the status of immigrant. Karim portrayed the positioning of immigrants as an obstacle, which relegated them to undesirable jobs with low social capital (such as CD vendors) and hindered their access to positions that garnered respect. He seemed to depict a sense of belonging that was contingent on the roles a given community occupied in a society. This was made obvious by his juxtaposing the respected professions of police officer, mayor, and pilot, to which blacks had access in France, with the eschewed profession of street vending, one of the few job options available to African immigrants who entered Italy, especially for those without papers.

It is also important to note that just like Professore, Karim chose to use the English word "black" instead of the Italian *nero* or the French *noir*. As stated earlier, code-switching for this charged word could either be a sign of avoiding a taboo word or a way of connecting to the black diaspora, where the concept of blackness originated from an African American theoretical framework.[42] Regardless of Karim's actual intent, the use of the word "black" offered an additional geographical and historical context to the conversation that would not have existed if he had used the word *nero*.

The case of Abi is a more obvious example of language use and transnational understandings of belonging. Abi, the dancer whose encounters with race were analyzed earlier, showed how her racial experiences in different countries influenced her opinions of those countries, which in turn affected her desire to learn the official languages of these places. She is an interesting example because in her interview she wanted to spend most of the time talking about her experiences outside Italy. Traveling with a dance troupe, she had been all over Europe as well as the United States.[43] When I interviewed her in Rome, almost a year into her stay there, she juxtaposed a predominantly negative experience in Italy with a positive connection to the United States and Spain. Uncomfortable speaking Italian even though she could get by in that language, Abi communicated with me primarily in French. She made it very clear throughout her interview that she disliked Italy because of what she viewed as racist treatment. Meanwhile, Abi did not speak of the United States in terms of racism but rather emphasized the cultural connection that she felt with it: "Les Etats-Unis, c'est meilleur. Parce que j'aime les Américains. J'aime les danses. J'aime le blues. J'aime tout, quoi. . . . L'Italie, c'est un peu difficile. Il y a du racisme, trop." (The United States, it is better. Because I love Americans. I love the dances. I love the blues. I love everything, you know. . . . Italy, it is a bit difficult. There is too much racism.)[44] For a dancer like her, the connection with music suggested an investment in the culture that translated into an investment in the language: "Quand j'étais aux Etats-Unis, franchement, je parlais anglais" (When I was in the United States, frankly, I spoke English). In other words, the use of certain languages is a way to express citizenship and belonging. It has affective tones, which show the affective character of citizenship.

Other incidents also indicated how Abi's opinions of a receiving country influenced her attitudes about language. She described her relationship with Spain and Spanish in similar terms to her experience of the United States and English. She had a positive time in Spain, which helped account for the high volume of Spanish used throughout her interview. She felt that there was no sort of hierarchy between her and Spaniards when she lived there, as seen in the following excerpt:[45]

    A:    Nous sommes *égual*, des Espagnols, des Sénégalais.
    M:    Et pour ça tu aimes, tu préfères la langue espagnole?
    A:    Oui, à cause de ça, franchement.
    M:    C'est intéressant.
    A:    Et puis, je ne vois pas là-bas le racisme. Même s'il y en a.

    [A:    We are *equal*, Spanish, Senegalese.
    M:    And for that reason you like, you prefer Spanish?
    A:    Yes, because of that, frankly.
    M:    That's interesting.
    A:    And I do not see racism there. Even if there is.]

Bonny Norton has framed investment in terms of the right to speak, and this right to speak is based on power relations.[46] Abi indicated her perceived position in the hierarchy of power relations by uttering "nous sommes égual," with *égual* seeming to be a mix of the French *égal* and the Spanish *igual*. She explicitly identified the link between this perceived equality and her love of the Spanish language. Through the wording of the last line in this excerpt, she also highlighted the fact that this was her experience, not necessarily the experience of others. She did not suggest that Spain was devoid of racism, just that she did not experience it.[47]

In the end, Abi came to her own conclusion that her difficulties with the Italian language were related to her feelings about Italy. She did so by comparing her experiences of the United States and English with her experiences of Italy and Italian:[48] "*Io vivo con italiens dieci mesi e non parlo biene italiano*.[49] *Non so* **por qué** ... parce que moi, j'ai fait Amérique, trois mois. Mais je parle l'anglais plus qu'italien. Je sais pas. Oui. Parce que j'aime." (*I live with Italians for ten months and I don't speak Italian well. I don't know* **why** ... because I was in America three months. But I speak English more than Italian. I do not know. Yes I do. Because I like it.) It was the love of the English language as well as the positive experiences in the United States that propelled her to learn English. The converse was true for Italian.

### Beyond New York City:
### "Black is black. They don't know where you're from."

I stepped off the subway at the Woodhaven Boulevard stop. It was my first time in this part of Queens. The station dumped me out in front of a giant mall, so I decided to take a shortcut through the shops and emerged on the other side. I navigated the unfamiliar streets of the residential neighborhood that flanked the mall. There was so much space in Queens. The buildings were newer than the brownstones I frequented when conducting interviews in Brooklyn. And while Manhattan had tall residential high-rises, I found the residences currently in front of me, with their larger footprints, more imposing in the way they took up space.

I looked down at the address that Julien had scribbled in my notebook the previous day when he invited me to this after-church potluck hosted by one of the members of the Senegalese Catholic Association. Once at my destination, I approached the intercom and scrolled through the names. The buzzer granted me entrance, and I took the elevator to the fourteenth floor. A little child opened the door, looked me up and down, shrugged, and let me in. I did not recognize anyone at first and felt as if I was crashing a party. Then Julien emerged from the balcony and, in his boisterous way, called to me from across the room. The noisy chatter that had been ricocheting against the walls came to an abrupt halt. It seemed that everyone was curious to know who I was even if they had not let on to their curiosity when I first arrived.

Once I had been introduced, various people came to me to extend their greetings. They inquired about what church I attended, and I mumbled something about being in town from Seattle, not wanting to go down that route. The host handed me a plate of chicken with *yassa* sauce and a glass of wine—which was a departure from the nonalcoholic interactions with my Muslim informants—and Julien led me out to the balcony. It was a decent-sized balcony but nonetheless overflowed with people. Julien quickly explained my interest in interviewing people about their linguistic habits, and after distributing audio release forms, I began recording. I figured it would be a productive exercise to hear multiple perspectives about language use at once. Only a few minutes in, however, the conversation quickly turned from linguistic practices into a heated debate about France's continued involvement in Senegal.

I had simply asked if anyone had lived in France before coming to the United States. One of the men (A), in his early thirties, loudly answered that he did not like France. I asked him to explain, which instigated a chorus of responses from the whole group, and from one particular man (B):

A:   Because they oppress us.
M:   How so?
A:   Since my great-great-great-grandfather.
B:   We were colonized by the French.
A:   It's like the same clash you have between African Americans and the white people. That's the same thing.

> B:    And they're still in Africa. Why don't they want to leave Africa? Why they still in Africa? . . . So they're still in Africa, using their power, their politic in Africa, making decisions. . . . My question is why French people still in Africa? Why? You know.
>
> A:    Because they want to suck you to the last bone.[50]

The young man (A) who first shared his disgust with France described France as an oppressor and conveyed the historical weight of this oppression by evoking his great-great-great-grandfather. This familial and generational tie suggested that in his mind not much had changed since the colonial period. In a way, this argument mirrored Karafa's earlier discussion of the oppressive nature of the French language that persists long after the decolonization of Senegal. Soon afterward, another man (B), around the same age, made the role of colonization explicit. "A" and "B" continued to co-construct this narrative of (post)colonial oppression, as "B" questioned France's continued involvement in Africa and "A" offered the metaphor of consumption through the image of being devoured by someone with an insatiable appetite.

As "A" explained his theories on why the French continued to meddle in West African affairs, arguing that France needed access to the region's natural resources, Sandra (S), an African American woman dating one of the men in the group, began talking about the cultural imposition of the French before being cut off by another man (C). "C" was taking an opposing view about the source of Senegal's current problems, having already blamed Senegal's leaders for their woes. He then stated that using the past to explain the present was unproductive:

> A:    That's why they can't leave us alone.
>
> S:    They teach you their culture—
>
> C:    Maya, you're African American, aren't you?
>
> M:    Yes.
>
> C:    [*to Sandra and "A"*] I disagree. You know why? Because I'm tired of when I hear you know, this is the past, people are talking about slavery. Slavery is over.
>
> A:    HELL NO!
>
> S:    Hell no.
>
> A:    I say loud and clear. HELL NO!

By this point, about fifteen people were yelling over one another. While a couple of people understood where "C" was coming from, that there was a need to move on, the majority provided anecdotal evidence for why the past was never just the past.

An analysis of this excerpt shows how "C" highlighted my identity as African American in order to make the connection between the United States' current racial issues and the institution of slavery. Just as "A" did in the earlier turn of talk, "C" suggested the similarities of this relationship with that of Senegal and colonialism. However, while he used a similar tactic, his argument could not have been more different from that of "A." This divergence of opinion caused both Sandra and "A" to issue resounding rebuttals as they raised their voices and repeated each other. This debate, which started off as a simple discussion of language attitudes, morphed into a lengthy dispute in which the legacies of slavery and colonialism converged. In addition to the theme of historical baggage and its influence on present-day experiences, which we saw earlier in the chapter, this exchange also pointed to global racial formation.

Whether it is in Paris, New York, Rome (e.g., Ndiaga evoking the African American experience to explain his own racialized existence in Italy), or anywhere else in the world, everyday people are invested in global racial identity formation. My data show a complex negotiation of what it means to be black, to be a citizen of a particular country, to be an immigrant or perceived an immigrant, to be an outsider, and to be a member of cultural groups whose borders are constantly in flux. Through this negotiation, various interviewees in all three sites tapped into this idea of black cultural citizenship.[51] From Professore's evocation of civil rights icon Dr. King to Faatu decrying the erasure of slavery in French history textbooks to the comparison between American slavery and French colonialism over supper in Queens, shared histories emerged.

Later on in the debate in Queens, the participants steered the conversation to comparing racial discrimination in the United States and France. Through personal anecdotes, forty-five-year-old Charlotte gave various perspectives on how it was easier to succeed in the United States than in France as a black person: "[In America] let's say I'm trying to take care of my business, and nobody is bothering me. In France, you can walk on the street and have immigration tell you, 'Hi, how are you? Can we have your papers, please?'"[52] And while there was evidence of racial profiling by police in the New York data, this profiling was not tied to immigration matters, at least in the experiences of those I interviewed.[53]

Charlotte also showed how attitudes about language played a key role in comparing experiences between France and the United States:

> You don't go to France because you aren't going to have the same
> opportunities. It's much easier to succeed here [the United States] than
> to succeed in France . . . because even if you have the language as a
> barrier, the country has more opportunities for immigrants. People who
> come here, all you have to do is believe. It's another state of mind. It's

another way of thinking . . . while in France, even if you have the highest ambition, you always have hurdles to go over, all the way, because of your skin. No matter how well you speak the language. No matter how well you speak French, when you do the interview on the phone, the job is granted. When you get to the place of those people, you don't have the job, because they didn't think, even if you had the French accent and everything, that that was a black person talking on the phone.[54]

Charlotte corroborated examples from the Paris data in chapter 2 where Lucie, Jean-Paul, and Ngirin read specific incidents of attacks on their language use as surreptitious attacks on their racial identity. This hostile environment impeded feelings of belonging, which in turn stymied any meaningful integration. Charlotte's musings indicated how a negative reception in France, along with the policy shifts that, since the 1970s, directed migration away from France, weakened the pull of the former colonial power, and problematized the nature of postcoloniality particularly as it pertains to language.

While Charlotte explained her reasons for preferring the United States to France, she argued that there was still rampant racial discrimination in the United States, such as in corporate America. "C," who was still playing the contrarian role, suggested that this was an issue that targeted African Americans specifically and did not concern Africans in America in the same way. He was juxtaposing black with African American in much the same way that Mariama and Julien recounted how some African Americans separated black from African. Charlotte swiftly shot him down: "Black is black. They don't know where you're from. They don't know." For Charlotte, black racial formation emerged from the shared lived experiences of race that Africans and African Americans encountered in the U.S. context. At the same time, the discussion also demonstrated the nuances between these groups as well as the slippages and messy overlaps among the conceptualizations of black, African, and African American. In fact, this argument led the group to change focus and highlight the divide between African Americans and Africans in America.

While scholarly research has analyzed this divide between Africans and African Americans,[55] it has not theorized where language fits in. Shaking his head, Julien argued: "The problem is, we blacks, or African Americans, or from Africa, we are not together. We are not doing together. If we work together, we succeed. You see the Spanish people? They together, no matter what. Even if they're black-skinned, if they speak Spanish, they are Spanish. . . . We are divided. That's why all the time we fail."[56] Julien's conceptualization of Latinx as a group that bands together even when confronted with its heterogeneity indicated his desire to learn from what he considered a success story. By wanting to emulate this conceptualization of Latinx, he showed the relationality of race that did not need a white center as the only point of negotiation. Furthermore, he saw language in this context as a way to transcend skin color and level the divisions forged through racial stratification.[57]

Julien was not the only one to focus on the power of language in smoothing out divisions. Soon after Julian had spoken, a young man who had been relatively quiet throughout the discussion chimed in by remarking that anglophone African immigrants had an easier time being accepted into the African American community than Senegalese immigrants because of their linguistic background: "The Nigerian or the Ghanaian or whoever speaks English from Africa, when they come here they fit very well. They fit faster. You know why? Because they speak English." He was echoing Samba's argument that his sister Madina struggled to fit in not because she was African per se but because she was a French-speaking African. While people such as Charlotte pointed to the linguistic pressure in Paris as a barrier to integration and acceptance by society at large, this man called into question the linguistic barriers erected by a specific subset of the New York City population. For him, in the very particular context of African/African American relations, shared language rather than shared blackness granted African immigrants acceptance. Whereas Julien positioned the Spanish language as a tool of inclusion in spite of racial differences, this young man was positioning the English language as an inclusionary force that carried more weight than racial similarities. In other words, from different perspectives they both exhibited the ways in which language eclipsed race in their minds.

## CONCLUDING THOUGHTS

Often in discussions on immigration, government officials and media in the host country champion notions of integration. There are expectations for the migrant community to do everything in its power to assimilate the host country's cultural norms. The three sites, however, offer different models of integration that those in my study have learned to navigate. They engaged with these different geopolitical contexts and the immigration laws and policies that have emerged. Many of them found that France expected the highest level of assimilation, the United States occupied the opposite end of the spectrum, and Italy fell somewhere in between. This chapter furthered the discussion about how Senegalese's understandings of racialized and linguistic identities fit into national discourses of the host countries with regard to immigration and integration.

In Paris, the French government and dominant discourses throughout the country placed pressure on immigrants to integrate and to behave in a way that reflected a very specific version of Frenchness and French national identity. However, this pressure to assimilate was disingenuous because racial, religious, and linguistic identity markers precluded many Senegalese from convincingly claiming Frenchness. They would never be more than *français d'origine sénégalaise*. This rejection was particularly painful because many people who participated in this study were actually French citizens; a long-standing relationship existed between France and Senegal that influenced language ideologies and cultural conceptions; and there was the looming presence of French national discourse with its colorblind ideology, which falsely convinced some people that they could achieve acceptance and, therefore, integration.

In Rome, race and citizenship status were conflated such that someone who was black was automatically assumed to be an immigrant. However, compared to those in Paris, the informants in Rome did not seem as bothered by this distinction because they themselves identified primarily as immigrants. The overwhelming majority of them saw their stay in Italy as temporary—as an opportunity to make money to send back to Senegal. They were not too concerned with integrating into Italian society, and they did not conceptualize Italy as their home. However, just because Senegalese seemed more accepting of the immigrant label in Rome than in Paris did not mean that they were not offended by this marginalization. Abi's preference for the United States and Spain based on her experiences suggested that this desire for onward mobility came as much from Italy's disinterest in being a receiving country as it did from a Senegalese cultural imaginary that relished the ability to be mobile.

The New York data, meanwhile, demonstrated the usefulness of having a space where a person felt he or she belonged. Little Senegal represented a place where being Senegalese and expressing global Senegality did not mark someone as an outsider or an intruder. While both France and the United States have tumultuous racial histories that continue to harm and marginalize their nonwhite and immigrant populations, in America the existence of communitarianism, which is discouraged in France, helps combat the danger of minorities being rendered invisible. According to my informants, speaking Senegalese languages and wearing Senegalese styles allowed them to tap into the Senegalese diaspora and reap the benefits that a sense of community creates in harsh environments. However, as Diop warned, there must be a balance. Although he saw nothing wrong in displaying pride in diverse cultural backgrounds, he also recognized a need to fit within the larger society and invest in the receiving country as much as the home country. As the younger generation of Senegalese migrants pointed out, learning and using English was one of the easiest ways to invest in their new space as well as take advantage of symbolic capital. It also combated the stigma associated with being labeled a French-speaking African.

While this chapter looked at reflections on immigration and integration in three locales, it also shed light on how Senegalese understood language ideologies, racial identity, and societal belonging through transnational perspectives. Similar to the ways in which Denis Provencher's informants combined multiple discourses (Anglo-American perspectives on sexuality, French republican tradition, and queer French tradition) to discuss sexuality, my informants relied on Senegalese understandings of ethnic/racial identity, French theorizations of race/nationhood, and American constructions of race/multiculturalism to position themselves locally, nationally, and globally.[58] Highlighting Senegalese mobility, they offered comparative critiques of each locale based on experiences they had had in other places or through stories they had heard from other travelers. They talked about how language ideologies at the societal level affected the desire and ability to integrate (e.g., Charlotte comparing the United States and France), how personal experiences dictated which languages they wanted to learn and how the relationship to these languages influenced their view of society (e.g., Abi's comparison of Italy, Spain, and the United States), and how a shared language could be worth more than other shared identity markers (e.g., the English language holding more cachet than blackness among African immigrants).

Furthermore, discussions showed how both local and global environments influenced racial formation. Some of my informants conveyed how their construction of a racial identity was mainly developed in predominantly white spaces, such as in the three sites of my research project.[59] For instance, both Professore and Diop, in Italy and the United States respectively, began to understand their blackness in the midst of a specific racialized social imaginary. Others, however, articulated how racial formation was forged through a wider lens. For instance, "A" juxtaposed the plight of the Senegalese dealing with a French presence in Senegal with the clash between African Americans and white people in the United States. By doing so, he foregrounded not only the existence of racial perceptions in Senegal but also a racialized experience shared by blacks in the United States and Senegalese in a French-dominated Senegal.[60] In other words, even before migrating, these interviewees had highly developed views and beliefs concerning race even in majority-black spaces such as Senegal, and these ideas were put into greater relief once migrating to majority-white spaces.[61] It was this long-term reflection on postcolonial relations that caused this group of Senegalese to engage in a raucous debate about race, history, and political sovereignty at the after-church potluck. Through historical connections, political positioning, and diasporic cultural formation, this global Senegalese community was continuing a tradition of Afro-Atlantic dialogues by defining and redefining who they were and who they would become in a transnational context.

# 4

# LEVERAGING LANGUAGE

## Multilingualism and Transnational Identity Formation

A few days after I moved to Paris for fieldwork, I called Duudu, an old friend of my host family in Dakar and at that point one of my only connections to the Senegalese community in Paris. He greeted me warmly on the phone, having been expecting my call. Duudu invited me to his family's home in Choisy-le-Roi, a southeastern suburb of Paris. The following day, I caught the RER C line at Saint-Michel and followed the left bank of the Seine until I arrived at the Choisy-le-Roi station. From there I meandered through the neighborhood for about a mile until I reached their home.

When I arrived on the eleventh floor of their apartment building, Nafi, Duudu's wife, opened the door and invited me in. She had just returned from the preschool across the street, where she worked. Duudu had a braced left leg propped up on a pillow. He was currently on sick leave from his job as a manager at a fire insurance company after a car accident had left him with a broken leg. He motioned for me to sit down in an ornate wooden armchair next to the sofa, making me feel like quite the guest of honor. Nafi brought me some fresh ginger juice and then sat down next to Duudu to join the conversation. As I considered their relatively comfortable life in France, with secure employment, paid sick leave, and an inviting home to welcome guests, I thought about how this picture challenged some of the negative images used to portray immigrants. In telling me their story, they would highlight many positives: the agentive strategies they used to move through transnational spaces, the ways in which language was a source of both pleasure and utility, and how they identified with and benefited from being multilingual.

Now in their fifties, Duudu and Nafi had moved to Paris eighteen years earlier. They were raising their four children, three of whom had been born in France. Duudu grew up in a Pulaar-speaking family in Saint-Louis after his parents migrated from bordering Mauritania. Nafi was born in Fouta, in northern Senegal, and was from a Pulaar-speaking family as well. After Duudu graduated from college, the two of them moved to Mauritania, where Duudu built a successful accounting business. However, border tensions between Mauritania and Senegal in the late eighties caused them to feel socially excluded. Mounting violence from the Mauritania-Senegal border war prompted them to move to France, where both of them eventually became French citizens through "reintegration."[1]

As the conversation turned to languages, Duudu reflected on his linguistic repertoire and the opportunities that his environment had given him:

> Nous avons de la chance d'avoir fait les écoles françaises donc nous avons appris le français. Nous avons tété cette langue qui est le pulaar, dès la naissance. Nous avons aussi grandi au Sénégal où on parle couramment le wolof, donc ça devient un *melting pot* où entre nous c'est n'importe quoi. On bascule du français au wolof au pulaar en moins de trois minutes. On ne sait même pas ce qu'on parle. Ça devient du ragoût, quoi.

> [We are lucky to have been provided French schooling so we learned French. We suckled this language, which is Pulaar, from birth. We also grew up in Senegal, where Wolof is spoken fluently, so it has become a *melting pot* where among us anything could be spoken. We switch from French to Wolof to Pulaar in less than three minutes. We don't even know what language we're speaking. It becomes a stew, you know.]

Duudu mentioned the different relationships he had with each language. French was the language of school, and Wolof the language of society. In describing Pulaar, he conjured the image of nourishment, equating the maternal language with feeding from a mother's bosom: "nous avons tété cette langue" (we suckled this language).[2] Duudu presented a positive description of this ability to switch between languages by framing the discussion with the word *chance* (luck). For him, being born in a place where he could utilize three languages was good luck. He then conveyed a sense of teetering back and forth (*basculer*) with his depiction of switching between languages. The words "melting pot" and *ragout* evoked the image of a simmering stew with various ingredients, circling back to the idea of nourishment that *téter* captured. However, in using an English loan word, "melting pot," which signifies diversity in the French-language context, he went beyond the food metaphor to emphasize the multicultural aspect of multilingualism.

I asked Duudu if he felt like a different person with each language he spoke. He answered: "Quand on maîtrise ces trois langues là, ça devient un jeu, quoi. Quand on parle le français, quand on parle le wolof, quand on parle le pulaar, on sait que dans la tête on est toujours sénégalais." (When we master these three languages, it becomes a game, you know. When we speak French, when we speak Wolof, when we speak Pulaar, we know that in our head we are always Senegalese.) By calling multilingual usage *un jeu* (a game), he underscored the notion of language play, the joy and creativity that emerges from the ability to manipulate multiple languages. Furthermore, he demonstrated how multilingualism is an integral part of Senegalese identity. It is therefore not so much that speaking multiple languages accesses multiple identities but that speaking multiple languages accesses a decidedly Senegalese identity whose Senegality comes precisely from this multilingualism.[3]

His migration to France helped him realize how his multilingualism, which was an important part of him, was not necessarily recognized in the same way in this new context: "Quand on vient en France, on est obligé de changer [sa façon de penser] parce qu'il y a des choses qui sont valables au Sénégal mais qui ne le sont pas ici" (When one comes to France, one is obligated to change [one's way of speaking] because there are things that are valuable in Senegal that are not here). Duudu was referring both to distinct traits in his French (vocabulary, accent, and other features that marked him as foreign) and to the rampant use of multilingualism. French societal language ideologies champion monolingualism and a very specific image of what French language should be.[4] For some informants, the pressure to speak French "perfectly" could impede conscious decisions to code-switch if they assume they will be labeled as less competent for their multilingualism.[5] Even in environments in France where multilingualism is more accepted, being able to speak African languages such as Wolof or Pulaar does not hold the same currency as speaking European ones in the eyes of French people. Perhaps because of these considerations, out of all three sites, I had substantially fewer examples of code-switching in Paris, where informants were the most interested in being labeled as competent speakers of the official language, French.

However, although using multiple languages in general and African languages in particular was worth less in the French context, both Duudu and Nafi worked hard to make sure that their children spoke not only these home languages but also English and other languages that would prove useful in the Senegalese diaspora. To them, the ability of their children to communicate within and across both African and European languages meant that they were building symbolic capital among the global Senegalese community. And there were other Senegalese in Paris who also focused on building and using multilingual repertoires because of the power it afforded them, particularly in making claims on global Senegality.

This vignette illustrates many of the issues that arose in my conversations with Senegalese in Paris, Rome, and New York—matters that have not previously been a focal point in research on Senegalese migration. Senegal is an avowedly multilingual country, as evidenced in multiple instances, from the more than twenty national languages protected by the constitution to the everyday usage of multiple languages in public and private spaces. A person raised there becomes very adept at using languages strategically, and there is a relatively robust body of literature on language use and politics in Senegal.[6] At the same time, research has been done on Senegalese outside Senegal, mainly through migration studies whose works primarily concentrate on the reception of migrants in the host country, their continued contact with Senegal, and the existence of transnational networks and support systems.[7] Just as in research on and discussions about Africans in diaspora, the focus is usually on labor, where the mobility of modern Africans is theorized through an economic lens. Unsurprisingly, migration research on Senegalese is primarily interested in the economic reasons that prompt people to migrate and the flow of goods and capital between Senegal and various global destinations.

What is missing from the literature is an approach to migration research through a sociolinguistic lens. Presuming that the linguistic gymnastic skills that have been documented in Senegal accompany those Senegalese who migrate to other countries, my interest lies in determining exactly how code-switching and multilingualism in these new contexts operate. The ability to utilize many languages often makes legible various formulations of identity, such as when Ndiaga, Professore, and Abi signaled racial othering and a lack of belonging through code-switching. While the previous chapters homed in on some of the trials and tribulations Senegalese experience with regard to negotiating identity and claiming legitimacy in European and American spaces, particularly as it pertained to blackness, not all interactions between the people in my study and their new environments should be viewed as stressful and trying. Nor were they always positioned as powerless. In previous chapters, I have noted moments when people expressed control over their situations. This chapter now aims to highlight more clearly the agency that many people have claimed and the symbolic capital they have amassed.

This chapter concretely shows how multilingualism plays a role in the Senegalese cultural imaginary and how emphasis on this multilingualism offers a new perspective on transnational identity. Many of my informants not only focused on where they came from, where they were presently, or where they were going. They also emphasized their transience—a transience assisted through multilingualism. In this specific formulation of identity, they forefronted the journey itself and the freedom they had to move between borders. Importantly, these borders are transnational in a double sense, for we will see examples of people crossing from one nation to the next and also, through performance, crossing from one nationality to the next as they negotiate identity through humor and language. By using multiple languages and their respective vernaculars, the Senegalese position themselves globally through complex linguistic formations. In the following pages, I foreground the pleasures and competencies attached to language use that were revealed in my interviews with multilingual, mobile Senegalese in Paris, Rome, and New York. While recognizing the multiple and differing experiences, I also find commonalities in each site and across sites. This exploration of the relationship between multilingualism and migration uncovers one of the most compelling images: that of the multilingual traveler, a transnational construct that explains a positive phenomenon that is absent from previous scholarly discussions on Senegalese in the diaspora.

## THE MULTILINGUAL TRAVELER: THREE SITES, THREE SNAPSHOTS

### New York: "L'uomo perfetto"

On a muggy summer day, I exited a crowded subway and walked along one of the large tree-studded boulevards that ushered me into the heart of Little Senegal. Aminata's description of this neighborhood was becoming alive before my eyes. Wafting through the air, the sounds of Wolof mingled with the smells of seasoned fish and fried plantains. Passers-by, decked out in multicolored wax prints, greeted each other in multilingual exchanges. Upon arriving at the terrace of a Senegalese-French restaurant, I noticed a man about to sit down at one of the sidewalk tables. He was wearing the white-cotton button-down shirt with red batik trim that fit the description that thirty-seven-year-old Ousseynou had texted me. As I approached, he greeted me with a huge smile. "So you're the one that's asking people about language?" he asked in French. Guilty as charged, I laughed, and he motioned me to sit. As we were engaging in small talk, the waiter (W) arrived and, addressing Ousseynou (O) in Wolof, asked, "Sénégalais nga?" (Are you Senegalese?) through both the content of his words and his language choice. Continuing in Wolof, he then asked me if I spoke any Wolof, implying that he knew I wasn't Senegalese. I participated in the basic Wolof greetings before switching to French. From his first interactions with us, the waiter conveyed his assumptions about who we were through his language choices and modes of address. I mentally noted that I should ask him later if he would be interested in an interview. As the waiter moved on to his next clients, Ousseynou and I continued our small talk. I learned that he was a taxi driver, he was originally from Dakar, and he had spent the last nine years in New York. I then commenced the interview. While there was a well-established precedent concerning multilingual interviews throughout my data collection, I was not prepared for the thrilling linguistic turn that the conversation would take. It was this moment that led me to focus on the concept of the multilingual traveler.[8]

| | |
|---|---|
| M: | *Quelle est votre langue préférée?* |
| O: | Italiano. |
| M: | Italiano? *Vous parlez* italiano? |
| O: | Io parlo bene italiano. |
| M: | Sì? Perché? |
| O: | Perché sono andato in Italia e ho fatto tre anni in Italia. |
| M: | Dove in Italia? |
| O: | Io stavo a Roma— |
| W: | [*waiter interrupts*] Parlano italiano? |
| O: | **Yes**. Este li è italiano, **too**. [ *points to waiter*] |
| M: | Sì? |
| O: | **Yeah**. |
| M: | È interessante. Perché ho fatto la stessa ricerca a Roma. A Parigi ed a Roma. . . . L'italiano è la tua lingua preferita? |
| O: | Preferita, sì. |
| M: | Perché? |
| O: | Per me, l'italiano è una lingua romantica. Quando la gente parla italiano, io, quando sento un italiano parlare . . . mi sento bene. . . . |
| M: | Sì. Come hai imparato l'italiano? |
| W: | Sei italiana? |
| M: | No. Ho vissuto a Roma. |
| W: | Sì? |
| M: | Sì. Lì ho imparato l'italiano. |
| W: | . . . io ho studiato anche l'italiano in Italia. |

M:     Dove esattamente?

W:     Vicino a Pisa. E tu?

O:     Roma.

W:     Roma? OK.

O:     . . . Ma *ça fait huit ans* **ma ngi fii leegi**.

W:     Ora io sono qui da cinque mesi.

O:     Cinco mesi? Ah.

W:     Cinque mesi che sono qui.

M:     Ah, OK.

W:     Però io sono laureato in lingue.

M:     Anch'io.

W:     Perciò ho studiato lingue. Inglese, francese, spagnolo, portoghese.

M:     Anch'io!

W:     Sì! . . .

O:     Un perfetto uomo che parla tutto.

[*waiter smiles and continues working*]

O:     *Ah, oui.*

[*I laugh*]

O:     *Tu as vu hein? Ça c'est les Sénégalais.*

M:     *Oui oui. C'est incroyable.*

O:     *Les Sénégalais aiment voyager, aiment apprendre des langues. Tu vois?*

M:     *C'est ça! C'est intéressant.*


[M:     *What is your favorite language?*

O:     Italian.

M:     Italian? *You speak* Italian?

O:     I speak Italian well.

M:     Yes? Why?

O:     Because I lived in Italy. I spent three years in Italy.

M:     Where in Italy?

O:     I was in Rome—

W:     [*waiter interrupts*] You are speaking Italian?

O:     **Yes**. This one there is Italian, **too**. [*points to waiter*]

M:     Yes?

O:     **Yeah**.

M:     This is interesting. Because I did the same research in Rome. Paris and Rome. . . . Italian is your favorite language?

O:     Favorite, yes.

M:     Why?

O:     For me, Italian is a romantic language. When people speak Italian, I, when I hear an Italian speak . . . I feel good. . . .

M:   Yes. How did you learn Italian?
W:   You are Italian?
M:   No. I lived in Rome.
W:   Yes?
M:   Yes. I learned Italian there.
W:   . . . I also studied Italian in Italy.
M:   Where exactly?
W:   Near Pisa. And you?
O:   Rome.
W:   Rome? OK.
O:   . . . But *it's been eight years* **I am here now.**
W:   I've been here for five months.
O:   <u>Five</u> months? Ah.
W:   Five months I'm here.
M:   Ah, OK.
W:   But I graduated with a degree in languages.
M:   Me too.
W:   For that reason I studied languages. English, French, Spanish, Portuguese.
M:   Me too!
W:   Yes! . . .
O:   A perfect man who speaks everything.
[*waiter smiles and continues working*]
O:   *Oh yes.*
[*I laugh*]
O:   *You see, eh? That is how the Senegalese are.*
M:   *Yes yes, It's incredible.*
O:   *The Senegalese love to travel, love to learn languages. You see?*
M:   *That's it! It's interesting.*]

Ousseynou's reflection supported my sense of the way so many in the Senegalese diaspora imagine themselves. Many of my interviewees had lived in several countries and displayed pride in the ability to move, adapt, and learn the local language. He put his finger on something fundamental about this cultural self-perception, and both what he said and how he structured his discourse shed light on this thoughtful theorization of global Senegality.

Ousseynou code-switched to answer the question on language preference, a move that resulted in the dominant language of the conversation changing to Italian. Upon overhearing us, the waiter interjected in Italian, further driving home the virtues and ubiquity of migration and multilingualism among Senegalese. Ousseynou went on to explain why he loved the Italian language, which he described as romantic, and which caused him to feel great when he heard it. Whether he was playing into known stereotypes of Italian or came to this conclusion of his own accord, he had a positive visceral reaction to Italian and expressed the joy that accompanied his using it.

I was also struck by the ownership claims that both he and the waiter made on Italian language and identity. There was a certain embodying of national identity happening, evidenced by Ousseynou saying in a mix of Spanish and Italian, "Este li è italiano" (this one there is Italian) when referring to the waiter. This national identity claim was juxtaposed with the waiter's earlier assumption that Ousseynou was Senegalese, obvious from the language used to address him. The waiter also asked if I was Italian, entertaining this as a possibility, even though I did not look like a traditional Italian. This is an important point because my research from Rome showed how difficult it was for people of color to claim an Italian identity even if they had Italian citizenship and/or were fluent in Italian. His affording me the opportunity to be Italian coupled with Ousseynou's calling him Italian indicated a certain negotiation of Italianness that was connected to our respective Italian-speaking abilities.[9]

At the same time, both Ousseynou and the waiter signaled what they viewed as an emphatically Senegalese identity in the way they spoke and switched between various languages. Ousseynou proved just how pervasive code-switching was when he used Italian, French, and Wolof effortlessly in the line "Ma *ça fait huit ans* **ma ngi fii leegi**" (But *it's been eight years* **I am here now**). In his next turn of talk, he used Spanish and Italian when verifying "Cinco mesi?" (Five months?). Meanwhile, at this point in the conversation the waiter decided to respond only in Italian even though he had been switching between French and Wolof. It was impossible to predict which language would be used. While it is true that the majority of the world is multilingual and in these societies code-switching is an expected phenomenon about which many people do not think twice, Ousseynou acknowledged the positive nature of this ability with his remark, "Un perfetto uomo che parla tutto" (A perfect man who speaks everything). Furthermore, he put this multilingual identity front and center when he explained, "Ça c'est les Sénégalais" (That is how the Senegalese are). The Senegalese, according to him, differentiated themselves by their love of travel and languages. These were quintessential aspects of their global Senegality and evidence of an accumulation of symbolic capital.

Later in the conversation, Ousseynou discussed why, as a taxi driver, he wanted to learn Spanish:[10] "Por **me, è** muy interesante de hablar muchos *different languages* . . . si le client entre dans ma voiture, je dis, '¿Cómo estás? ¿Muy bien?' They say 'Ah OK, ¡tu hablas español!' Tu vois?" (For **me, it is** very interesting to speak many *different languages* . . . if the client gets in my car, I say,

"How are you? Very good?" *They say, "Ah OK, you speak Spanish!"* You see?)
Creating a space of linguistic hospitality, he sought to put his clients at ease,
many of whom spoke Spanish. But it was not only what he said that suggested
the multilingual identity he tried to cultivate; it was also how he said it, smoothly
switching between several languages in this short excerpt and throughout the
longer interview, that illustrated the privileged nature of multilingualism.

Thirty-eight-year-old mechanic Bouba displayed a similar versatility in
languages. Born in Dakar to a Bambara-speaking father and a Pulaar-speaking
mother, Bouba learned Wolof by playing with the neighborhood children.
He went to trade school in Morocco for three years and then decided to go to
Switzerland to work for two years. He returned to Senegal, where he remained
for seven years, working for an Italian firm part of that time. When I interviewed
him, he had been in the United States for two years with the hope of getting a
degree from an American college or university, but he had found the cost of
education in the United States to be prohibitive. Bouba conveyed how both his
linguistic experience in Senegal and his moving to different places allowed for
multilingual language learning:[11] "Je *parlo italiano* mais **just a little bit** parce
que je travaille avec des Italiens au Sénégal. . . . Mais ici, quand je suis venu aux
États-Unis, ici j'ai pas mal de travail avec des Espagnols." (I *speak Italian* but
**just a little bit** because I work with Italians in Senegal. . . . But here, when I
came to the United States, I work quite a bit with Spaniards.) Bouba exhibited
a willingness to adapt linguistically, having learned some Italian because of his
work environment in Senegal and wanting to learn Spanish because of the
work environment here in the United States. Just like Ousseynou, he showed
while telling. Although he admitted to speaking only a little Italian, he was con-
fident in his French and English speaking abilities and demonstrated how he
used these skills to his advantage.

For instance, he described how his French was useful with his current job at
a restaurant: "Mon *big boss*, il ne parle pas français. Maintenant, quand il veut
quelque *translation*, il m'appelle, pour que je puisse faire cette *translation*. Ça c'est
fort pour moi. C'est pour cela que j'aime bien mon idéologie."[12] (My *big boss*, he
doesn't speak French. Now, when he wants some *translation*, he calls me so that
I can do that *translation*. That's important for me. That's why I like my ideology.) Bouba thus provided tangible evidence to support his ideology about the
importance of multilingualism. For him, anywhere he went he would adapt to
his immediate surroundings. This ability to adapt, facilitated by his access to
different languages, minimized borders that often constrained other people.
His focus on translation highlighted how he mastered the liminal space between
languages, ensuring his ownership of symbolic competence. By gaining strength
through this cultivated linguistic ability, Bouba had transcended restrictions

that could be imposed on him for being a foreigner, a non-native speaker, or an immigrant.

Both Bouba and Ousseynou explained the utilitarian purposes of speaking multiple languages, as their abilities proved useful for their jobs. However, they blurred the boundary between speaking for utility and speaking for pleasure. Bouba conveyed the pride he felt that someone in a position of authority had to rely on him. In referring to his boss as "big boss," he accentuated the power dynamic between them: the boss might be more important, but he needed Bouba's superior language skills. So while his skills served a utilitarian purpose, they were also a source of pleasure. The situation was similar for Ousseynou. As a taxi driver, he was required to have only limited communication skills. As long as the destination address was understood, there was little need to be able to communicate more extensively. However, he derived pleasure from creating a good environment for his clients, achieving what many informants deemed as a quintessential Senegalese value: *teranga*, or hospitality.[13] Furthermore, Bouba and Ousseynou both obtained pleasure from two other key tenets of global Senegality, being mobile and multilingual, therefore fitting into their conception of a true diasporic Senegalese.

### Paris: The Businessman as the Model Multilingual Traveler

On a weekly basis in Paris, I would satisfy my hunger for authentic Senegalese cuisine at a restaurant in the northern part of the city. While I sometimes conversed with the loquacious owner, Nyambi, most of my conversations revolved around the musings of the waitress, Ndella, and her most loyal patron, Boubacar.[14] The TV, which was always on Senegalese channel RTS1, was consistently blaring in the background, providing fodder for discussions of current events. In fact, the two of them were constantly providing a running commentary, taking the stories that the Senegalese newscasters presented and interjecting their own colorful critiques. The hot topic on this particular day was the currency devaluation in Guinea, and Boubacar was musing that he could probably buy a whole village there because of the current exchange rate. As someone who had introduced himself to me as "businessman extraordinaire," he was often explaining both his actual and his desired business ventures.

During lulls in their comedic recaps of the news, I usually interspersed questions about language. When I asked them about language preferences, Ndella (N) and Boubacar (B) agreed that while they were partial to Wolof, no language competed with English globally:[15]

> B:    *L'anglais c'est mieux parce que dans le monde entier on parle anglais.*
> N:    *. . . J'aime bien l'anglais.*

B: Dafa neex, *quoi.* Làkk bu neex la.

N: Torop.[16]

B: Boo déggee, loo wax ci tubaab,[17] soo ko waxee ci *anglais* day neex.

N: Yow, dégg nga *anglais?*

B: *Bien sûr* dégg naa anglais. Man ma def *cinq ans en Hollande.* **Businessman** bu déggul *anglais?*

N: Loolu, moom, dëgg la.

B: Suba nga dem fenn. Beneen nga dem fenn. Bu yàggee nga dégg *anglais.*

[B: *English is better because the whole world speaks English.*

N: *. . . I like English.*

B: It's beautiful, *you know.* It's a beautiful language.

N: So beautiful.

B: If you understand, everything that you say in French has a beautiful translation in *English.*

N: Do you speak *English?*

B: *Of course* I speak *English.* I spent *five years in Holland.* **A businessman** who doesn't speak *English?*

N: That's true.

B: Go somewhere tomorrow. The day after, someplace else. Soon you will understand *English.*][18]

Boubacar's theorization of a businessman identity contributes to the overarching theme of the multilingual traveler. He conveyed the ephemeral nature of the businessman who changed locations from day to day: "Suba nga dem fenn. Beneen nga dem fenn. Bu yàggee nga dégg *anglais.*" (Go somewhere tomorrow. The day after, someplace else. Soon you will understand *English.*) It was through travel that one could learn English—a language that was essential for successfully conducting business—and add to a linguistic repertoire. He suggested that this language learning was as natural to the businessman as the need to migrate. The use of *bien sûr* (of course) indicated that not knowing English would be unlikely for a person who identified as a businessman. Furthermore, using the anglicism "businessman" instead of *homme d'affaires* indexed America and its position as a major powerhouse in international affairs and global capitalism.[19]

He also implied the global importance of English by mentioning his English usage in the five years he spent in the Netherlands, a country that was not officially English-speaking. He did not learn Dutch, so I assume knowing English was sufficient for the time he spent there. This disinterest in learning Dutch does complicate the image of the multilingual traveler that we saw in Ousseynou's discussion of learning languages, where there was certain joy in just being able to communicate with people in their most comfortable language. Perhaps because Boubacar was so invested in his identity as a businessman, his interest in English overrode an investment in a more general multilingual identity. Additionally, Boubacar seemed to take a more pragmatic approach to language learning, acquiring the language that would serve him most, and Dutch did not meet this criterion.

Nevertheless, Boubacar not only reflected on the usefulness of English; he also discussed English from an aesthetic point of view. He described English as beautiful: "Làkk bu neex la" (It's a beautiful language). He then compared French and English, showing that whatever he said in French could be beautifully translated into English: "Boo déggee, loo wax ci tubaab, soo ko waxee ci *anglais* day neex" (If you understand, everything that you say in French has a beautiful translation in *English*). In this case, he shared a common intrinsic motivation with Ousseynou, who felt great when learning Italian. For Boubacar, the beauty of the English language warranted its acquisition. He indicated that both the aural aesthetics of English and the fact that it could succinctly convey a message, which was particularly useful in business negotiations, contributed to its beauty. In short, Boubacar reiterated many of the attitudes about the English language that surfaced throughout my research, namely, its usefulness, its global importance, its aesthetic appeal, and its distinction as a language that everyone wanted to learn. Therefore, while English was deemed useful in a variety of contexts, this utility existed in concert with the pleasure it bestowed on those who spoke it.

Hakim was not a self-made businessman like Boubacar, but he performed market research for a supermarket and had his own thoughts on multilingualism and traveling that conveyed both utility and fulfillment: "C'est un enrichissement, le fait d'être plurilingue. Parler le wolof, français, anglais, arabe, et aussi une autre langue, ça permet une fois dans un autre pays de s'intégrer. . . . C'est une ouverture dans le monde, c'est une ouverture en soi-même. On en profite." (It is an enrichment, being multilingual. Speaking Wolof, French, English, Arabic, and other languages, too, allows one to integrate once in another country. . . . It's a window to the world, a window to the self. We take advantage of it.) Hakim's use of words such as *enrichissement* and *profiter* evoked notions of wealth accumulation, but in this case, wealth was measured not in money but in symbolic capital. Multilingualism allowed for integration and therefore acceptance in foreign lands. While most of the discussions on integration in my data had been framed negatively, as an elusive goal that was racially restricted, Hakim chose to highlight successful integration made possible through the ability to use languages. Hakim also underscored notions of mobility. Integration is usually confined to specific locales, but Hakim's list of multiple languages and his failure to name a country in particular suggested that integration was possible in multiple sites. With access to languages, people could move freely and effortlessly while simultaneously growing personally by gaining insight about themselves.

For the restaurateur Nyambi, a businessman himself, this mobility was a cultural trait that was quintessentially Senegalese: "Mais l'immigration sénégalaise est culturelle d'abord. Le Sénégalais, c'est quelqu'un dans le départ. . . . C'est un peuple qui voyage, un peuple qui s'en va." (Senegalese immigration is cultural, above all. A Senegalese person is constantly departing. . . . We are a people who travel, a people who leave.) Nyambi gave me a history lesson about the mobility of Senegalese who migrated all over West Africa, then to France, and then finally to the United States and Italy. With each wave, they reached further and further shores. The image he painted of someone being *dans le départ* was quite poetic in French. Signaling their constant movement, he positioned Senegalese people within the act of departing, in that transitional space between two places. It was as if departure itself were a place one could inhabit. He reinforced this image through repetition, tweaking the verb ever so slightly while retaining its general meaning and the phrase's rhythm: "un peuple qui voyage, un peuple qui s'en va." In other words, he rhythmically conjured movement through his linguistic construction. Just like Ousseynou in New York with his depiction of the Senegalese as consummate multilingual travelers ("Ça c'est les Sénégalais"), Nyambi foregrounded what he also viewed as Senegalese people's most indispensable trait.

## Rome: "Sempre in giro"

Karim, the head dancer and owner of his eponymous dance school, was leading a group of predominantly mid-twenties Italian women in a Sabar routine. They were accompanied by a full drum troupe with Dakar-native Idi at the helm. I was trying to follow along, hoping that the West African dance course from my time living in Dakar seven years prior would at least allow me to keep up. By the end of the hour, I was one massive puddle of sweat, a perfect state for an introduction with a possible interviewee. A close friend of mine had brought me to the class, and afterward she took me to meet her friends Karim and Idi. As I explained my research, Idi perked up. "I know just the person," he said in fluent Italian. He was referring to thirty-year-old Bachir, described as *una persona importante* (an important person). Beatrice, Idi's Italian dance partner, inquired about the nature of his importance. Idi simply explained that Bachir knew a lot of things. The difficulty was that he would be hard to pin down. Apparently, Bachir had returned the previous day from Switzerland and was going to Turin the following day. He had been in France the previous month.

Idi summed up perfectly what we were thinking: "Lui sta sempre in giro" (He is always on the move).

To be *in giro* denotes that someone is out and about, always moving. When I finally located Bachir, who was splitting his time between Rome, northern Italy, and Paris, I asked him why he had come to Italy in the first place and why he was always in motion. He paused for a moment and replied thoughtfully:[20] "Vengo perché magari venendo qui posso fare un cambiamento. Quello che ti **dispinge**—ti spinge,[21] quello che *te pousse à partir, ça n'a rien à voir à la fin. . . . C'est un besoin profond de vouloir arriver à quelque chose de plus concret. De donner sens à ta vie, même si ta vie a déjà son sens.*" (I come here because perhaps coming here I can make a change. That which **spaints** you—pushes you, that which *pushes you to leave, it doesn't matter in the end. . . . It is a deep need to want to arrive at something more concrete. To give sense to your life, even if your life already makes sense.*) Bachir saw movement as a natural process that gave life meaning. As he tripped over the word *dispingere* (spaint), a made-up word in Italian, which was a mistake he seemed to correct instantly with the Italian word for push, *spingere*, he switched to French to conclude his thought. It was as if he needed French, the language he could speak more comfortably, in order to provide a philosophical description of this need to migrate. The move from Italian to French mimicked his spatial movement between countries as he searched for some intangible prize.

Many other interviewees in Rome also underlined the propensity of Senegalese to travel and speak multiple languages. When I asked Karim why he had moved to Italy, he detailed a long history of migration and language acquisition. He was born to a Sereer family and grew up in Kaolack, a region in central Senegal. He spoke both Wolof and Sereer at home, which he described as a normal occurrence in a country like Senegal. His village was predominantly Sereer-speaking, but because there were so many different ethnic groups nearby, Wolof was the lingua franca. He also began to learn French in elementary school. At eighteen, armed with three languages, he moved to Dakar and worked toward a degree in languages at the university. He knew he never wanted to stop learning languages and decided to add English and Spanish to his repertoire. He considered his English imperfect but decent. He then laughed as he thought about how the Spanish he had learned in college quickly disappeared when he moved to Italy.

Karim explained how moving to Italy was simply a linguistic opportunity: "Volevo imparare un'altra lingua. Voglio imparare tutte le lingue possibili. Venendo qua, posso vedere il sistema, come è. . . . Se tu non viaggi, non sei ricco. Se non viaggi, non sai chi sei." (I wanted to learn another language. I want to learn all the languages possible. Coming here, I can see the system, how it is. . . . If you don't travel, you are not rich. If you don't travel, you don't know who you are.) Karim had been living in Paris for four years before moving to Rome, where, when I met him, he had been for three years. By having moved from rural Senegal, to Dakar, to Paris, and then to Rome, Karim was following the migration pattern that Nyambi had described to me months earlier. While Karim had depicted Bachir as *sempre in giro*, he was not doing too badly himself. I was also struck by how he philosophized mobility and multilingualism in a way similar to Hakim's. It was through travel that one could become rich from experiences as well as achieve self-awareness. Italy, in particular, was a self-directed study abroad opportunity for many of my interviewees.

Ondine, a twenty-six-year-old actress from Dakar who had been living in Rome for five years, emphasized the citizen-of-the-world figure that many of my interviewees embodied. She boasted about having done *tanti giri nel mondo* (so many trips throughout the world), including journeys to the Netherlands, Spain, and Italy. Drawing the connection between travel and language, she remarked, "È molto importante parlare tante lingue. È importantissimo perché come noi siamo cittadini del mondo, facciamo giri a qualsiasi paese. È importante anche studiare altre lingue." (It's very important to speak many languages. It is extremely important because since we are citizens of the world, we go around to any country. It is also important to study other languages.) With *noi siamo cittadini del mondo*, she moved from talking about herself to including Senegalese in general, who are socialized to travel and acquire languages. Ondine used the superlative *importantissimo* only twice in her interview, and both times it was to argue the significance of multilingualism. Speaking multiple languages grants access to the world, and in return the world gives opportunities to speak. Mobility and multilingualism exist symbiotically.

In addition, there is also the ludic aspect of multilingualism whereby people I interviewed in Rome conceived of using different languages in a conversation as a game such as we saw with Duudu's description of code-switching as *un jeu* (a game).[22] For instance, Ibou referred to the ability to speak multiple languages as *uno sport* and the desire to leave his country as a means to *fare esperienze fuori* (have experiences outside the country). Thirty-six-year-old Ndour, who had spent a decade in Rome, echoed this sentiment when talking with Senegalese in Italy: "Quando ci vediamo, non è che parliamo wolof. Parliamo in italiano. Io ho un amico con cui lavoro. Tante volte parliamo wolof, ma tante volte anche parliamo italiano perché ci piace parlare in italiano. Scherziamo un po'." (When we meet, it is not that we speak Wolof. We speak in Italian. I have a friend at work. We often speak Wolof, but we also speak Italian because we like to speak in Italian. We joke a bit.) The phrase *scherziamo un po'* means to joke or to play around, conveying a similar meaning as the word *sport*. The focus on playing with multiple languages highlights the very nature of symbolic competence. Even though he was more comfortable speaking Wolof, he would sometimes speak Italian for the joy of speaking it. His friend and he had more than one language at their disposal, so they could choose a random language to speak at any given time. Sometimes there is meaning in language choice; sometimes just having the choice is what gives the experience meaning.

A major thread in the research both on multilingualism in Senegal and on Senegalese migration to the West is the utilitarian nature of various choices. In the former, people choose certain languages to display particular allegiances or express certain identity markers. In the latter, people learn a language in order to secure employment. Motivations are understood in terms of the purposes they serve. While these reasons cannot be discounted, more is happening. Utility and pleasure coexist. Ousseynou explicitly described Italian as a romantic language, while Boubacar noted the beauty of English. Meanwhile, Ibou, Ndour, and Duudu expressed the pleasure attached to language play. These reflections forefront just how nuanced a person's relationship to language is. Furthermore, these experiences offer a space for Africans to reflect on joy, a notion that is often absent from research on Africa and Africans.

## PERFORMING IDENTITIES

Through different types of linguistic expression, my interviewees simultaneously performed and formed identities in a variety of spaces. From the use of multilingual humor in a Senegalese restaurant, to the creation and consumption of multilingual hip-hop in Paris, to the negotiation of identities via multilingual exchanges and music in a Senegalese enclave in New York and across the diaspora, language was central to how these communities made sense of and claims to their local and global environments.

Places such as restaurants and cafés can serve as fertile space for identity formation. It was evident in my research how important cafés, restaurants, cultural centers, and shared meals at home were to the sense of self and belonging in Senegalese communities. In each site, I found people debating the nature of life over meals. Most of these times, I did not instigate these conversations but was a curious bystander. Often the discussions became slightly heated as the participants enjoyed engaging in enthusiastic repartee. These sites served not only as a space of creative freedom but also as a laboratory where one could test ideas and receive feedback.[23] Indeed, the café-as-laboratory was very much in evidence, particularly in the aforementioned Senegalese restaurant in Rome.

Similarly, music offers a space for cultural expression and a site of identity formation. Listening to music is both an individual and a collective practice where listeners simultaneously experience lyrics, melodies, and rhythms at a personal level (feeling emotions and engaging the senses) and at a societal level (aligning oneself with a group that shares musical tastes).[24] Through the production and consumption of music, people make a variety of identity claims. For instance, in exploring musical traditions in black communities in Britain, Paul Gilroy has triangulated the construction of blackness across the Atlantic world: "This musical heritage gradually became an important factor in facilitating the transition of diverse settlers to a distinct mode of lived blackness. It was instrumental in producing a constellation of subject positions that was openly indebted for its conditions of possibility to the Caribbean, the United States, and even Africa."[25] Music thus offers a way for people to see how others interpret lived experiences and to construct narratives of sameness and difference regardless of geographic location.

The recent memoirs of former Ghanaian president John Dramani Mahama and former French minister of justice Christiane Taubira attest to the power of music, language, and black identity formation. Mahama reminisces about how music across the continent and the world helped him articulate who he was and how he belonged.[26] From the ability of Miriam Makeba to coax people around the world to sing along to "Pata Pata" in Xhosa to Mahama's friends substituting James Brown lyrics with words from Gonja, Dagbani, or pidgin, linguistic and cultural diversity were feeding the global black experience and creating a space for cultural exchange between black America and Africa.[27] Meanwhile, Taubira connects some of the same musical icons with big names in black liberation (e.g., Angela Davis and the Black Panthers). For instance, she writes, "Le swing furieux de James Brown m'a révélé une impétueuse vérité, enfouie, négligée jusqu'alors, étouffée peut-être. *Say It Loud, I'm Black and I'm proud*." (The furious swing of James Brown revealed to me an impetuous truth, buried, neglected until then, smothered perhaps. *Say It Loud, I'm Black and I'm proud*.) As high school students in Cayenne in the late sixties, her classmates and she would use this imperative to proudly and unapologetically exclaim that they were "black and beautiful."[28]

Instead of face-to-face conversations in cafés that produce complex discussions of identity and belonging, these musical interactions happen through a cultural medium disseminated globally. As Simon Frith acknowledges, "What makes [music] special for identity . . . is that it defines space without boundaries."[29] In what follows, I consider the role of gathering spaces, such as restaurants, musical events, and cultural centers, in supporting Senegalese identity formation abroad. Here, too, we will see the same blending of utility and pleasure that the multilingual traveler evokes, with perhaps even more focus on pleasure, since these types of spaces are focal points for coming together and sharing. These vignettes, analyzed from a linguistic perspective, interrogate how different sites foster identity formation and performance in transnational spaces.

## A Senegalese Restaurant in Rome as a Site of Humor

Thinking back on my three months in Rome, I am struck by the amount of laughter that pervades my memories. Central to my experience was the secret Senegalese restaurant. It had no official name. It officially did not exist. In fact, there was nothing official about it. It was tucked behind a storefront that had an odd assortment of beauty products, newspapers, and various other things. The lights were always so dim that I doubt anyone walking by would have assumed it was open. It was as if the proprietors were trying *not* to sell things.

But for those in the know, it opened up a portal to the most authentic Senegalese space I encountered in my three sites. At the end of a long hall was a back room with a few tables, loads of chairs, and a TV hanging from the wall. At all hours of the day, a raucous group of regulars would feast on *ceebu jen* and other typical Senegalese dishes. Food wasn't placed on plates, as you would expect in established Senegalese restaurants in Paris and New York, but on a large platter. Just as is customary in any house in Dakar, people would sit around and shovel rice into their respective mouths with their right hands. This establishment could barely be considered a restaurant. It was as if Kolle, the owner, simply opened her home to all her friends and received a nominal tip to help cover the costs of the raw materials.

This space acted as a haven, an anomaly in the hustle and bustle of immigrant life in Rome. Those who ate here were not outsiders. They truly belonged. And in this relaxed setting, the laughter, jokes, and teasing flowed endlessly. On a cold day in February, the patrons were particularly feisty, most likely because it was the first time in two decades that Rome had seen snow. The owner Kolle (K) was presently scolding Biondo (B) in a raised tone of voice because of his behavior. Victoria (V), the Italian woman married to Idi, was also present:[30]

> K:  Waaw, baax na. **Hai sentito?** Baax na. Moytul rekk. *Comme que* dangay tas rekk, negal ba nga dem sa kër, nga def ko fa. *Problème* nga ma naral indil. Bàyyil li ngay def.
>
> B:  *Est-ce que* am nga *assurance?* . . . [*Kolle is mad and doesn't respond anymore. Biondo turns to Victoria*] **Allora, che dici? Tutto a posto?**
>
> V:  **Ma sì::::.**
>
> B:  Ana waa kër ga?
>
> V:  **Bene. Hai visto la neve?**
>
> B:  **Mamma mia.**

> [K:  Yes it's fine. **Did you hear me?** It's fine. Watch out. Since you want to break it, wait until you get home to do it. Don't create *problems*. Stop what you're doing.

B:     *Do* you have *insurance?* . . . [*Kolle is mad and does not respond anymore. Biondo turns to Victoria*] **So, what's going on with you? Everything OK?**

V:     **Of cou:::rse.**

B:     How's the family?

V:     **Good. Did you see the snow?**

B:     **My word.**]³¹

Kolle said rather sarcastically to Biondo: "Waaw, baax na. **Hai sentito**, baax na?" (Yes it's fine. **Did you hear me?** It's fine.) This whole section of the conversation had been in Wolof, so the contrast with Italian was quite stark. It was as if she were stressing her sarcasm by bracketing it with Italian. Switching to Italian to say "You hear" gave voice to her words by drawing attention to the sense of hearing. Meanwhile, Biondo was able to add emphasis through his multilingual usage as well: "*Est-ce que* am nga *assurance?*" (*Do* you have *insurance?*) He used question markers in both French and Wolof when *am nga* would have been sufficient by itself. He could have just as easily said, "Est-ce que tu as de l'assurance?" but that would have constituted a complete rupture with the Wolof-speaking conversation. The presence of the French word *assurance* was not surprising because it was a French borrowing in Wolof. However, the French question marker was unnecessary because *am nga* already indicated that a question was being asked. This redundancy succeeded in emphasizing either the joking nature of his question or the question itself.

Once Kolle refused to speak to him any further, Biondo turned his attention to Victoria, changing languages to show that he had changed interlocutors. However, he was not finished with Wolof. After greeting Victoria in Italian, "tutto a posto?" (Everything OK?), he mirrored that greeting with a standard one in Wolof, "Ana waa kër ga?" (How's the family?). Victoria answered in Italian before moving the conversation to the topic of the day, the unprecedented snowfall in Rome. In signaling different interlocutors and different subject matters, code-switching offered a variety of discursive options.

The secret Senegalese restaurant was also a site where people could "try on" identities and not worry about how they would be received and perceived. For instance, one day Moustapha, whom I had not met before and never got a chance to formally interview, acted out his version of an Italian. In taking a bite of his meal, he dramatically declared: "Buonissimo. Buonissimo. Come gli italiani. Mamma mia, che buo:::no. Come, come hai fatto per prepararlo così, eh?" (Delicious. Delicious. Like Italians. Wow, how goo:::d. What did you do to prepare it like this, huh?) In his mind, he was behaving like an Italian and signaled this evocation of the Italian spirit by saying *come gli italiani* (like Italians).

He exaggerated the words by extending the vowels in *buono*, by repeating the
superlative, which in turn emphasized its weight, and by using a phrase that the
Senegalese I interviewed in Rome had adopted with vigor, *mamma mia*. He was
performing his version of an Italian who enjoyed his meal and used phrases
that he assumed an Italian would use. His use of Italian was almost theatrical,
seemingly emphasizing a particular brand of Italianness.[32] Moustapha's exag-
gerations captured the voice that he imagined for the stereotypical Italian,
highlighting how he was engaging with his new environment.

On another day, Biondo (B) and Kolle (K) were watching a video of two
well-known West African artists, Youssou Ndour from Senegal and Rokia
Traore from Mali. In this excerpt, they were midway through their conversation, which was almost entirely in Wolof:[33]

K:   Wa ji booko xoolee.
B:   *Oh che bella, mamma mia, guarda gli occhi. Che belli.*
K:   Gisoo ki ànd ak ki toog. Xam nga, ñoom, bu ñu àndee ak Afrikan
     ba dugg si biir Afrik yi, dañuy bég. Mungi bég xam nga di ree rekk.
     [*watches video*]

[K:  This guy, if you look at him.
B:   *How beautiful, my word. Look at the eyes. How beautiful.*
K:   Look at that one sitting there. You know, them, when they are
     with Africans, among Africans, they are happy. He is so happy,
     you know, he's laughing nonstop. [*watches video*]][34]

As Kolle was describing a guy in the video in Wolof, Biondo momentarily
switched to Italian when Rokia Traore appeared. He started fawning over her
beauty. But why did he do so in Italian? Gesticulating wildly, he spoke in exaggerated tones, suggesting that the language switch signified a voicing of what he
might see as the prototypical Italian male in the presence of a beautiful woman.
He used the seemingly prerequisite *mamma mia* and focused on a body part, the
eyes. He repeated the word *bello* to accentuate her beauty. Again, this voicing
of Italian seemed to create a performance of an Italian identity, at least his
conceptualization of a male Italian identity.

These two examples demonstrated cultural and national identity performance through voicing. The following excerpt goes even a step further by not
only appropriating certain cultural and national characteristics but also initiating
a mindful discarding of a national identity. Questions of identity were evoked
consciously in natural conversation and in a manner that played on words and
languages in a creative way. In the following conversation, Idi (I), a friend (F),

and Bachir (B) were joking about being Senegalese over a meal at the Senegalese restaurant:[35]

> I:    Non mi piacciono i senegalesi, e per questo io ho tornato[36] italiano adesso. Capito? [*everyone laughs*] I senegalesi parlano troppo, capito. Hai visto questo?
>
> F:    Chi è italiano? Sei italiano?
>
> I:    Sì.
>
> F:    Meno male. <u>Boy,</u> *yow yaa doon naan fii?*
>
> I:    Non è male che cosa?
>
> F:    Perche sei italiano adesso. Noi siamo dei senegalesi, capito?
>
> B:    **Je suis fier d'être sénégalais.**
>
> F:    *Wax ko si* **italien.**
>
> I:    Ecco, io, grazie a tutti—
>
> F:    *Jox ko si ndox mi mu naan si* **italien.**
>
> I:    *Bokkul si* **italien.**
>
> F:    *Waaye benn la.*
>
> I:    *Asstaf four la.*[37]

> [I:    I don't like the Senegalese and therefore I've become Italian now. Understood? [*everyone laughs*] The Senegalese talk too much. Understood? You've seen this?
>
> F:    Who's Italian? You are Italian?
>
> I:    Yes.
>
> F:    Thank goodness. <u>Boy,</u> *wasn't it you who was drinking here?*
>
> I:    What thing isn't bad?
>
> F:    Because you are Italian now. We are Senegalese, understood?
>
> B:    **I am proud to be Senegalese.**
>
> F:    *Say it in* **Italian.**
>
> I:    Listen, I, thanks to everyone—
>
> F:    *Give him some water so he can drink it in* **Italian.**
>
> I:    *That is not part of* **the Italian language.**
>
> F:    *It's the same thing.*
>
> I:    *Forgiveness from God. / It's not true.*]

While the conversations at the restaurant were normally in Wolof unless a non-Wolof speaker was being addressed, it made sense for Idi to begin this topic in Italian since he was discarding his Senegalese identity. Since he had decided he did not want to be Senegalese because they talked too much, he claimed an Italian identity. The friend challenged Idi by suggesting he was drunk for saying such a thing, using the word "boy" to address him, a word taken from English but which had been appropriated in Wolof. He also light-heartedly said something to the effect of "thank goodness" with "meno male." This phrase in context could also mean "good riddance." However, either through a misinterpretation or a play on words, Idi transformed "meno male" into "non è male" in his next turn. The other person's response suggested an "us versus him" framework. *Noi* (we) included all Senegalese, but Idi had now defected, which was not necessarily a bad thing in the friend's mind.

Although this exchange was obviously in jest, for there was laughing in the background and a lack of seriousness in their voices, Bachir's interruption "Je suis fier d'être sénégalais" (I am proud to be Senegalese) conveyed a need to voice pride in his identity. It was surprising that Bachir would use French to profess his Senegalese heritage when he typically spoke in Wolof and had discussed in other conversations how French as a colonial language was an imposition. While it was unclear why he made his assertion in French instead of Wolof, it reiterated what many of my interviewees claimed: being Senegalese involved being able to move between space and language.

Meanwhile, for the people present, Italianness had transformed from being simply an identity marked by the language spoken to being an identity that encompassed every aspect of living. For instance, the friend told Idi to drink the water in Italian. Idi retorted by arguing that drinking was not included in the Italian language, an argument that the friend dismissed. As if this exchange and the languages used were not interesting enough, Idi got the last word, electing to use Arabic to do so. While possible translations include "Forgiveness from God" or "God forbids," a more context-specific translation is "it's not true." In other words, Idi decided to negate his friend's words once more.

The linguistic intricacy of this exchange mirrors the complexity surrounding where Senegalese fit in the discussions of *italianità* from the previous chapters. Even though Idi presented his claim on Italianness in a humorous manner, he showed that the nature of Italianness deserves to be negotiated. He stood in contrast to Bachir, who used the opportunity to reaffirm his global Senegality. Meanwhile the friend, through instigation, created a space where these reflections on identity and nationhood could flourish. What was most evident here was the dynamic nature of identity and the insistence that it be negotiated.

In a way, both Rome and the secret Senegalese restaurant foster an environment where this creative negotiation thrives. Because the phenomenon of Senegalese migration to Rome is relatively new when compared to other parts of the world or even other parts of Italy, there is less of a template for how a person performs, on the one hand, Italianness as a Senegalese and, on the other hand, global Senegality in an Italian space. Furthermore, this particular restaurant had become a perfect place for its patrons to express their existential perspectives through wit, jokes, teasing, reflection, and introspection among a community that encourages this identity formation to thrive. Providing a sociolinguistic counterpart to Benoît Lecoq's historical and Shachar Pinsker's literary analysis of café culture, these scenes at the Senegalese restaurant vividly exhibited how the playful manipulation of multiple languages affords people various strategies to simultaneously negotiate identity and convey humor.[38] By playing with multiple linguistic codes in order to cross borders and flaunt national representations, they wielded a considerable amount of symbolic competence.

### Identity Formation in Paris through Hip-Hop

I took the RER D north to Sarcelles for the first time. As with any trip into the Parisian *banlieue*, the scenery drastically changed as the train crossed the threshold from the center of Paris to the suburbs. The tall housing projects from the sixties towered over their surroundings, their stark presence and muted grays contrasting with the architectural image that Paris tends to export to the rest of the world. While the buildings became drabber, human presence inversely increased with color as a diversity of people and dress marked the streets. Sarcelles had hosted waves of immigration since *pieds-noirs* and Jews arrived during the Algerian War of Independence.[39] Boasting substantial numbers of people from France's Caribbean territories, West Africa, North Africa, and other parts of the world as well, Sarcelles represented a French diversity that existed but was not always visible or displayed to the outside world.

Abdu invited me into his apartment on the twentieth floor of his building. The sun was setting, leaving a constantly dimming light in its retreat. Abdu offered me a drink and a place to sit. As I sipped freshly made hibiscus juice, he thumbed through some flyers from past concerts and transported me into these memories with his vivid recollections of each experience. I used his musings as the point of departure for our interview. He was a fairly well-known rapper born in Dakar to an even better known Senegalese novelist. Paris had been his base for the last seven years. After he explained the importance of the French language according to his mother, the novelist, I asked him which language he preferred to speak.

As he thought about my question, he unconsciously twisted one of his locs between his index finger and thumb before replying that he felt close to both languages:[40]

> A:  En fait des deux langues je me sens proche. Le wolof, c'est mon identité quelque part. Et moi, je fais du rap en français mais c'est pas du rap français. La réflexion est en wolof. Les valeurs viennent

de là-bas. Ce qu'on a vécu. Les images sont en wolof. Mais le rap
est en français. Je mets des petits mots en wolof mais je ne peux
pas écrire comme un *guy* qui est né en wolof, qui a capté le wolof.[41]
Même mon accent, en fait. Je n'ai pas un vrai accent français ni
un vrai accent wolof.

M:    C'est problématique?

A:    Je ne sais pas si c'est un problème. C'est mon identité en fait. Je n'ai
      pas de complexes.


[A:    Actually I feel close to both languages. In some way, Wolof is my
      identity. And I rap in French but don't produce French rap. The
      reflection is in Wolof. The values come from there. What we have
      experienced. The images are Wolof. But the rap is in French. I put
      a few words in Wolof but I can't write like a *guy* who was born in
      Wolof, who grasped Wolof. Even my accent, actually. I do not have
      a real French accent or a real Wolof accent.

M:    It is problematic?

A:    I do not know if that's a problem. This is actually my identity. I
      have no complexes.]


Wolof was part of his identity even if he rapped in French. He spoke of *réflexion*.
He thought in Wolof, and his relationship with the world was in Wolof. He
conceptualized the world in Wolof because of his time spent in Senegal, because of how he was raised, even if he had grown up in a francophone family
and spent a large part of his childhood in France. Abdu identified with Senegal
and signaled a Wolof identity by using the occasional Wolof word in his music.

Meanwhile, the use of French afforded him a larger audience, allowing for
a fan base in the francophone world. As he put it, rapping in French permitted
him to reach Guineans, Malians, Swiss, Belgians, and so on. In addition to en-
abling him to capture a wider audience, using French also allowed him to pay
homage to a strong hip-hop francophone tradition. Although Abdu emphasized the importance of Paris as a francophone center and how his French-
language music brought together people from all over the francophone world,
he stressed the fact that while he rapped primarily in French, he did not produce French rap. In making this distinction, he staked a claim on the French
language while championing a Wolof sensibility.

As he described how he rapped, his eyes lit up. Grinning, he asked if I would
like to go with him to his band's jam session later that evening. After the interview, we proceeded to catch the RER D back to the center of Paris, switching
to the RER B at Gare du Nord. We arrived at Bagneux, a southern suburb of
Paris, about an hour later.

The jam session was fantastic. I got to see him interact with his musicians, backup singers, and manager. They all seemed to have a good rapport and even let me try my hand at free-style singing. I do not have a singing voice at all, but it was nice that they humored me. A few weeks later, I witnessed their rehearsal transform into a live concert at a decent-sized venue in the Eleventh Arrondissement. The show was sold out to an ethnically diverse group of fans who cheered and sang along to the music. As he performed, I took note of his multilingual usage and how he expressed identity through his language choices. For instance, at one point Abdu engaged his band and the crowd simultaneously:[42]

A:    J'ai envie de partager, tu vois, aujourd'hui, tu vois, cette scène avec tous ceux qui sont là. Ce que je voudrais . . . je vais lui donner mon micro et il va traverser.

B1:   OK.

A:    Vous pensez que c'est possible? Vous pensez que c'est possible?

B1:   C'est possible. C'est possible.

B2:   *Hold up, hold up, hold up.* Abdu. Abdu. *Hold up.* Abdu, ça c'est quoi, ça? Ça, ça, ça c'est quoi?

A:    C'est Af-roots.

B2:   Ça veut dire que ça parle de nos *roots*, quoi.

A:    Oui, c'est ça.

B2:   *Yeah, you know the deal. Afroroots. It's coming soon.*

[A:    I want to share, you see, now, you know, this scene with all the people here. What I would like . . . I'll give him my microphone to pass around.

B1:   OK.

A:    You think it's possible? You think it's possible?

B1:   It's possible. It's possible.

B2:   *Hold up, hold up, hold up.* Abdu. Abdu. *Hold up.* Abdu, what is this? What, what, what is this?

A:    It's Af-roots.

B2:   It means that it speaks of our *roots*, you know.

A:    Yes, that's it.

B2:   *Yeah, you know the deal. Afroroots. It's coming soon.*]

During the concert, Abdu rapped and spoke to the crowd predominantly in French, corroborating the language discussion in his interview. He addressed the crowd but was engaged in dialogue with two band members. In an attempt to include the crowd in his musical creation, he planned to give them a voice by passing a microphone to them for the last song of the evening. What was striking was the code-switching between French and English that the second band member employed. He entered the conversation by using English. In this first turn of talk, the band member moved between English and French at sentence boundaries.[43] However, in his second turn of talk, he switched within a single sentence, substituting the English word "roots" for the French word *racines* while keeping the French possessive adjective *nos* before using the French discourse marker *quoi*. While Abdu responded in French, in the next turn of talk, the band member switched completely to English.

In using both French and English, the group was signaling two symbolic hip-hop centers. They went beyond the francophone hip-hop tradition, valorizing its African American English-language origin. When I asked Abdu in his interview if he often used English, he responded: "Pas trop. Soit qu'il y a des mots intraduisibles comme 'lyrics' ou des mots en jargon de hip-hop qui sont la base." (Not too much. Either when there are untranslatable words such as "lyrics" or hip-hop jargon, which is the main source.)[44] While Abdu limited his English usage in concerts, he acknowledged the underlying presence of English and its influence on the hip-hop medium.

When the band member entered the conversation with "hold up, hold up, hold up," there was nothing happening previously to warrant the switch. He appeared to engage in metaphorical code-switching, in which the metaphorical "world" of the variety was that of hip-hop. I am particularly led to this reading because of the word "roots." Hip-hop is a global phenomenon with local inflections, connected by an appreciation for African American culture. The word "roots" is a term packed with all sorts of meanings, many of which relate to a type of African identity.[45] The band member highlighted this link to Africa when he said, "Afroroots." If one applies the Markedness Model to this reading of code-switching, one can argue that the band member signaled his desired affiliation with American hip-hop culture as well as a sense of Pan-Africanism and diasporic connection.[46]

Whereas Jesse Shipley sees hip-hop as granting membership in a global community and in particular a black cosmopolitan world, I contend that hip-hop also offers a form of multilingual travel. Bayo Holsey touches on hip-hop's ability to grant access to an "imagined cosmopolitanism" even for those without the means to travel; my work shows the compelling perspective that the linguistic implications connected to music offer in theorization on hip-hop and cosmopolitanism.[47] Abdu situated himself in a hip-hop tradition with ties to English language and African American culture, a francophone space that was explicitly not French (*pas du rap français*) but that relied on the French language for maximum reach, and a Wolof sensibility (*la réflexion est en wolof*) conveyed through the occasional Wolof word thrown in the mix. He therefore refused to be limited by any one language in order to tap into all the different facets of his identity as a person and a performer. In other words, a hip-hop artist such as Abdu was a multilingual traveler of sorts. Through multilingual expression, he transported his listeners to the multiple metaphorical worlds that hip-hop evoked and situated his various identity markers within these spaces.

## Negotiating Identity through Language in New York City and Beyond

The Senegalese Association's headquarters in Harlem would often rent out its space to the community for cultural events. Madina, Ndiaye, and the rest of the women I had been following decided to move their fund-raising efforts from Madina's home in Brooklyn to the heart of the Senegalese community in Upper Manhattan.[48] I arrived early to this de facto cultural center and sat down near the back, trying to remain as inconspicuous as possible. However, most people had dressed up in their finest *boubous* and headscarves for the occasion, so my lack of finery made it hard to blend in. A framed photo of Macky Sall, the newly elected president of Senegal, was hanging above the door, and a little girl, no older than three, had just taken the mic and was trying to rouse the sparse crowd into joining her in a round of "Old MacDonald." Ndiaye, spotting me in the corner, took a break from setting up to welcome me. She sat down beside me to catch her breath, and a different little girl plopped down beside her. She put her arm next to Ndiaye's and asked whose skin was lighter. Ndiaye calmly asked her why it mattered since both of them were beautiful shades of brown. She then went on to explain the expansiveness of the African diaspora in a way that the little girl could understand, effectively modeling what her organization seeks to do when they take youth to Senegal.

While this nonprofit was firmly rooted in New York and established as a way for black youth in America to learn about and travel to Senegal, the founders of the organization soon realized the interest that Senegalese youth had in learning about America. Madina foregrounded its core mission as a facilitator of intercultural interaction: "It is literally an intercultural movement because there are people who are from the African diaspora here who want to know more about the culture back in Senegal, West Africa, and then in Senegal, West Africa, they also want to learn more about what's here, about our history as African Americans and what we've been through. So it's literally like an intercultural exchange program." Throughout the year, participants in New York attend a Saturday arts and education program. Then, each summer a group of predominantly Senegalese American youth as well as college interns for the organization travel to Dakar and participate in a variety of classes with Senegalese youth and instructors. They collaborate on arts projects that incorporate theater, dance, drumming, singing, filmmaker, and visual arts. For Madina's brother, Samba, this is the perfect "opportunity to make connections between Senegalese American youth and Senegalese youth." While an arts education was originally this organization's main focus, teaching English in Senegal has become a crucial aspect of the summer program. As Ndiaye noted, "I'm step coordinator. But we also teach like everything. Everybody teaches English."[49] The demand for English instruction is huge, with the Senegalese participants relishing the fact that they can learn American English.

Throughout my data, interviewees remarked about the interest that people in Senegal, particularly youth, took in American English. Omar speculated why this might be the case: "People in Senegal, they love the English language. Trust me. When somebody, when you're walking around the street, you speak English because people think English is cool. Then it's associated with this American power. You know. And then people think that when you're speaking it, you are yourself cool. Then you are representing the American kind of like powerness quote unquote." America's primacy throughout the world materializes in the form of language choice. Even though students learn British English in Senegalese schools and traditionally British English has a higher prestige factor than American English at a global level, positive attitudes concerning American English have gained ground.[50] According to Omar, America indexes power and being hip, both of which can be achieved through the English language, as long as that English is American English.[51] Furthermore, language through African American culture allows for Americanness and coolness in ways that other practices might not. African American cultural production, particularly through hip-hop, contributes to the rising prestige of American English across the globe. While chapter 1 explored how Senegalese who had learned British English in Senegal needed to navigate various American English varieties once they arrived in New York City, this chapter focuses on the current ways in which Senegalese encounter these Englishes while still in Senegal.[52]

Some informants seemed to employ or hear others employ Black Stylized English (BSE) in Senegal, which was often learned through hip-hop and rap music. For instance, fifty-three-year-old Aliou, who had spent half his life in New York, corroborated Ibrahim's findings about motivation in learning BSE: "The younger generation speaks a little bit of English. They all want to speak English because of the music, all that rap. They want to understand what they are talking about." Mariama illustrated this phenomenon when she recounted an experience of intercultural communication with her cousin in Senegal:

> We couldn't really communicate. . . . He spoke hardly any English and I spoke hardly any Wolof, and we were trying to understand each other

through music. And so, hip-hop came on and he was singing Snoop Dogg's "I Wanna Love You," but the explicit version.[53] And you could just tell that he didn't understand what he was singing but he was just excited to be able to sing it for me, because it was like uh, yes I understand American music. I like American music. I know this song. But then I was like, oh no, that's a bad word. I tried to get him to understand that, you know, F-bomb, dropping it like that.

This excerpt shows the importance of hip-hop not only as a motivation for learning English but also as a tool in English-language acquisition and for mitigating linguistic barriers to a certain extent.[54] While the explicit nature of the song made Mariama feel somewhat uncomfortable, she recognized what the song signified to her cousin: something that connected him to his American family and that positioned him as a consumer and practitioner of American and specifically African American culture.[55]

Many Senegalese diasporans living in America and elsewhere in the world as well as Senegalese people living in Senegal have access to and share an interest in an African American cultural production that influences language attitudes and identity formation. While the analysis of Julien's example in chapter 1 shed light on how his desire to fit into specific communities in New York dictated the type of English he attempted to speak, Mariama's cousin in Dakar demonstrated how hip-hop travels across borders to engage potential speakers in English-language learning. Furthermore, her cousin aligned himself with a particular pan-African identity that emerged through African American cultural consumption.

However, Senegalese youth are not just consuming African American cultural production; they are producing their own versions as well, effectively entering into a transnational dialogue. Mariama explained, "During my few times [in Senegal] I've seen videos of Senegalese version of 50 Cent. Senegalese version of Lil Wayne . . . the way they look would definitely be very very nearly identical to 50 Cent or Lil Wayne." Although rapping predominantly in Wolof, these Senegalese rappers imitate popular U.S. rappers, appropriating their mannerisms and copying the visual aesthetics in their music videos. For instance, Mariama, Sonia, and Diallo showed me a video called "Home Party" by Senegalese rapper Baby Izi, an autotuned song in Wolof and English, which sounds and looks like Meek Mill's "House Party." Pulling out their smartphones, they proceeded to watch the videos side by side and offer critiques as we sat on the stoop of Madina's house in Brooklyn. The women described Baby Izi as the spitting image of Lil Wayne, giving details about all the ways in which Baby Izi tried to imitate Lil Wayne (e.g., similar hat, glasses, hairstyle, autotuned voice). They recognized how these Senegalese artists have affiliated with American hip-hop artists, often borrowing visuals and sounds from multiple artists at once, but they also acknowledged the local flavors that these same artists have injected into this image.[56]

Just as in Gilroy's conceptualization of Britain, where cultural representation of blackness allowed disparate groups to feel a part of something, people in Senegal are now relying on African American cultural exports to feel connected to these specific notions of blackness.[57] It is therefore not only skin color and a once-shared history that create feelings of belonging; the co-construction of black culture across the Atlantic also contributes to this belonging. However, multiple trips across the Atlantic are happening because Baby Izi, as an imitator of American culture, is not just being consumed in Africa; he is also being consumed in America. As the women in my study watched this Senegalese rapper emulate American rappers Meek Mill and Lil Wayne, they were importing African cultural production to help them theorize about their own identities as Africans in America. In Gilroy's rumination on music and subject positions in the black Atlantic world, he seems to deemphasize the importance of Africa in this diasporic dialogue: Africa is last on his list of locations and introduced with an air of surprise (*even* Africa). Yet there were multiple examples in my data where Africa was front and center in diasporic theorization.[58]

The women's discussion of hip-hop not only points to how culture can foster a sense of inclusion. The role of language, particularly multiple languages, is central to their theorization. In addition to the women's critiques of Baby Izi, as I was talking to Aminata (A) and Diallo (D) later about their thoughts on code-switching, Diallo perked up and offered an anecdote about how her observation of the Nigerian rapper Wizkid opened her eyes to her own language use. While she at first thought there was something wrong with switching not just between languages but also between dialects, she had since realized how pervasive the practice was and now saw it as a positive ability:

> D:    My best friend is African American. When I'm talking to her in English, it's like English with slang, a hood English. But when I talk to let's say my sister-in-law, and I'm talking to her in English, it's like I have an accent. Even though I'm speaking in English, I have an accent. I never realized . . . I was watching this artist, his name is Wizkid, he does the same exact thing. When he's in Nigeria he has the like Yor, Yorba, Yor—
>
> M:    Yoruba?
>
> D:    Yoruba accent. When he speaks in English, he has the accent. But when he's with the artists over here like Chris Brown, he has the hood accent. I'm like, wow, like we really do do that.

A:    We all do that. We all do that.

D:    We do that. Turn it on and off.

Diallo looked to performers she respected not only to seek answers for why she did the things she did but also to seek permission in a way. It is as if she were saying, "If it's good enough for Wizkid, it's good enough for me." For those in my study who were not always comfortable with the marginalized position they inhabited, often marked by the languages they spoke, the clothes they wore, their country of origin, their skin color, and so on, it was important to have various role models. Diallo found an unlikely role model in Wizkid. In this instance, Diallo was relying on interactions between Africans and African Americans in both Africa and America to help her make sense of her own life and how she belonged in multiple contexts.

People such as Diallo negotiate their blackness and their Africanness, relying not only on American conceptualizations of race or black culture but also on a global formation of blackness. While in chapter 2 Lucie demonstrated how black people in France have often failed at claiming cultural citizenship even when they have actual citizenship as well as the French-language skills so evocative of French identity, Diallo showed how black cultural citizenship offered a different type of belonging and inclusion that she could access through music and multilingual practices. For Diallo, a complex linguistic repertoire gave her access to claiming membership in a black cosmopolitan world.

Furthermore, as we saw with Abdu in Paris, hip-hop is doing more than just offering inclusion; through language use it allows one to travel to different metaphorical worlds. Moreover, I argue that travel can be more than just metaphorical; the connection between hip-hop and multilingualism opens up the possibility of actual physical travel. As a Nigerian, Wizkid is somewhat restricted in his global mobility. As a well-known hip-hop artist, Wizkid enjoys a status that confers access to countries that might have balked at admitting him were he not famous. Mariama's cousin had been learning English through hip-hop in order to feel connected to his family in the United States and to invest in a medium that holds significant symbolic capital; however, he could also be using hip-hop as his socialization into a multilingual traveler. This experiment in language learning signals aspirations to see the world and speak multiple languages. Even as a young kid, he might already be thinking about how he could move to other countries, just as many of his family members have done. In addition, the cousin displayed the same type of pleasure that Ousseynou and Boubacar did when speaking a foreign language. He found joy in listening to music that pleased him all the while supplementing his English-language learning in a way that was probably more enjoyable and engaging than the way he learned English at school.

## CONCLUDING THOUGHTS

The excerpts in this chapter provided insight into the myriad ways in which the people in my study made sense of where they fit in their immediate communities, in society at large, within the Senegalese diaspora, and in the larger African diaspora. In addition to other cultural markers, it was through language that they negotiated and renegotiated their positionality and the identity claims that they made. The use of multiple languages allowed them not only to communicate with a wide range of people in a variety of situations but also to explore and champion different identities to create a sense of belonging and to express joy. Whether it was the humorous performance of Idi, who discarded his Senegalese identity for an Italian one when he wanted to get a rise out of his friends, or the pensive reflection of Abdu, who recognized the various messages that he could send when rapping in specific languages, the people I interviewed were acutely aware of the power that language afforded them. Through global Senegality, they were embodying the transnational multilingual subject.

The specific contexts influenced how and where multilingualism was expressed. In Paris, while many of the people I interviewed professed the belief that multilingualism was important, actual multilingual usage did not necessarily reflect this belief. The data I collected were overwhelmingly in French only. This could partially be because of the demographics of the informants in Paris, some of whom were French of Senegalese descent and only spoke French fluently. It could also be the settings in which I interviewed people. Many of the natural conversations were recorded in mixed company where speaking a language such as Wolof would be unlikely out of respect for people who would be kept out of the conversation. However, I would argue that there is also a desire to prove French linguistic competence in a society that places such importance on speaking standard French. Furthermore, the places where multilingualism was abundant in Paris either catered to a Senegalese crowd such as the Senegalese restaurant, where the patrons replicated linguistic phenomena that one would expect to find in Senegal, or they catered to a more cosmopolitan crowd such as Abdu's hip-hop concerts, where he relied on a variety of hip-hop traditions and the languages associated with them.

Of all three sites, the Rome data was the most robust regarding code-switching. This was partially due to linguistic repertoire: everyone I interviewed spoke Wolof, and most people had some knowledge of both French and Italian. In addition, Italian societal language ideologies seemed to be less concerned with the speaking of Italian than ideologies in France with regard to French. If they were with monolingual Italians, most informants would try to speak only Italian out of respect for their interlocutor, but they did not convey the sense that code-switching was a negative phenomenon. Abi was the only person who highlighted being attacked linguistically for speaking a language other than Italian. Moreover, the spaces in which I recorded conversation were conducive to multilingualism. When Senegalese and Italians were engaged in conversation, either at the Senegalese restaurant or when attending West African dance classes, the Italians were consciously placing themselves in predominantly Senegalese domains. These were Italians who showed great affinity to Senegalese culture, and some were even learning Wolof. It was, therefore, not surprising that Wolof would be mixed in with Italian. However, Italian was frequently used in situations where only Senegalese were present. In these instances, I assumed the informants would speak in a manner similar to what one would find in Dakar or other cities in Senegal: a Wolof heavily influenced by French along with other Senegalese national languages. However, in places such as the Senegalese restaurant, hearing Wolof mixed with Italian was a common occurrence.

The New York City data also contained many instances of code-switching. New York City was more like Paris in the number of American and French citizens of Senegalese descent, respectively; however, in New York there did not seem to be the same amount of pressure to speak only English as there was in Paris to speak only French. That is not to say that English was not important. As we saw throughout the book, several people remarked that speaking English allowed people to diminish the immigrant stigma or stake a claim on "American" blackness. At the same time, they also extolled multilingualism, particularly in the multilingual enclave of Little Senegal, where Wolof and French could be heard as often as English. Depending on one's interlocutor (older-generation Senegalese, younger-generation Senegalese, Senegalese American, African American), different types of linguistic repertoires served different purposes.

Many of the people in this study, however, did not just employ different linguistic repertoires based on the situation; they also proudly created and maintained an overarching identity, that of the multilingual traveler, that transcended geographic location. So while Dominic Thomas demonstrates how francophone literary production shows the ability of West Africans to travel to France to acquire cultural capital, my research broadens the scope, arguing that Senegalese do not just stop with French or France but set the whole world and the world's languages in their sights.[59] In other words, through stories of migration and mastery of language, they forge a figure of a Senegalese that is unbounded by geographic borders or linguistic boundaries, amassing symbolic capital with each country visited and each language learned. For people like Ousseynou, this was the quintessential Senegalese—someone who loved languages, loved to travel. This was *l'uomo perfetto*. Senegalese people living abroad export this image to the world. They also display the possibilities of physical travel, leading by example. Multilingualism offers the potential for both physical travel and the pure pleasure of inhabiting a fantasy (e.g., the romantic Italian or the cool American). Multilingualism thus not only fashions identity, but at the same time this linguistic multiplicity fuels aesthetic art.

Therefore, through multilingual practices in which people actively negotiate identity as well as through the sharing of cultural production where people signal particular aesthetics, those in the Senegalese diaspora control their narrative. They are not just members of marginalized communities dealing with the latent effects of slavery and colonialism; they also express mobility, creativity, and agency as they tap into a transnational cosmopolitanism that champions multilingualism and global identity formation. In other words, through this transnational multilingual subjectivity, they are acquiring a symbolic competence that flips the script on host countries' image of migrants as lacking qualities that make them desirable in specific national contexts. Instead, they are creating and owning identities that express what is important to them in a global context—across borders and languages.

# Epilogue

A week after I interviewed Ndiaga for the first time, he asked to meet with me again. He sent me a text telling me he had reflected on some of my questions and wanted to share his thoughts. It was an unseasonably hot day in February, so we met at the same park near my apartment, and as we sat down on a bench facing a fountain, he politely turned the tables on me. As I listened to his questions, I thought how refreshing it was to be the interviewee for once.

He wanted to know what it was like to go up to strangers and earn their trust to the point that they opened up to me. We had a mutual friend, an Italian anthropologist PhD student, who initially put us in touch. He laughed and told me that he used to call her 007 because he suspected her of being either an undercover cop or a journalist. He explained that while Senegalese do their best to express *teranga* (hospitality), when they are living in places where they often feel excluded, they are wary of people questioning them. However, he confided that my questions put him at ease right away. No one had ever asked him about the languages he spoke and his feeling toward these languages. These issues had remained on his mind the whole week.

When we met for the last time at the beginning of May, after three months of weekly chats at cafés or parks, we reminisced about our conversations. Ndiaga had been quite forthcoming during these meetings, and his stories captured the range of human emotions. We reflected on the comical frustration he had felt his first week in Rome, eight years prior, when he tried to buy eggs at the store but failed because the word for eggs in French sounded nothing like the word in Italian and his pantomiming left much to be desired. He expressed disappointment when recalling racialized incidents experienced in Rome and nostalgia for his life and family in Senegal. But just as importantly, he relived his successes, such as when he was able to communicate in Italian for the first time or when he made his first Italian friend. He also told me how his favorite question from my interview was when I had asked him in which language(s) he dreamed. He admitted to having spent these past three months paying attention to his dreams and was happy to report that he always dreamed in Wolof. He appreciated the question because it caused him to take note of an aspect of his life he had always taken for granted.

As we said our final goodbye, he thanked me for giving him an opportunity to share his linguistic experiences, and I expressed gratitude for his time and candor. When I think back on the more than eighty interviews I conducted in Paris, Rome, and New York, I marvel at the complexity of these life histories, with their intricate trajectories, linguistic experiences, and elaborate networks. I see the complicated ways in which the people I interviewed simultaneously navigated national, racial, migrant, linguistic, postcolonial, and global identities, exposing the nuances and various perspectives of identity formation as well as its constant evolution. I also realize the diversity of viewpoints. Although there were those who cherished their mobility and lack of attachment to a specific place, others struggled for inclusion in their adopted countries, while still others kept looking back to what they considered their homeland, Senegal.

By recounting their linguistic autobiographies, my interviewees could step back and make sense of their experiences from a different perspective. Through the power of storytelling, they taught me their conceptualizations about mobility and multilingualism. They foregrounded the role of languages in their lives, which shed light on how and why they moved. While so much of what we hear about migrants is filtered through national discourses bemoaning their presence and calling for restriction on their movement, this book has sought to privilege their voices and center their perceptions of the migrant experience. The fact that so many Senegalese view themselves as cosmopolitan world travelers challenges the Western conceptualization of Africans in the West as nothing more than migrants forced to move because of economic necessity.

The first interviews began almost a decade ago, and in many ways the world is a much different place. The blatant bigotry and intolerance that national discourses have tried to attribute to fringe political groups have become more mainstream. The governments of several European countries have moved or are in the process of moving to the far right on platforms guided by xenophobic, anti-immigrant, and anti-Muslim sentiments. Since mid-2016, the United Kingdom has been negotiating Brexit. In 2017 Marine Le Pen's National Front, historically France's most successful Far Right Party, made it to the second round of the presidential election.[1] In early 2018, the city of Macerata in Italy was forced to come to terms with the drive-by shooting of six African immigrants by Luca Traini, a municipal-level Northern League candidate. This violent display of racism and xenophobia was a harbinger for things to come as far-right populist parties received about 50 percent of the vote in the 2018 general elections. The migrant crisis then reached new heights when far-right Matteo Salvini, Minister of the Interior, barred the rescue ship *Aquarius* carrying more than six hundred migrants from docking on Italian soil in June 2018. According to polls, the majority of Italians support hardline stances such as this one.[2]

Meanwhile, the United States continues to alienate its most marginalized and vulnerable populations. Since 2017, under the helm of President Trump and the Republican Congress, the United States has started realizing isolationist goals such as trying to build a wall at the Mexican border, refusing asylum cases from certain Muslim-majority countries, and more vigorously deporting immigrant populations. At the same time, the political discourses of racism and exclusion have intensified. For instance, in 2017 the Federal Bureau of Investigation branded Black Lives Matter and other activists seeking social justice reform with the newly created label of Black Identity Extremists, which justifies increased surveillance and possible prosecution. This designation is particularly problematic considering that white nationalists have perpetrated the most violent offenses committed by extremists groups. In addition, Trump's comments depicting Haiti and African nations as "shithole" countries in early 2018, followed by a ban on Haitians applying for low-skilled working visas, demonstrate how racial animus is influencing national policy. Exclusionary rhetoric is particularly notable in the change to the mission statement of the United States Citizenship and Immigration Services, which removed the words "America's promise as a nation of immigrants." However, this rhetoric pales in comparison to the lived experiences of abuse and dehumanization that migrants have encountered amid the Trump administration's "zero tolerance" policy of separating children from parents in efforts to deter border crossings, which created public outcry in June 2018. I would be interested to see how my interviewees' conceptualizations of racial and immigrant identities have changed amid outward and all-encompassing displays of white nationalism and inhumane treatment of migrants. It is more important than ever to give voices to marginalized groups.[3]

Research such as the exploration that was undertaken in this book has potential implications for policy, both in language and migration, in a world that in some ways seems to be pushing back against the forces of globalization.

This type of study can give both host nations and migrant communities a new perspective in approaching a number of issues related to migration, language policy, and integration. Policy makers who are made aware that the highly specific and complex nature of each immigrant community–host nation relationship affects integration are more likely to write policy that reflects this understanding. Moreover, agencies that work on the ground level with migrants can be informed about what sort of context-dependent factors influence second language acquisition among the specific migrants with whom they work. Just the short conversation I had with the immigration lawyer in Rome showed that many different people charged with the integration of foreign populations are looking for any information that can make their jobs easier. Providing both migrants and host-country members with detailed reflections on immigration and language attitudes is one step forward in easing tensions and promoting intercultural awareness. There is an urgent need for such nuancing of our understanding of migrant identities given the plight of asylum seekers and others migrating to different parts of the world. Policy makers could benefit from additional comparative, ethnographic studies.

In sum, what people say and how they speak offer meaningful insight into the relationship between self, language, and social context. Looking at identity markers in the specific social and historical contexts of each site further problematizes our understanding of identity formation and boundary negotiation vis-à-vis language attitudes and use. Comparative studies should become a central part of SLA research because they put into relief many concepts that are not as accessible in research on single sites or single groups. By the same token, approaching diasporic and transnational research through a sociolinguistic lens adds nuance and valuable perspectives to migration, critical race, and cultural studies. By speaking about experiences with language, people have a platform to share their voices. The often-glum picture of migrants or other marginalized groups is countered by stories of creativity, agency, reflection, and resilience in order not to diminish the struggles that people encounter in often-hostile environments but to change the terms of the conversation. Incredible aesthetic and creative possibilities are also fueled precisely by these conditions. As members of the Senegalese diaspora move not only through space but also through language, they express the pride, shame, happiness, displeasure, hope, dismay, and myriad other emotions that convey the human condition.

Appendixes

Notes

Bibliography

Index

# Appendix A: Senegalese Informants in Paris

| No. | Name | Age | Date of interview | Sex | Place of birth/childhood | Maternal languages | Additional languages spoken | Education | Years in France | Countries lived in |
|---|---|---|---|---|---|---|---|---|---|---|
| 1 | Duudu* | 54 | Oct. 2, 2009 | M | Saint-Louis | Pulaar | French, Wolof, Arabic | Some college | 18 | Senegal, Mauritania, France |
| 2 | Ouria | 45 | Oct. 4, 2009 | F | Senegal | Wolof | French | Some high school | 25 | Senegal, France |
| 3 | Nyambi | 50s | Oct. 8, 2009 | M | Dakar | Wolof | French, ~English | High school diploma | 26 | Senegal, France |
| 4 | Nafi | 50s | Oct. 17, 2009 | F | Fouta (northern Senegal) | Pulaar | Wolof, French, ~English | Some primary school | 18 | Senegal, France |
| 5 | Djibril | 25 | Oct. 18, 2009 | M | Northern Senegal | Soninke | French, Pulaar, Wolof | Some high school | 7 | Senegal, France |
| 6 | Latif | 27 | Oct. 20, 2009 | M | Kedougou (southeastern Senegal)/ Saint-Louis | Pulaar | Mandinka, Wolof, French, ~English | Master's degree | 1 | Senegal, France |
| 7 | Yasirah | 22 | Oct. 30, 2009 | F | Senegal | Wolof | French, ~English, ~German, ~Chinese | In college | 2 | Senegal, France |
| 8 | Ndella | 45 | Nov. 3, 2009 | F | Dakar | Wolof | French, ~English | Some high school | 19 | Senegal, France |
| 9 | Boubacar | 40s | Nov. 3, 2009 | M | Dakar | Wolof | French, English | High school diploma | 20 | Unknown |
| 10 | Sébastien* | 28 | Nov. 8, 2009 | M | Dakar | French | Wolof, Spanish, English, ~German | Bachelor's degree | 8 | Senegal, United States, France |

| | | | | | | | | | | |
|---|---|---|---|---|---|---|---|---|---|---|
| 11 | Dib | 27 | Nov. 8, 2009 | M | Dakar | Wolof, French | ~English, ~German | Bachelor's degree | 3 weeks | Senegal, France |
| 12 | Ngirin with Sandrine | 38 | Nov. 21, 2009 | M | Touba (central Senegal) | Wolof | French, ~English | High school diploma | 7 | Senegal, France |
| 13 | Vera | 22 | Nov. 23, 2009 | F | Dakar | Jola | Wolof, French | In college | 2 months | Senegal, France |
| 14 | Jean-Paul | 32 | Nov. 23, 2009 | M | Monrovia/Dakar | French | English, Wolof, ~German | Master's degree | 11 | Senegal, Liberia, Ireland, France |
| 15 | Abdu* | 31 | Nov. 25, 2009 | M | Dakar | French | Wolof, ~English | High school diploma | 7 | Senegal, France |
| 16 | Karafa | 50s | Nov. 26, 2009 | M | Southern Senegal | Wolof | French, Mandinka, Pulaar, Jola, Portuguese, ~Spanish, ~English | Bachelor's degree | 30 | Senegal, France |
| 17 | Lucie | 31 | Nov. 27, 2009 | F | Marseille | French | Wolof | Bachelor's degree | 31 | France |
| 18 | Soulou (notes) | 22 | Nov. 30, 2009 | M | Senegal | Mandinka | French, Wolof, ~English | Some high school | Unknown | Senegal, France |
| 19 | Riquet student | 22 | Dec. 1, 2009 | M | Senegal | Unknown | Unknown | Unknown | Unknown | Senegal, France |
| 20 | Tambo (notes) | 27 | Dec. 2, 2009 | M | Senegal | Mandinka | ~French | Some primary school | 8 | Senegal, France |
| 21 | Faatu | 28 | Dec. 3, 2009 | F | Paris | Jola | French, ~English, ~Spanish | Bachelor's degree | 28 | France |
| 22 | Salif | 23 | Dec. 7, 2009 | M | Dakar | Wolof | French, English, ~Arabic, ~Spanish, ~German | Working on master's | 4 | Senegal, France |

(Appendix A continued on next page)

| No. | Name | Age | Date of interview | Sex | Place of birth/childhood | Maternal languages | Additional languages spoken | Education | Years in France | Countries lived in |
|---|---|---|---|---|---|---|---|---|---|---|
| 23 | Yasmina | 27 | Dec. 8, 2009 | F | Paris | Wolof | French, German | Bachelor's degree | 27 | France |
| 24 | Hakim | 35 | Dec. 8, 2009 | M | Dakar | Wolof | French, English, Spanish | Bachelor's degree | 2 | Senegal, France |
| 25 | Ali | 25 | Dec. 8, 2009 | M | Dakar | Wolof, French | English, ~German | Bachelor's degree | 8 | Senegal, France |
| 26 | Chantal | 25 | Dec. 12, 2009 | F | Marseille | French | English, ~Chinese, ~Spanish, ~German, ~Wolof | Bachelor's degree | 25 | France |
| 27 | Ajuma (b. Niger) | 27 | Dec. 13, 2009 | M | Niger/Dakar | Zarma, French | Wolof, English, ~Hausa | Master's degree | Unknown | Senegal, Niger, France |
| 28 | Momar (notes) | 30s | Dec. 14, 2009 | M | Senegal | Pulaar | French, Wolof | No formal education | 15+ | Senegal, France |

\* Indicates principal informant.

\*\* Place of birth is by the smallest unit known. In most cases it is by city. It is by region if the city is unknown and by country if the region is unknown.

~ Limited speaking ability.

*Supplemental Interview Data:*

**language instructors:**

1.  Thérèse interview      Oct. 30, 2009
2.  Anastasie interview      Nov. 4, 2009
3.  Anouk interview      Nov. 27, 2009
4.  Dorothée interview      Dec. 2, 2009

5. Louise interview
   (notes)                                           Dec. 10, 2009

**public servants:**

1. Huong from Secours Populaires Français
   (nonprofit organization)                          Dec. 4, 2009; Dec.10, 2009

**additional recordings:**

1. AESGE (Senegalese Student Association)
   conference                                        Oct. 24, 2009
2. conversation with Boubacar and Ndella            Oct. 27, 2009
3. Wolof class (beginning and intermediate)         Nov. 14, 2009
4. class on race at EHESS                            Nov. 18, 2009
5. Senegalese Business Association meeting
   with various panelists                            Nov. 21, 2009
6. screening of film on *les foyers*                 Nov. 24, 2009
7. class at Espace Riquet                            Dec. 1, 2009
8. conference on teaching French
   to migrants                                       Dec. 9, 2009

**demographic breakdown of Senegalese informants:**

nineteen men, nine women

aged 22–54

mean age 31

fourteen in their twenties, six in their thirties, three in their forties, four in their fifties

maternal languages spoken were French, Wolof, Pulaar, Jola, Mandinka, Soninke, Zarma.

# Appendix B: Senegalese Informants in Rome

| No. | Name | Age | Date of interview | Sex | Place of birth/childhood | Maternal languages | Additional languages spoken | Education | Years in Italy | Countries lived in |
|---|---|---|---|---|---|---|---|---|---|---|
| 1 | Kati | 27 | Feb. 10, 2010 | F | Paris | Pulaar, French | English, Italian | Bachelor's degree | 6 months | France, Italy |
| 2 | Bachir | 30 | Feb. 12, 2010 | M | Senegal | Wolof | French, Italian, ~Latin | Unknown | Unknown | Senegal, Italy, Switzerland |
| 3 | Ndiaga* | 36 | Feb. 14, 2010 | M | Matam (northeastern Senegal)/Dakar | Pulaar | Wolof, French, Italian, | Some primary school | 8 | Senegal, Italy, France |
| 4 | Ibou* | 42 | Feb. 19, 2010 | M | Fouta (northern Senegal)/Saint-Louis | Pulaar | Wolof, French, English, Italian, ~Russian | High school diploma | 12 | Senegal, Italy, France |
| 5 | Alfa | 39 | Feb. 25, 2010 | M | Dakar | Wolof | Italian, French, ~English | Some college | 11 | Senegal, Italy, France |
| 6 | Ndour | 36 | Feb. 27, 2010 | M | Fatick (central Senegal)/Dakar | Wolof, Pulaar | Sereer, French, Italian, English, ~Spanish | JD | 10 | Senegal, Italy |
| 7 | Karim | 32 | Mar. 2, 2010 | M | Kaolack (central Senegal)/Dakar | Sereer, Wolof | French, English, Italian, Spanish | Some college | 3 (4 in France) | Senegal, Italy, France |
| 8 | Anta | 26 | Mar. 7, 2010 | F | Dakar | Wolof | French, Italian | Bachelor's degree | 5 | Senegal, Italy |
| 9 | Ngoné | 23 | Mar. 7, 2010 | F | Dakar | Wolof | French, ~Italian | Some high school | 2 | Senegal, Italy |

| # | Name | Age | Date | Sex | City | Native language(s) | Languages | Education | Years | Countries |
|---|---|---|---|---|---|---|---|---|---|---|
| 10 | Ablaay | 40 | Mar. 8, 2010 | M | Casamance | Jola, Wolof | French, Italian | High school diploma | 5 | Senegal, Italy |
| 11 | Ondine | 26 | Mar. 11, 2010 | F | Dakar | Wolof, Mandjak | French, Italian, ~English | Some high school | 5 | Senegal, Italy |
| 12 | Naza | 36 | Mar. 13, 2010 | F | Dakar | Jola, Wolof | ~Pulaar, French, Italian | Some primary school | 5 | Senegal, Italy |
| 13 | Balla | 42 | Mar. 28, 2010 | M | Kaolack | Wolof | French, Italian, English | Some college | 5 | Senegal, Italy |
| 14 | Abi | 35 | Mar. 28, 2010 | F | Kaolack | Mandinka | Wolof, ~Bambara, French, ~Italian, ~Spanish | Some high school | 1 | Senegal, Italy, Spain |
| 15 | Badu | 32 | Apr. 2, 2010 | M | Dakar | Wolof | Italian, ~French, ~English | Some primary school | 9 | Senegal, Italy |
| 16 | Kolle | 32 | Apr. 10, 2010 | F | Dakar | Wolof | French, Italian | Some primary school | 7 | Senegal, Italy |
| 17 | Ndao | 35 | Apr. 10, 2010 | M | Dakar | Pulaar | Wolof, French, Italian, ~English, ~Greek | Some high school | 10 | Senegal, Italy, Greece |
| 18 | Idi* | 33 | Apr. 10, 2010 | M | Dakar | Wolof | Italian, ~French | Some primary school | 6 | Senegal, Italy |
| 19 | Biondo with friend | 34 | Apr. 10, 2010 | M | Dakar | Wolof | Pulaar, English, French, Italian | Unknown | 5 | Senegal, Italy, France |
| 20 | Isidore | 32 | Apr. 17, 2010 | M | Diourbel (central Senegal) | Wolof | Pulaar, Portuguese, French, Italian, English | High school diploma | Unknown | Senegal, Italy, Portugal |

(*Appendix B continued on next page*)

| No. | Name | Age | Date of interview | Sex | Place of birth/childhood | Maternal languages | Additional languages spoken | Education | Years in Italy | Countries lived in |
|---|---|---|---|---|---|---|---|---|---|---|
| 21 | Alasaan | 30s | Apr. 23, 2010 | M | Dakar | Wolof | French, Italian, ~English | Unknown | 3 | Senegal, Italy |
| 22 | Keita | 33 | Apr. 23, 2010 | M | Dakar | Wolof, Bambara | French, Italian, English, ~Spanish | Some primary school | 10 | Senegal, Italy, Spain |
| 23 | Djenebou | 27 | Apr. 23, 2010 | F | Senegal | Wolof, Mandinka | ~French, ~Italian | Unknown | 4 | Senegal, Italy |
| 24 | Amath | 35 | Apr. 23, 2010 | M | Louga (northern Senegal) | Wolof | Italian | Unknown | 11 | Senegal, Italy |
| 25 | Professore w/ Ndiaga | 40 | Apr. 24, 2010 | M | Fouta/Saint-Louis | Wolof | French, Italian, English, Spanish | Master's degree | 5 | Senegal, Italy |

* Indicates principal informant.
** Place of birth is by the smallest unit known. In most cases it is by city. It is by region if the city is unknown and by country if the region is unknown.
~ Limited speaking ability.

*Supplemental Interview Data:*

**language instructors and public servants:**

1. Speranza interview    Feb. 16, 2010
2. Arietta (sociologist) (notes)    Apr. 28, 2010
3. Silvia (lawyer)    Apr. 29, 2010

**additional recordings:**

1. dance class with Idti    Feb. 11, 2010
2. conversations at the Senegalese restaurant    Feb.12, 2010; Mar. 26, 2010; Apr. 6, 2010; Apr. 10, 2010; Apr. 16, 2010

3. Classe Media (similar to a GED course) — Feb. 16, 2010
4. elementary Italian class — Feb. 17, 2010; Feb. 24, 2010; Mar. 3, 2010; Mar. 10, 2010; Mar. 17, 2010; Apr. 7, 2010; Apr. 14, 2010; Apr. 21, 2010; Apr. 28, 2010
5. dance class with Karim — Feb. 24, 2010
6. dance performance with Idi — Feb. 26, 2010
7. day of the immigrant protests — Mar. 1, 2010
8. conversation between Karim and friends during interview — Mar. 2, 2010
9. conversation (Ablaay's house) between Bachir, Ablaay, and friend — Mar. 2, 2010
10. Senegalese dance performance — Mar. 23, 2010
11. conversations at Abi's house — Mar. 28, 2010
12. conversation with Ibou and French couple — Mar. 31, 2010
13. language instruction for immigrants — Apr. 13, 2010
14. conversations with Ndiaga — Apr. 17, 2010
15. drumming performance at a Sans Papiers rally — Apr. 17, 2010

**demographic breakdown of Senegalese informants:**

seventeen men, eight women

aged 23–42

mean age: 33

five in their twenties, sixteen in their thirties, four in their forties

maternal languages spoken: Wolof, Pulaar, French, Jola, Bambara, Mandinka, Mandjak, Sereer.

| No. | Name | Age | Date of interview | Sex | Place of birth/childhood | Maternal languages | Additional languages spoken | Education | Years in the U.S. | Countries lived in |
|---|---|---|---|---|---|---|---|---|---|---|
| 1 | Aliou | 53 | July 8, 2014 | M | Dakar | Wolof | English, ~Arabic | Bachelor's degree | 26 | Senegal, United States |
| 2 | Moussa | 58 | July 11, 2014 | M | Dakar | Pulaar | French, Jolla, ~Wolof, ~English | Primary school | 13 | Senegal, United States |
| 3 | Aminata | 24 | July 12, 2014 | F | Dakar | Wolof | French, English | In college | 5 | Senegal, United States |
| 4 | Diallo | 23 | July 12, 2014 | F | New York City (Harlem) | English | Wolof | Bachelor's degree | 23 | United States |
| 5 | Ndiaye | 24 | July 12, 2014 | F | New York City (Bronx) | Wolof, English | French, Serer | Bachelor's degree | 24 | United States |
| 6 | Mariama | 26 | July 12, 2014 | F | Oakland/Dakar | Wolof, ~Pulaar | English | Master's degree | 20 | Senegal, United States |
| 7 | Madina* | 27 | July 12, 2014 | F | New York City (Brooklyn)/Dakar | Wolof, English | ~French | Master's degree | 15 | Senegal, United States, France |
| 8 | Sonia | 25 | July 12, 2014 | F | New York City | English | ~Spanish, ~Wolof | Bachelor's degree | 25 | United States |
| 9 | Fatoumata | 31 | July 16, 2014 | F | Dakar | Wolof | French, English | Bachelor's degree | 14 | Senegal, United States |
| 10 | Julien* | 34 | July 17, 2014 | M | Casamance | Mankanya | Wolof, French, English, ~Kriol | Master's degree | 1 | Senegal, United States |
| 11 | Ablaye | 33 | July 19, 2014 | M | Senegal, parents from Guinea | Pulaar | Wolof, Jolla, Mandingo, English, French, ~Greek, ~Latin | Bachelor's degree | 13 | Senegal, United States |

| | | | | | | | | | | |
|---|---|---|---|---|---|---|---|---|---|---|
| 12 | Dija | 21 | July 19, 2014 | F | Senegal | English | Wolof, ~Spanish | In college | 21 | Senegal, United States |
| 13 | Marieme | 50s | July 20, 2014 | F | Senegal | English | ~Wolof | Bachelor's degree | 50+ | Senegal, United States |
| 14 | Samba | 31 | July 20, 2014 | M | South Carolina | English | ~Wolof, ~Spanish, ~French | Master's degree | 31 | United States |
| 15 | Omar* with Daphne | 31 | July 23, 2014 | M | Saloum (western Senegal)/Saint-Louis | Wolof | French, English, Mandinka, Arabic, ~Sereer, ~Pulaar | In master's program | 3 | Senegal, United States |
| 16 | Diop | 51 | July 26, 2014 | M | Louga | Wolof | French, English | Quranic school | 26 | Senegal, United States |
| 17 | Tapha | 17 | July 26, 2014 | M | New York City (Harlem) | English | Wolof, ~French | In high school | 17 | United States |
| 18 | Charlotte | 45 | July 27, 2014 | F | Casamance | Sereer | Wolof, French, English, Spanish, ~Portuguese | Bachelor's degree | 20 | Senegal, United States, France |
| 19 | Vivienne | 40 | July 27, 2014 | F | Casamance | French | Wolof, English | Bachelor's degree | 5 | Senegal, United States, France |
| 20 | Laurent | 30 | July 27, 2014 | M | Casamance | Pulaar | Wolof, French, English | Some college | 5 | Senegal, United States |
| 21 | Papy | 56 | July 28, 2014 | M | Niger/ Senegal | French | Wolof, English | Some high school | 23 | Senegal, Niger, United States |
| 22 | Ousseynou with waiter | 37 | July 29, 2014 | M | Dakar | Wolof | French, English, Italian, ~Spanish | Some primary school | 9 | Senegal, United States, Italy |

(Appendix C continued on next page)

| No. | Name | Age | Date of interview | Sex | Place of birth/childhood | Maternal languages | Additional languages spoken | Education | Years in the U.S. | Countries lived in |
|-----|------|-----|-------------------|-----|--------------------------|--------------------|-----------------------------|-----------|-------------------|--------------------|
| 23 | Joseph | 33 | Aug. 5, 2014 | M | Dakar, mother from Cape Verde | Jola | French, Wolof, ~Serer, ~Pulaar | Associate's degree | 5 | Senegal, United States, France |
| 24 | Amadou | 29 | Aug. 7, 2014 | M | Saloum, Saint-Louis | Wolof | French, English, Arabic, ~Pulaar | Master's degree | 2 | Senegal, United States |
| 25 | Idrissa | 31 | Aug. 10, 2014 | M | Casamance/ Dakar | Mankanya | Wolof, French, English, Jola, Mandinka, Pulaar, Kriol, ~Spanish | Master's degree | 2 | Senegal, United States |
| 26 | Bouba | 35 | Aug. 18, 2014 | M | Dakar | Pulaar, Bambara | Wolof, French, English, ~Italian | Trade school | 2 | Senegal, United States, Morocco, Switzerland |
| 27 | David | 46 | Aug. 23, 2014 | M | Dakar, mother from Cape Verde | Kriol, Wolof | French, English, ~Spanish | Bachelor's degree | 21 | Senegal, United States, France |
| 28 | Khadidiatou | 54 | Aug. 26, 2014 | F | Banjool, Gambia/ Dakar | Mandinka | Wolof, English, ~French | High school diploma | 25 | Senegal, Gambia, United States |
| 29 | Khady | 46 | Aug. 29, 2014 | F | Saint-Louis | Wolof | French, English, ~Spanish | Some primary school | 15 | Senegal, United States |

\* Indicates principal informant.

\*\* Place of birth is by the smallest unit known. In most cases it is by city. It is by region if the city is unknown and by country if the region is unknown.

~ Limited speaking ability.

*Supplemental Interview Data:*

**additional recordings:**

| | | |
|---|---|---|
| 1. | Brooklyn fund-raiser | July 12, 2014 |
| 2. | fund-raiser at a Senegalese cultural center in Harlem | July 15, 2014 |
| 3. | Queens dinner with members of the Senegalese Catholic Association | July 27, 2014 |
| 4. | Korite celebration | July 28, 2014 |
| 5. | African market in Little Senegal | Aug. 29, 2014 |
| 6. | laundromat in Harlem | Sept. 2, 2014 |

**demographic breakdown of Senegalese informants:**

sixteen men, thirteen women

aged 17–58

mean age: 36

one in his teens, eight in their twenties, ten in their thirties, four in their forties, six in their fifties

maternal languages spoken: Wolof, Pulaar, Serrer, English, French, Mankanya, Jola, Bambara, Mandinka, Kriol.

# Notes

## INTRODUCTION

1. All names of my interviewees have been changed, including this nickname. In this particular case, the pseudonym chosen reflects his studious nature.

2. The character Celie says, "I'm poor, black, I may even be ugly, but dear God, I'm here! I'm here!" Spielberg, *Color Purple*. For the quotation of Celie's statement in the film, see https://www.quotes.net/mquote/11088. This exchange with Ndiaga and Professore will be analyzed in depth later.

3. A major subplot of the novel and the film is Celie finding the letters that her sister Nettie has been writing her about her experiences living in Africa with companions who turn out to be Celie's biological children.

4. In addition to foregrounding race, *The Color Purple* (as both a novel and a film) focuses heavily on gender, an identity marker that I do not analyze in detail in this book. Lauren Berlant discusses the intersections of gender and race throughout the novel in "Race, Gender, and Nation."

5. Buggenhagen, *Muslim Families in Global Senegal*; Carter, *States of Grace*; O. Kane, *Homeland Is the Arena*; Riccio, "*Toubab* and *Vu Cumprà*"; Robin, *Atlas des migrations ouest-africains*; Schmidt di Friedberg, "L'immigration africaine en Italie"; Stoller, *Money Has No Smell*; Tall and Tandian, *Migration irrégulière des Sénégalais*.

6. Literary criticism includes D. Thomas, *Black France*; Cazenave, *Afrique sur Seine*; Rofheart, *Shifting Perceptions of Migration*. Literary production includes Camara, *L'enfant noir*; C. H. Kane, *L'aventure ambiguë*; Socé, *Mirages de Paris*; Diome, *La préférence nationale*.

7. See Toma and Castagnone, "What Drives Onward Mobility?," for a look at the Senegalese propensity for migrating to multiple destinations. Meanwhile, Balibar and Wallerstein's *Race, Nation, Class* explores the phenomenon of cultural racism to show how national identities in Europe are structured through race.

8. Among themselves, Senegalese focus more on ethnic affiliations such as Wolof, Sereer, or Fulani to denote difference.

9. I interviewed twenty-eight people of Senegalese descent in Paris, twenty-five in Rome, and twenty-nine in New York City. I collected the Paris data from October through December 2009, the Rome data from February through April 2010, and the New York City data from June through August 2014.

10. Cohen, *French Encounter with Africans*, 167. In fact, French contact with West Africa dates as far back as the fifteenth century, but the first trade port was established in Saint-Louis in 1659. Mamadou Diouf distinguishes between *habitants* or *originaires*, who were Africans (either full-blooded or mixed) living in the Four Communes and could access French citizenship, and *indigènes*, who were Africans living outside those four locations. Only those with enough wealth were granted French citizenship. Diouf, "French Colonial Policy of Assimilation," 672. See also Wilder, *French Imperial Nation-State*, for more information.

11. According to Johnson, Catholic missionaries brought Western education to Senegal as early as the 1630s. By the early twentieth century, state-run institutions also provided instruction in order to better indoctrinate Senegalese with the ideals of the French Republic. In addition, as Johnson has argued, "France extended her schools with the intention of training new clerks, messengers and schoolteachers." Johnson, *Emergence of Black Politics*, 139.

12. McLaughlin, "Dakar Wolof," 159.

13. The national education system is modeled on the French system. French is the only language of instruction.

14. According to article 1, part 2, of the constitution from July 7, 2001, "La langue officielle de la république du Sénégal est le français. Les langues nationales sont le diola, le malinké, le poular, le sérère, le soninké, le wolof et toute autre langue nationale qui sera codifiée." (The official language of the Republic of Senegal is French. The national languages are Jola, Malinké, Pulaar, Sereer, Soninké, Wolof and any other national language that will be codified.) Ball and Morley, *The French-Speaking World*, 35. See Trudell, "Practice in Search of a Paradigm," for information on how indigenous languages become recognized by the government through the process of *codification*. By 2014, twenty-one languages had been recognized. For more information, see Ministère de l'Éducation Nationale, *Élaboration d'une politique d'éducation*, 65.

15. French-language statistics are provided by the OIF's study "La francophonie dans le monde: 2006–2007." French-speakers usually live in large cities, such as Dakar or Saint-Louis. Additionally, men are more likely than women to know and speak French. As for Wolof, the percentage of speakers is considerably greater than the 43 percent of the population who are ethnically Wolof. For further discussion, see Cissé, "Langues, État et société," 101, 105.

16. In "Diglossia," Charles Ferguson coined the term to explain the cleavage between "high" and "low" varieties of a single language, while in *The Sociology of Language*, Joshua Fishman expanded the definition of diglossia to include separate languages in a common geographical area. The situation is further complicated in Senegal, where in

some contexts French and Wolof represent high and low languages, respectively, and in other contexts Wolof becomes the high language next to the low status of other national languages. See Calvet and Dreyfus, "Urban Family," and Schürkens, "Le rôle du français," for discussions of the diglossic situation in Senegal.

17. For more information, see Cruise O'Brien, "Shadow-Politics of Wolofisation"; Cruise O'Brien, "Langue et nationalité"; and McLaughlin, "Haalpulaar Identity."

18. See Diop, *Nations nègres et cultures*, and Warner, "Limits of the Literary," for more information. A few decades later, Senegalese novelist Mame Younousse Dieng wrote one of the first novels in Wolof with her 1992 book *Aawo bi* (The first wife).

19. Ngũgĩ wa Thiong'o's *Caitaani mũtharaba-Inĩ* (Devil on the cross) from 1980 is the first modern novel in Gĩkũyũ.

20. Thiong'o, *Decolonizing the Mind*, xiv; Thiong'o, *Something Torn and New*, 17–19.

21. Cissé, "Languages, État et société," 101. Ethnic groups include the Lebou, the Jola, the Mandinka, and the Soninke, among others. See McLaughlin, "Haalpulaar Identity," for further discussion of Wolof as a colonizing language.

22. "Pure Wolof" is a direct translation of the Urban Wolof phrase "Olof piir" to refer to Wolof spoken in rural regions. Presumably, there is no one "pure" variety of Wolof, but the term has come to mean any Wolof that is not influenced by French: "Set off against the 'deep Wolof' (olof bu xóot) spoken in Baol and Cayor, the Wolof heartlands, Dakar Wolof is seen by many as an impure language because of its extensive borrowing of French lexical items. Paradoxically, the urban Wolof term for olof bu xóot is olof piir, or pure Wolof, piir being derived from the French word *pur*." McLaughlin, "Dakar Wolof," 163.

23. Swigart, "Cultural Creolisation," 179.

24. In its most simplistic definition, code-switching is the use of "varied combinations of two or more linguistic varieties." Gardner-Chloros, *Code-Switching*, 4. In "Two Codes or One?," Swigart explores whether speakers of Dakar Wolof are code-switching between two languages or speaking one language heavily influenced by French. McLaughlin, arguing the latter, relies on Myers-Scotton's notion of matrix language and embedded language where "one of the two languages involved in codeswitching or code-mixing can be said to be the matrix language in that it supplies the overall morphological and syntactic structure of the discourse, while the embedded language supplies lexical items that can be plugged into the matrix structure." McLaughlin, "Dakar Wolof," 160.

25. In fact, sociolinguistic research has long since challenged the notion of distinct languages. For more information, see Creese and Blackledge, "Translanguaging and Identity," and Blommaert and Rampton, "Language and Superdiversity."

26. Even those Senegalese who do not speak French probably speak multiple languages, usually Wolof and at least one of the other national languages.

27. For instance, there is extensive research in sociolinguistics and English-language education on the place of English alongside various national languages in India. See Ramanathan, *English-Vernacular Divide*.

28. McLaughlin, "Senegal," 89–90.

29. Blommaert argues that "multilingualism is a feature of sociocultural diversity, often associated with migration, and sensitive to influences at both macro- and micro-levels, leading to highly complex, 'messy' and hybrid sociolinguistic phenomena that defy established categories. To start with the macro-levels: migration as a force behind

multilingualism compels analysts to consider *mobile* people—people who do not stay in the place where their languages are traditionally used, to put it simply—whose linguistic resources and communicative opportunities are affected by such forms of mobility." Blommaert, "From Mobility to Complexity," 4.

30.  See MacGaffey and Bazenguissa-Ganga, *Congo-Paris*; Tall and Tandian, *Migration irrégulière des Sénégalais*; and Maher, "Barça or Barzakh," for discussions of how migrating is a type of rite of passage that allows migrants, particularly men, to return to Senegal transformed into mature and cosmopolitan men. See research by Riccio, "Talkin' about Migration," and Rofheart, *Shifting Perceptions of Migration*, for conceptualizations of migration in Senegalese popular culture such as through *mbalax* and hip-hop music.

31.  Riccio, "West African Transnationalisms Compared"; O. Kane, *Homeland Is the Arena*; Cole and Groes, *Affective Circuits*.

32.  The 2016 INSEE report, "La localisation géographique des immigrés," which considers census data from 2012, states that immigrants make up 8.7 percent of the population in France, and Paris with its surrounding suburbs is the most popular destination; 38 percent of all immigrants in France live there. According to the 2017 INSEE report, "Étrangers—Immigrés en 2014," which considers census data from 2014, there are 92,000 Senegalese in metropolitan France, of which 10,000 live in the Paris region. Because France does not take racial or ethnic statistics of its citizens, it is impossible to know how many people of Senegalese descent reside there.

33.  Carter, *States of Grace*; Riccio, "Senegal Is Our Home"; O. Kane, *Homeland Is the Arena*; Robin, *Atlas des migrations ouest-africaines*; Schmidt di Friedberg, "L'immigration africaine en Italie."

34.  Riccio, "Senegal Is Our Home," 78.

35.  The figure provided by the ISTAT 2016 census shows 101,207 Senegalese residents or 2.0 percent of the total foreign population. Senegal is the most represented sub-Saharan African country. This number marks a huge increase from the 80,989 in the ISTAT 2010 report. Rome has historically been an important destination for southern migration and, more recently, foreign immigration. Presently, 13.2 percent of Rome's population is composed of migrants, which is somewhat higher than the 8.3 percent foreign-born population in Italy at large (roughly 5 million foreigners out of over 60 million people). The 2016 census calculated 377,217 foreigners out of a population of 2,864,731 living in the city of Rome. More information can be found at Demo.istat.it.

36.  Much literature examines Senegalese migration to northern Italian cities (e.g., Carter's focus on Turin in *States of Grace* and Riccio's look at Bergamo in "Migranti per il co-sviluppo" and at Ravenna and Rimini in "More than a Trade Diaspora").

37.  The number tends to fluctuate between twelve thousand and twenty thousand depending on the year. This statistic also does not take into account the descendants of enslaved Africans, many of whom came from the Senegambia region beginning in the seventeenth century. Both O. Kane, *Homeland Is the Arena*, and Stoller, *Money Has No Smell*, offer detailed discussions of relatively recent Senegalese migration to New York.

38.  Semple, "City's Newest Immigrant Enclaves." Currently, 37 percent of the city's 8.5 million inhabitants are foreign born. New York is also a majority-minority city with less than 45 percent of the population being white according to the U.S. Census Bureau, 2012–2016 American Community Survey 5-Year Estimates. Racial statistics are present only for New York City since neither the French nor the Italian government collects official census data based on race.

39. McClintock, "Angel of Progress," 87, 97.

40. While 79 percent of Senegalese migrate to only one country in Europe, 10 percent continue on to a second European country, and 11 percent return to Senegal. This is most likely a conservative estimate because "those still in their first European destination at the time of the survey may remigrate to another European country or return to Senegal at a later date." Toma and Castagnone, "What Drives Onward Mobility?," 77. Of those who participate in onward migration, 40 percent arrive in France first, followed by migration to Spain and Italy. However, the opposite trend occurs as well with 25 percent starting in Italy or Spain and continuing on to France.

41. Glick Schiller, "Centrality of Ethnography," 105.

42. According to the World Bank's Bilateral Remittance Matrix 2017, Senegal received over $2.2 billion in remittances in 2017. People in France sent back the biggest chunk at $647 million. Italy was second with $425 million. Spain was third with $302 million. The United States came in seventh, behind the Gambia, Mauritania, and Gabon, at $85 million. These remittances statistics show the presence of the Senegalese diaspora throughout Africa as well as in the Americas and Europe. For the purposes of this project, I have chosen to focus only on the Senegalese diaspora in the West because I am interested in the racial aspect of migration discourses that is heightened in majority-white spaces. I have chosen the United States instead of a country such as Spain, which is higher on the remittance list, because I wanted to include English as both a global language and a national language. In addition, it is important to highlight the difference in racial formation projects across the Atlantic.

43. The internet through platforms such as YouTube, Facebook, Twitter, and Wordpress allows for increased access and a larger variety of perspectives; however, these are not the texts with which literary and cultural studies most readily engage.

44. C. L. Miller, *Theories of Africans*, 24.

45. As we saw with Thiong'o, even those African authors who make a concerted effort to write in African languages often acquiesce to the pressures of European languages' monopoly on the literary market. Christopher Miller expounds on how African authors engage with this global market: "This literature continually uses devices such as footnotes, parentheses, and character-to-character explanations in order to provide the reader with necessary cultural information. Due to the conditions in which this literature arises—notably the limited literacy and knowledge of French throughout 'francophone' Africa—readers of a francophone text cannot be presumed to be local. Every time an author uses a phrase like 'here in Africa,' a *non-Africa* is revealed to be at play in the writing and reading process. A degree of 'otherness' is inscribed in any text which addresses itself to a world that is construed as outside." C. L. Miller, *Theories of Africans*, 6.

46. According to Shih, "Broadly speaking, cultural and political discourses undergirded by European republican ideology, especially in France, have posited the political and analytic lens of race as differentialist, divisive, and even illiberal, when in fact discrimination is rampant under the unacknowledged but highly operative sign of race. . . . Race is such an *American* issue! French-derived critical theory has continued, in the United States academy, to relegate race to the margins, and theories of race developed in ethnic studies and other disciplines continue not to be recognized as theory." Shih, "Comparative Racialization," 1348.

47. Shih, "Comparative Racialization," 1360.

48. Provencher, *Queer French*, 193.

49. Canagarajah frames the book as such: "This handbook endeavors to home in on the language/mobility nexus so that interdisciplinary scholars can take stock of the emergent scholarship for critical reflection and further development. . . . The handbook doesn't feature scholars from other fields in the humanities and social sciences (such as comparative literature, geography, sociology, or anthropology) who are engaged in studying mobility, though their work has significantly influenced the scholarship and theorization of applied linguists represented here." Canagarajah, *Routledge Handbook*, 1.

50. For a general discussion on language ideologies, see Woolard and Schieffelin, "Language Ideology." For information on AAVE in particular, see Milroy, "Language Ideologies," and Spears and Hinton, "Languages and Speakers." See Cruise O'Brien, "Shadow-Politics of Wolofisation"; Cruise O'Brien, "Langue et nationalité"; and McLaughlin, "Haalpulaar Identity," for information on multilingualism in Senegal.

51. Haugen, "Dialect, Language, Nation." Abbé Grégoire's report on regional languages at the time of the French Revolution claimed that 46 percent of the 26 million people had no ability to speak French and that only 11 percent had complete control of the language. For a detailed discussion of the report, see Certeau, Julia, and Revel, *Une politique de la langue*, or Lodge, *French*.

52. According to Rebecca Posner, "The standard language is viewed in the French tradition as a *trésor*, a *patrimoine*—an institution, which has been elaborated and perfected over time." Posner, *Linguistic Change in French*, 11.

53. For discussions concerning anxiety, see Coppel, "Les Français et la norme linguistique," and Drewelow and Theobald, "Comparison of the Attitudes." Archibald argues that some people who have sought citizenship have been turned down because of their insufficient linguistic abilities. Archibald, "La langue citoyenne," 19.

54. According to John Staulo, "[France] had experienced a central political force that radiated order and unity throughout the entire country at rather early stages in their aspiration for national political and linguistic unity. Italy on the other hand obtained its political unity only in the second half of the nineteenth century and for centuries had political forms of government that tended to fragmentize each region into separate and permanent linguistic entities." Staulo, *Other Voices*, 8–9.

55. Even if standard Italian has made major gains in the past two decades, recent statistics show that the use of standard Italian is still only slightly over 50 percent when people are at home or with friends. According to ISTAT, "From 1995 to 2012 the prevailing use of Italian in the family increased by about 10 percentage points (from 43.2 percent in 1995 to 53.1 percent in 2012), by 10.3 percentage points the proportion of those who use Italian language with friends (from 46.1 percent to 56.4 percent), and by 13.4 percentage points the use with strangers (from 71.4 percent in 1995 to 84.8 percent in 2012). The sole use of dialect, especially within the family, declined quite significantly over time: between 1995 and 2012 the percentage of those who spoke dialect only in their families decreased from 23.7 percent to 9 percent; from 16.4 percent to 9 percent when speaking with friends and from 6.3 percent to 1.8 percent when speaking with strangers." ISTAT, "Usage of Italian Language."

56. For instance, Donald Carter recounts the difficulties of one of his informants: "One Senegalese migrant, a recent arrival to Italy who was educated in French schools all his life and was working in construction in Italy, once complained: 'This language is so difficult, Italian. At work my boss is Piedmontese and so he speaks Piedmontese.

Another is Sicilian and he speaks only Sicilian. With all these languages, how am I to learn Italian?'" Carter, *States of Grace*, 143–44.

57. According to Ronald Schmidt, "The 'official English' movement—known to its detractors and some supporters as the 'English-only' movement—formally began on a national level on April 27, 1981, when Senator S. I. Hayakawa (R-California) introduced into the Senate a proposed amendment to the Constitution that would have designated English as the sole official language of the United States. A similar proposed constitutional amendment has been introduced in each Congress since that time, although none has come to a vote on the floor of either house." Schmidt, *Language Policy and Identity Politics*, 28.

58. Gonzalez, *Language Ideologies*, introduction; Schmid, "Politics of English Only."

59. Roberts, "Listening to (and Saving) the World's Languages."

60. Carter, *States of Grace*.

61. See O. Kane, *Homeland Is the Arena*; Buggenhagen, *Muslim Families in Global Senegal*; Riccio, "*Toubab* and *Vu Cumprà*," for Senegalese migration scholarship that has focused extensively on religious identity formation. While religion was discussed in some of my interviews, race was ever present. Perhaps my own racial identity contributed to this desire to discuss race. Perhaps the sociopolitical climate during the time of these interviews made my interviewees want to participate in the conversation on race.

62. Omi and Winant, *Racial Formation*, 102, 115.

63. Norton, "Language, Identity"; Norton, *Identity and Language Learning*; Rampton, *Crossing*.

64. Kramsch, "Privilege of the Non-Native Speaker"; Kubota, "Rethinking"; Lippi-Green, *English with an Accent*.

65. Rosa and Flores, "Unsettling Race and Language," 3.

66. Ibrahim, "Becoming Black," 353.

67. According to Ibrahim, "[The African youths in the study] access Black cultural identities and Black linguistic practice in and through Black popular culture, especially rap music videos, television programs, and Black films." He argues that this type of language learning is not so much about mastering the language as it is about making a statement about identity: "It is a way of saying, 'I too am Black' or 'I too desire and identify with Blackness.'" Ibrahim, "Becoming Black," 359, 351.

68. Fanon, *Black Skin, White Masks*, 18.

69. Sarkozy, "Le discours de Dakar."

70. The version posted on the governmental website is no longer accessible. *Le Monde* has reproduced the speech but without the word "history" capitalized.

71. Mbembe, "L'Afrique de Nicolas Sarkozy." See D. Thomas, *Africa and France*, for further exploration of Sarkozy's speech and discussions of the relationship between France and Africa.

72. For further discussion, see Hargreaves, *Multiethnic France*, and Lloyd, "Concepts, Models and Anti-Racist Strategies."

73. See Lozès, "Black France," for a discussion of housing and employment, and Constant, "Invention of Blacks in France," for one concerning legitimacy.

74. Patrick Lozès, founder of CRAN (Conseil représentatif des associations noires de France / Representative Council of France's Black Associations), has expounded on the tension surrounding *noir*, a word that has "long been taboo in the French political vocabulary, perhaps because it referred to a reality that no one wanted to face. In a

country that considers itself the 'land of human rights,' it is difficult, even shameful, to admit that millions of citizens suffer massive discrimination on a daily basis, limiting their access to housing, employment, education, credit, creating businesses, and leisure activities." Lozès, "Black France," 103.

75. Pap Ndiaye has discussed the paradox for visible minorities: "Les Noirs de France sont individuellement visibles, mais ils sont invisibles en tant que groupe social et qu'objet d'étude pour les universitaires. D'abord en tant que groupe social, ils sont censés ne pas exister, puisque la République française ne reconnaît pas officiellement les minorités, et ne les compte pas non plus." (Blacks in France are individually visible, but they are invisible as a social group and an object of scholarly study. As a social group, they supposedly do not exist, since the French Republic does not officially recognize or count minorities.) Ndiaye, "Pour une histoire des populations noires," 91.

76. Calling into question a tradition that has focused solely on the role of social structures in the formulation of a national identity, Didier and Éric Fassin have shown how "la question sociale est aussi une question raciale" (social issues are also racial issues). Fassin and Fassin, *De la question sociale*, 13. The chapters in Trica Danielle Keaton, Denean Sharpley-Whiting, and Tyler Stovall's edited volume demonstrate how "blackness in France is primarily a response to and rejection of anti-black racism. To be Black is, above all, to be targeted by such racism and to develop strategies to resist it." Keaton, Sharpley-Whiting, and Stovall, *Black France / France Noire*, 3.

77. Focusing on the migration of people and their identities in the works of authors from a variety of francophone African countries and time periods, Dominic Thomas explores the "transnational constituencies that have emerged from colonialism and immigration [to offer] new ways of thinking about the symbiotic dimension of relations and population flows between France and the francophone world." He connects colonialism and postcolonial immigration as well as French and African histories by using what he calls a transcolonial approach in order to "account for blackness in its multiple expressive forms in France as a lived experience, particularly since these questions have, until recently, been ignored in France." D. Thomas, *Black France*, 3, 206.

78. Christina Lombardi-Diop and Caterina Romeo mark the Italian colonial period from its first formal colony in Eritrea in 1890 to its loss of Libya as well as Albania and the Dodecanese Islands in 1943: "In the period between 1890–1943, Italy claimed colonial rights over Eritrea, Somalia, parts of Libya, Ethiopia, the Dodecanese Islands, and Albania." Lombardi-Diop and Romeo, introduction to *Postcolonial Italy*, 1.

79. Ben-Ghiat and Fuller, *Italian Colonialism*, 1. See Barbara Sòrgoni's "Racist Discourses and Practices" for a discussion of systemic racism in the administration of the Ethiopian colony.

80. See Gramsci, *Southern Question*, for a discussion of the North-South divide. Importantly, Nelson Moe argues that in the northern imaginary, the South has represented "both 'Africa' and *terra vergine*, a reservoir of feudal residues, sloth, and squalor on the one hand and of quaint peasants, rustic traditions, and exotica on the other." Moe, *View from Vesuvius*, 3.

81. Verdicchio, *Bound by Distance*, 28.

82. Gillette, *Racial Theories in Fascist Italy*.

83. According to David Ward, Italy's failure to reconcile its fascist past has repercussions for current formulations of Italian national identity. In looking at various types of Italian cultural production, such as graffiti found around Rome, he has traced the

evolution of contemporary racist arguments concerning immigration. Ward, "'Italy' in Italy," 91.

84. Khouma's "Io, nero italiano" is a prime example. See Brioni, *Somali Within*, for more information.

85. Omi and Winant, *Racial Formation*.

86. The racial dimension of slavery was evidenced in the 1640 ruling in which John Punch, an African, was sentenced to lifetime slavery after being caught escaping indentured servitude, while the two white escapees caught with him were punished only by a few additional years of indentured servitude. Furthermore, Leon Higginbotham has argued that by the mid-seventeenth century, white colonists "were already beginning to establish a process of debasement and cruelty reserved for blacks only." Higginbotham, *In the Matter of Color*, 26.

87. Louisiana, a French colony until the Louisiana Purchase, had relied on the Code Noir since 1724. While ensuring some rights to enslaved people, the code, dating back to 1685 in other French colonies, also codified the link between blackness and slavery. Similarly, in 1723 Virginia governor William Gooch justified the denial of voting rights to free blacks, finding it necessary "to fix a perpetual brand upon negroes and mulattos by excluding them from the great privilege of a freeman." Allen, *Invention of the White Race*, 242.

88. See Ross, "Multi-Level Bayesian Analysis," for an exploration of racial bias in policing; Gray, *Watching Race*, and Means Coleman, *Say it Loud!*, for media representation; and Alim, Rickford, and Ball, *Raciolinguistics*, and Flores and Rosa, "Undoing Appropriateness," for the relationship between race and linguistic norms. For instance, calling attention to power dynamics, Flores and Rosa theorize that raciolinguistic ideologies "produce racialized speaking subjects who are constructed as linguistically deviant even when engaging in linguistic practices positioned as normative or innovative when produced by privileged white subjects." Flores and Rosa, "Undoing Appropriateness," 150.

89. See Stoller, *Money Has No Smell*, and Zeleza, "Diaspora Dialogues," for a discussion on relationships between Africans and African Americans. Clarke and Thomas's *Globalization of Race* explores the difficulties that arise when diasporas clash.

90. Marable and Agard-Jones, *Transnational Blackness*, 3.

91. Fouquet, "Construire la Blackness depuis l'Afrique."

92. Fila-Bakabadio explains, "Au-delà des liens continus des Africains-Américains avec d'autres peuples noirs, le terme blackness peine à s'extraire d'une lecture étatsunienne et conduit souvent à réifier la race, voire à penser une unicité des peuples noirs qui n'existe pas" (Beyond the continuing links of African-Americans with other black peoples, the term blackness is difficult to extract from a US reading and often leads to a reification of race and a unity of black peoples that does not exist). Fila-Bakabadio, "Photographie et géographie corporelle," 23.

93. Pierre and Niauffre, "L'Afrique et la question." Pierre also tackles the question of global racial formation: "My work reveals the long history of interaction that was not only facilitated by the active and conscious negotiations of people of African descent—on both sides of the Atlantic—but was also shaped by global social, economic, and political processes that have worked to inform racialized understandings of identity for these populations. As such, my aim has been not to limit my focus on complex negotiations in the contemporary making of African diasporic and African relationships, but to

reframe these negotiations both within a long historical durée of Afro-Atlantic dialogues and within processes of global racial formation." Pierre, *Predicament of Blackness*, 183.

94. Pierre, *Predicament of Blackness*, xii.

95. Another way to think about global racialization is through Shih's concept of the worldliness of race. According to her, "Because instances of racialization are situated in specific times and places, comparison between these instances may seem random or unrelated, but the colonial turn reveals potential and concrete relations among them. To think comparatively therefore is to think about the world where the colonial turn has left indelible marks—that is, to think the worldliness of race." Shih, "Comparative Racialization," 1349.

96. In translation theory, Paul Ricoeur describes linguistic hospitality as a site where "the pleasure of dwelling in the other's language is balanced by the pleasure of receiving the foreign word at home, in one's own welcoming house." Ricoeur, *On Translation*, 10. Furthermore, he argues that it is the paragon of all other types of hospitality. Ricoeur, *Reflections on the Just*, 116.

97. Anderson argues that the nation "is imagined because the members of even the smallest nation will never know most of their fellow-members, meet them, or even hear of them, yet in the minds of each lives the image of their communion. . . . In fact, all communities larger than primordial villages of face-to-face contact (and perhaps even these) are imagined." Anderson, *Imagined Communities*, 6.

98. They embody Françoise Lionnet and Shu-mei Shih's concept of the transnational, which "is not bound by the binary of the local and the global and can occur in national, local, or global spaces across different and multiple spatialities and temporalities." Lionnet and Shih, *Minor Transnationalism*, 6.

99. Bourdieu, *Distinction*, 291.

100. Kramsch and Whiteside detail what symbolic competence entails: "Social actors in multilingual settings seem to activate more than a communicative competence that would enable them to communicate accurately, effectively, and appropriately with one another. They seem to display a particularly acute ability to play with various linguistic codes and with the various spatial and temporal resonances of these codes. We call this competence 'symbolic competence.'" Kramsch and Whiteside, "Language Ecology in Multilingual Settings," 664. As an example of symbolic competence, Ana Celia Zentella points to New York Puerto Rican children growing up in El Bloque who use all the languages at their disposal in order to convey different meanings while taking pride in their unique ability to do so. Zentella, *Growing Up Bilingual*.

101. Kramsch, *Multilingual Subject*, 17. Kimberly Vinall further explains that it is through symbolic competence that second-language learners can gain "the potential to become aware of and critically reflect on and act on the crossing of multiple borders between linguistic codes and cultural meanings, the self and others, various timescales and historical contexts, and power structures." Vinall, "Got Llorona?," 5.

102. García, "Education, Multilingualism and Translanguaging," 140.

103. As Jan Blommaert and Ben Rampton argue, "There is now a substantial body of work on *ideologies of language* that denaturalizes the idea that there are distinct languages, and that a proper language is bounded, pure and composed of structured sounds, grammar and vocabulary designed for referring to things (Joseph and Taylor 1990; Woolard, Schieffelin, and Kroskrity 1998). Named languages—'English,' 'German,' 'Bengali'—are ideological constructions historically tied to the emergence of the nation-state in the nineteenth century, when the idea of autonomous languages free from

agency and individual intervention meshed with the differentiation of peoples in terms of spiritual essences (Gal and Irvine 1995; Taylor 1990)." Blommaert and Rampton, "Language and Superdiversity," 3–4.

104. Ofelia García and Wei Li explain how "a translanguaging approach to bilingualism extends the repertoire of semiotic practices of individuals and transforms them into dynamic mobile resources that can adapt to global and local sociolinguistic situations. At the same time, translanguaging also attends to the social construction of language and bilingualism under which speakers operate." García and Wei, *Translanguaging*, 18.

105. While the term "translanguaging" is an important conceptual tool, "code-switching" is a perfectly adequate term in referring to multilingual discourse and will be used throughout this book.

106. For García, multilingualism is the norm throughout the world, yet multilingual practices, especially in North America and Europe, are often framed as deficient forms of communication. She discusses how most scholarship on bilingualism takes place in North America, where in the public eye, bilingualism is often seen as detrimental to monolingual linguistic competence; however, the greatest linguistic complexity exists in sub-Saharan Africa and Southeast Asia. García, "Education, Multilingualism and Translanguaging," 142–43.

107. As Blommaert and Rampton contend, "Rather than working with homogeneity, stability and boundedness as the starting assumptions, mobility, mixing, political dynamics and historical embedding are now central concerns in the study of languages, language groups and communication." Blommaert and Rampton, "Language and Superdiversity," 3. See also Blommaert, "From Mobility to Complexity."

108. For instance, Tricia Redeker Hepner's anthropological study highlights the facets of transnationalism in a globalized world when she demonstrates how a postcolonial nation such as Eritrea can be both centralized and diffuse, nationalist and internationalist. Redeker Hepner, *Soldiers, Martyrs, Traitors, and Exiles.*

109. To further protect privacy, I also agreed to take notes instead of recording conversations when asked.

110. Appendix 1 provides demographic information on the informants in Paris.

111. Appendix 2 provides demographic information on the informants in Rome.

112. *Classe media,* which often attracts migrants, is similar to a class taken for a General Equivalency Degree (GED).

113. While the three principal informants were all well-educated people in their late twenties to early thirties, they interacted with and introduced me to a wide range of people with regard to age and education level. Appendix 3 provides demographic information on the informants in New York City.

114. See Norton, "Language, Identity," and Norton, *Identity and Language Learning,* for further discussion.

## CHAPTER 1. WHAT'S LANGUAGE GOT TO DO WITH IT?

1. See information about each informant, including when the interview took place, in the appendixes.

2. Norton, "Language, Identity," 411.

3. See France's official governmental website for more information: http://www .diplomatie.gouv.fr/en/french-foreign-policy/francophony/the-status-of-french-in -the-world.

4. For instance, see letter-writing scenes in Sembène's *La noire de . . .* (Black girl) and *Mandabi* (The money order).

5. Noting the "indelible marks" of colonialism, Dominic Thomas shows how this phenomenon affects francophone literary production as well: "Francophone writers have by definition been compelled to mediate their aesthetic and political projects through a linguistic domain that is inextricably linked to this historical context." D. Thomas, *Black France*, 82–83.

6. Indeed, the OIF estimates that by 2050, 80 percent of the world's projected 700 million French speakers will be in Africa and that French may become the second most widely spoken language on the planet. See more information at www.diplomatie .gouv.fr; www.francophonie.org.

7. In the case of Senegal, French is most often considered the official language with the term "national language" usually reserved for indigenous languages such as Wolof.

8. French West African territory included the present-day countries of Senegal, Mali, Mauritania, Guinea, Ivory Coast, Burkina Faso, Benin, and Niger. The federal capital, and therefore the residence of the governors-general of French West Africa, was in Saint-Louis first, then Dakar.

9. See Senghor, "Le français, langue de culture," for his thoughts on the French language and culture. See Ousmane Sembène's novel *Le dernier de l'empire* for a critique of Senghor's relationship with France and French.

10. Hakim specifically refers to West Africa, but he includes Central Africa when talking about the Congo.

11. The notion of Tarzan speech usually comes up in research on foreigner talk. See Ferguson, "Toward a Characterization," and Lipski, "'Partial' Spanish Strategies."

12. Fanon, *Black Skin, White Masks*.

13. In fact, in the song "Tout ceci ne vous rendra pas le Congo" (All of this will not give you the Congo back), Congolese Belgian rapper Baloji says, "Le Congolais reste le nègre de l'Afrique" (The Congolese are the n****s of Africa).

14. This term *Français de souche* appears often in my interviews and denotes white French people whose families have lived in France for at least several generations. Laurent Dubois translates it as "real" French people. Dubois, "République Métissée," 18 (scare quotes in the original).

15. It would be interesting to know if this situation is atypical. I have yet to find in the research other examples of speakers from an official-language setting arguing that their variety of a colonial language is better than that of speakers from the original colonizing country. (I am excluding settler-colonial settings such as the United States, Canada, and Australia, which would also be useful to explore, but which would require a different lens.) However, Yasukata Yano cites anecdotal evidence from personal communication in which Singaporean speakers of English question the validity of inner-circle speakers (those from the center) with regard to native-speakerness because they "feel that they are native speakers of English and they do have native speaker's intuition." Yano, "World Englishes," 122. See also B. Kachru, "Standards, Codification and Sociolinguistic Realism," for a discussion on the three circles of English.

16. Borrowing from political economy and referring to the English-speaking world, Canagarajah defines the center as "the industrially/economically advanced communities of the West, which sustain their ideological hegemony by keeping less-developed communities in Periphery status." Meanwhile, the periphery denotes "recent users of this

language, many of whom would display sound multilingual competence in many codes—including the Center's standard dialects as well as their indigenized variants of English—which they would use in contextually appropriate ways." Canagarajah, "Interrogating the Native Speaker Fallacy," 79.

17. We see a similar situation with Spanish in Latin America in which historical and social factors have bearing on contemporary understandings of prestige that could be applied to a revised understanding of center and periphery. For example, Ralph Penny states that because of Mexico City and Lima's position as the main administrative and cultural centers of Latin America, the speech in the highlands of Mexico and Peru became examples of prestigious varieties. The speakers of these two varieties could be seen as embodying center status compared to the rest of Latin America, whose status is more periphery. Penny, *History of the Spanish Language*, 23–26.

18. As Thomas asserts, "Colonial education and the dissemination of the myth of French universalism and cultural superiority created a logical desire among colonial subjects to travel to the metropole, the result of an acquired francocentrism that in turn contained the promise of cultural capital." D. Thomas, *Black France*, 51.

19. It should go without saying that people of color can speak standard French as well as white speakers; however, as the discussion in chapter 2 will show, value judgments about linguistic ability are often tied to race, regardless of speakers' linguistic competence, thus demonstrating the short-sightedness of colorblind ideologies.

20. There are a few notable cases of Italian speakers from the New York City data, including Bouba—the one person who was exposed to Italian while in Senegal—whose perspective I will analyze in detail in chapter 4.

21. The excerpt uses the following notation: Italian, *French*.

22. *Damme* in Romanesco; *dammi* in standard Italian.

23. Please refer to the International Phonetic Alphabet (IPA) for script bracketed by slashes.

24. While formal spelling rules for these languages exist, used mainly by linguists and some literary authors, most people just write them phonetically, which usually means using a Frenchified spelling that dates to the colonial era. McLaughlin, "Dakar Wolof," 167.

25. *Essetto* is the Romanesco version of the Italian word *eccetto*.

26. According to the Doxa surveys (one thousand interviews in 1974 and 1988, two thousand interviews in 1982), by 1988 40 percent of adult Italians spoke dialect with everyone at home compared to 34 percent speaking Italian at home with everyone. With friends and colleagues, 23 percent always spoke dialect with 31 percent always speaking Italian. Tosi, *Language and Society*, 29–30.

27. It would be worthwhile for future research to see if the Senegalese who have learned regional varieties view some as more prestigious than others.

28. Romanesco is most prevalent in the Trastevere neighborhood and is characterized by a more open and slower pronunciation. The prevalence of shortened forms of words is noted. K. J. Pratt, "Dialect of Rome," 168. Deaffrication of intervocalic /tʃ/ to /ʃ/ is also common. Loporcaro and Bertinetto, "Sound Pattern of Standard Italian," 135.

29. A similar study of Gambian attitudes to English—using the Gambia as a primary site—would be a useful future direction.

30. See Ager, "Identity, Insecurity and Image," for research on the threat of the English language. However, France's aversion to English is sometimes overstated.

According to a 2012 Eurobarometer report on languages in the European Union, 39 percent of respondents from France said they speak English well enough to hold a conversation, 57 percent said they use English occasionally, and 92 percent think English is one of the two most useful languages for children to learn. "Europeans and their Languages," 21, 44, 80.

31. There are plenty of examples in my interviews of how Italians do not learn English well, but the explanations are based not on a cultural disdain for English such as one finds in the data from Paris but on a perception that Italy is uninterested in multilingualism unless it specifically refers to Italian languages and dialects.

32. Although nothing in my data specifically supports these claims, further research on Senegalese attitudes about English as a postcolonial language would be quite productive. In addition, while my colleague's friends may bristle at the idea of going to the Gambia to learn English, the reality is that there is a long tradition of migration between Senegal and the Gambia. See Ngom, "Social Status," for more information. Furthermore, the Gambia sent $264 million to Senegal in 2017, placing fourth in annual remittances (behind France, Italy, and Spain), according to the World Bank's Bilateral Remittance Matrix 2017.

33. While there is very little scholarly work on English-language acquisition in Senegal, Fallou Ngom notes that intermittent British rule in Senegal and the Gambia in the eighteenth and nineteenth centuries is partially responsible for the influence of English. Ngom, "Social Status," 354. In addition, since Senegal follows the French educational model, it would make sense that one learns British English in school. Most discussions of foreign-language learning are found not in academic texts but in those for marketing. For instance, a study by the British Council has found that Senegal has the highest level of English competence of any country in West Africa. Sene, "Sénégal."

34. Having been priced out of rapidly gentrifying Harlem, many of the people I interviewed live deep in the Bronx or Queens.

35. Howe, "Negation," 185. New York is a major dialectal center with multiple hierarchies and registers. See Newman, *New York City English*, for a very detailed account of linguistic variation in New York City with regard to regional features as well as racial factors contributing to sociolinguistic variation.

36. Research in second language acquisition has specifically tackled the acquisition of nonstandard languages such as AAVE. For instance, Lynn Goldstein has investigated the motivation for a group of twenty-eight Latino boys in New York City to make AAVE versus SAE their target language. In doing so, she broaches the issue of what it means to make a sociolinguistic choice in learning a second language and what factors dictate the choice of the target language. She posits that language contact and feelings of identity play the biggest role in assimilation of different grammar points. Goldstein, "Standard English," 426.

37. Race is not the only factor that informants mentioned in language variation. For instance, Bouba remarked on both racial and regional differences: "The white people and the black people don't speak the same language. Or when you go to Alaska or when you go to Oregon, all the states here, the English is not like the same. I lived in Pennsylvania and the language is not like the same in other parts of the U.S." Throughout the data, there are examples of class and regional differences. However, most discussion of language variation is related to either race or education level.

38. McLaughlin, "Haalpulaar Identity."

39. The Casamance region, in particular, challenges the narrative of Wolof dominance. While a tiny minority nationally, the Jola are the dominant ethnic group of Casamance. Since the 1980s, Casamance has been home to a separatist movement seeking autonomy and even independence.

40. Technically, Pulaar is a term used to label the dialects of the Fulfulde language spoken by the Fulani and Toucouleurs in Senegambia, especially in the Futa Toro region along the Senegal-Mauritania border. Fulfulde is, in some sense, an international language since its dialects are spoken across a huge stretch of West Africa as well as in the diaspora, with varying degrees of intelligibility between them. However, it lacks a transdialectal standard comparable to Modern Standard Arabic, thus limiting the international reach of any one dialect. See Kane and Robinson, *Islamic Regime of Fuuta Tooro*, for more information.

41. The heart of Little Senegal, 116th Street traverses Harlem.

42. French is another lingua franca.

43. Aminata was speaking during her joint interview with Diallo.

44. However, French should be in moderation. As Swigart explains about Wolof use in Senegal, "The use of an urban variety such as Urban Wolof must be contrasted to the choice by educated speakers to use a European language by itself. . . . The use of French without at least some recourse to Wolof expressions or lexical items in a friendly conversation, or even in an informal discussion in the workplace, marks a Senegalese as assimile, a perhaps too willing victim of the French civilising mission. To speak French is desirable; to speak French too much is inappropriate. Most Senegalese do not wish to display that kind of admiration or closeness with the cultural 'centre' of colonial times." Swigart, "Cultural Creolisation," 179.

45. O. Kane, *Homeland Is the Arena*, 63–66.

46. As Harlem continues to gentrify and Senegalese communities in other boroughs attract new migrants, it will be interesting to see what this fragmentation does to Little Senegal. However, as long as the markets, stores, and restaurants survive, Senegalese all over the city will continue to flock to Harlem.

47. Carter, *States of Grace*; Riccio, "*Toubab* and *Vu Cumprà*."

48. Charbol, "Château Rouge."

49. Sébastien divulged that he was a Senegalese citizen with a French temporary residency card.

50. McLaughlin, "Dakar Wolof."

## Chapter 2. Speaking while Black

1. Secrétariat général à l'immigration et à l'intégration, "Réforme du contrôle de la connaissance de la langue française par les candidats à la nationalité" (Loi no. 94-665 du 4 août 1994). This requirement does not apply to stateless persons or political refugees. (Translation from https://www.legifrance.gouv.fr/Traductions/en-English/Legifrance -translations.) The United States also has a language requirement, with exemptions and accommodations based on age, time of residency, and disabilities. The English-language test requires the applicant to read one of three sentences correctly, write one of three sentences correctly, and communicate in English during the eligibility interview (see www.uscis.gov). Since 2012, applicants for residency in Italy must sign an integration agreement (*accordo di integrazione*), which includes either taking Italian-language classes or

passing an Italian-language test (see http://www.interno.gov.it/it/temi/immigrazione-e
-asilo/modalita-dingresso/accordo-integrazione-straniero-richiede-permesso-soggiorno).

2.  Linguistic legislation in France reflects societal attitudes concerning the value
placed on the French language, in particular, a standardized norm, which has historically
been important in France as a marker of societal cohesion. From legislation during the
revolutionary era that accentuated the need for a national language to 1882–83 Ferry
Laws, which ushered in an era of universal acquisition of the standard language, tying
language to a sense of nationality and duty to country is nothing new.

3.  Archibald, "La Langue Citoyenne," 19. The required level of language competence is B1: "Can understand the main points of clear standard input on familiar matters
regularly encountered in work, school, leisure, etc. Can deal with most situations likely
to arise whilst travelling in an area where the language is spoken. Can produce simple
connected text on topics, which are familiar, or of personal interest. Can describe experiences and events, dreams, hopes & ambitions and briefly give reasons and explanations for opinions and plans." Language competency levels have been put forth by the
Council of Europe, *Common European Framework of Reference for Languages*.

4.  Claire Kramsch has argued that native speakership "is more than privilege
of birth or even education. It is acceptance by the group that created the distinction
between native and nonnative speakers." Kramsch, "Privilege of the Non-Native
Speaker," 363.

5.  Kubota, "Rethinking the Superiority."

6.  In her sociolinguistic research on language attitudes and accent, Rosina Lippi-
Green describes how "the evaluation of language effectiveness—while sometimes quite
relevant—is often a covert way of judging not the delivery of the message but the social
identity of the messenger." Lippi-Green, *English with an Accent*, 17.

7.  The Alsatian *V* is pronounced /f/, which Diome conveys through the substitu-
tion of *V*s for *F*s in the script. See Keller, *German Dialects*, for more information on Alsatian
phonology.

8.  Diome, *La préférence nationale*, 86, 87; silent diatribe, 87–89.

9.  Diome's narrator encounters a very similar scenario when a woman refuses to
offer her a tutoring job because of the color of her skin: "Je veux une personne de type
européen; . . . je ne veux pas qu'on me bousille l'éducation de mon enfant" (I want a
European person; . . . I do not want my child's education to be ruined). The expression
*de type européen* is a euphemism for a white person that allows people not to say "white" in
a context where talking about race is taboo. The narrator then thinks to herself: "Madame
est française, il est vrai, mais elle n'a même pas son bac et s'estime incapable d'assurer le
soutien scolaire de sa fille. À cause de mes lèvres noires, qui du moins psalmodient la
langue de Vaugelas mieux que les siennes, elle me refuse le travail." (Madame is French,
it is true, but she does not even have her baccalaureate and considers herself unable to
provide school support for her daughter. Because of my black lips, which at least intone
the language of Vaugelas better than hers, she refuses to offer me the job.) Diome, *La
préférence nationale*, 91. The narrator's French linguistic skill is not enough to whiten her
black lips—to make her a French person—so she is denied employment on racial
grounds.

10.  Lucie was currently learning Wolof in order to feel more connected to the
country of her ancestors.

11.  Jean-Paul insisted on being interviewed in English in order to practice.

12. The Other evokes the postcolonial black subaltern. Gayatri Spivak's question of whether the subaltern can speak is particularly relevant when considering which languages are used, to whom those languages "belong," and how often speakers are illegitimated based on their backgrounds and therefore refused to be heard. Spivak, "Can the Subaltern Speak?"

13. Focusing primarily on how people's perceptions of accents influence interactions between native and non-native speakers, Lippi-Green warns that although all interlocutors have to work at successful communication, native speakers tend to shirk their communicative duties when speaking to non-native speakers such as by claiming they cannot understand someone's accent without actually trying. Lippi-Green, *English with an Accent.* Donald Rubin's study in which sixty-two American undergraduate students listened to a four-minute prerecorded lecture by a native English speaker from Ohio shows how listeners' perceptions of a speaker's ethnicity can influence listening comprehension. Half the group was shown a picture of an Asian woman and told the voice belonged to her, while the other half was shown a picture of a white woman. Not only did questionnaires show that the students thought the white woman was easier to understand; they also performed better on a listening comprehension test, even though all students listened to the exact same recording. Rubin, "Nonlanguage Factors."

14. Lippi-Green offers a similar conclusion: "The process of standardization and language subordination is concerned not so much with an overall homogeneity of language, but with excluding only *certain types* of language and variation, those linked to social differences which make us uncomfortable." Lippi-Green, *English with an Accent*, 121.

15. Lippi-Green, dissecting different ads and articles promoting good accents in the American context, shows that racism is a likely factor: "'Asian, Indian, and Middle Eastern accents and Spanish accents' are not acceptable; apparently French, German, British, Swedish accents are, regardless of the communication difficulties those languages may cause in the learning of English." Lippi-Green, *English with an Accent*, 146. In other words, these accents do not represent the Other in the minds of most Americans who see people coming from these countries as equals.

16. This is not to say that some sectors of the French population are not worried about the influence of the English language. For instance, la loi Toubon (The Toubon law), also called loi no. 94-665 du 4 août 1994, "Relative à l'emploi de la langue française," requires the use of French in official governmental publications, advertisements, workplaces, government-financed schools, and other contexts. Many scholars, such as Michele Belluzzi, have suggested that this law was particularly aimed at English and its influence on French language and culture. Belluzzi, "Cultural Protection." Dennis Ager looks in detail at Americanophobia. Ager, "Identity, Insecurity and Image." While many negative attitudes exist about the English language's influence in France, these attitudes seem restricted to the language. When it comes to negative attitudes about the people who speak English, expats from England or America do not seem to pose a threat to French society on an individual level.

17. Francien, the ancient dialect of Latin that would eventually become modern French, came from the monarchy and nobility in the Paris region; therefore, it is unsurprising that the descendent of this dialect would be the prestige dialect of present-day France. In work done by John Paltridge and Howard Giles on regional accents in France, the accent from Provence is seen as the most accented but comes second after the Parisian dialect in a hierarchy concerning positive attitudes about regional variation.

Paltridge and Giles, "Attitudes towards Speakers." Meanwhile, Lawrence Kuiper has found that Parisians ranked speakers from Provence twentieth out of twenty-four regions for correctness but first for pleasantness. Kuiper, "Perception Is Reality," 36.

18. Canagarajah, "Interrogating the Native Speaker Fallacy," 79.

19. Jean Beaman defines cultural citizenship as "a claim to full societal belonging by fellow members of one's community." Beaman, *Citizen Outsider*, 23. Her qualitative research on forty-five college-educated, second-generation North African adults in Paris demonstrates how high education level and social class did not translate into acceptance or the ability to fully integrate. They were seen as Muslim or North African, first and foremost.

20. Kington, "Italy's First Black Minister." See Jaksa's "Sports and Collective Identity" for a discussion on sports and national identity formation.

21. Kington, "Italy's First Black Minister." Kyenge, in discussing the hostile reception she and Balotelli have received at times, told Aldo Cazzullo: "Lo fischiano per lo stesso motivo per cui insultano me: perché siamo degli apripista. Lui il primo centravanti nero della nazionale, io la prima ministra nera. Tentano di indebolirci, ma non ci riusciranno." (They hiss and jeer for the same reason that they insult me: because we are trailblazers. Bolatelli, the first black center forward for the Italian national team, and I, the first black minister. They try to weaken us, but they will not succeed.) Cazzullo, "Kyenge." In this article, Kyenge also reflected on the argument that black Italians don't exist.

22. See Ben-Ghiat and Fuller, *Italian Colonialism*, for a detailed account of racial formation in Italy during the colonial period. Furthermore, in discussing how denial plays a role in Italian discourse on race, Alessandro Portelli has argued that part of the reason for the lack of introspection on the part of Italians with regard to race relates to how they position themselves (and have done so since colonization) as normal and unmarked: "Jokes and songs from the colonial period never oppose a White and a Black person, but always an *Italian* and a Black." Portelli, "Problem of the Color-Blind," 356.

23. While a critical mass of black voices in Italy might not have existed until recently, Africans have been in Italy for centuries. Sergio Tognetti's analyses of the Cambini Bank's account books show Florence's hand in the black African slave trade, while Nelson Minnich's work looks at the relationship between black Africans in Italy and the Catholic Church. Tognetti, "Trade in Black African Slaves"; Minnich, "Catholic Church." In addition to enslaved Africans, there are examples of prominent people in Italy's history who would be considered black by today's standards. For instance, historian Catherine Fletcher's *Black Prince of Florence* chronicles the life of Alessandro de' Medici and his rule of Italy from 1531 to 1537. The fact that very few people know or talk about Africans in Italy prior to the nineteenth century shows selective historical amnesia.

24. Lombardi-Diop and Romeo, "Introduction," 10.

25. Khouma, "Io, nero italiano," 3.

26. Kington, "Italy's First Black Minister."

27. Elisabetta Povoledo notes in "Slurs against Italy's First Black National Official" that "experts who track immigration issues say that more subtle and insidious forms of racism are pervasive in Italy as it struggles to come to terms with its rapidly changing demographics."

28. The excerpt uses the following notation: French, *Italian*, <u>English</u>, **Romanesco**.

29. *Vabbèh* means *va bene* (OK) in Romanesco. K. J. Pratt, "Dialect of Rome," 168.

30. Spielberg, *Color Purple*. For the quotation of Celie's statement in the film, see https://www.quotes.net/mquote/11088.

31. Jan-Petter Blom and John Gumperz describe metaphorical code-switching as a phenomenon in which switching languages "enriches a situation, allowing for allusion to more than one social relationship within the situation." Blom and Gumperz, "Social Meaning in Linguistic Structures," 408.

32. Gardner-Chloros, *Code-Switching*, 59.

33. The excerpt uses the following notation: French, *English*.

34. Ibrahim, "Becoming Black."

35. Ana Celia Zentella notes cases where those in her study switched languages to avoid a taboo word. Zentella, *Growing Up Bilingual*, 97.

36. Stovall, "Race," 211.

37. Trica Keaton argues that the use of "black" instead of *noir* in France connects speakers "to a U.S. type of consciousness permeating France and parts of Europe." Keaton, *Muslim Girls*, 7.

38. Furthermore, *The Color Purple* explicitly connects Africa with black America when Celie finds her sister Nettie's letters about her experiences living in Africa.

39. The excerpt uses the following notation: French, *Italian*, Spanish. The transcription and translation tries to convey the non-standard French that Abi used.

40. Referring to a study on Jamaican English in London, Penelope Gardner-Chloros writes "that code-switching is used . . . to 'animate' the narrative by providing different 'voices' for the participants in the incident which is described." Gardner-Chloros, *Code-Switching*, 3.

41. Butler, *Excitable Speech*, 2.

42. See Faloppa, *Parole contro*, for a historical and contemporary discussion of words to describe blacks in Italian.

43. According to Butler, "One comes to 'exist' by virtue of this fundamental dependency on the address of the Other. One 'exists' not only by virtue of being recognized, but, in a prior sense, by being *recognizable*. The terms that facilitate recognition are themselves conventional, the effects and instruments of a social ritual that decide, often through exclusion and violence, the linguistic conditions of survivable subjects." Butler, *Excitable Speech*, 5. Abi's existence was contingent on being recognizable as Other, an identity that was not welcomed by those who were taunting her.

44. Socé, *Mirages de Paris*, 34–35.

45. Socé, *Mirages de Paris*, 63–64.

46. Ibrahim, "Becoming Black."

47. Many but not all the people who participated were first- or second-generation Senegalese who had grown up in America.

48. See O. Kane, *Homeland Is the Arena*, and Stoller, *Money Has No Smell*. A similar antagonism exists in France between Afro-Caribbean and African communities seen through such cultural production as Alain Mabanckou's short story "The Fugitive." However, this phenomenon did not often arise in my data.

49. Paul Gilroy warns how the concept of diaspora can be misleading: "A myth of shared origins is neither a talisman which can suspend political antagonisms nor a deity invited to cement a pastoral view of black life that can answer the multiple pathologies of contemporary racism." Gilroy, *Black Atlantic*, 99.

50. Okwui Enwezor demonstrates this propensity to reduce Africa and Africans to

less than human status if not altogether erased: "For decades now, the photographic imaginary of Africa has circled the same paradoxical field of presentation: either showing us the precarious conditions of life and existence, in which case the African subject always appears at risk, on the margins of life itself, at that intersection where one is forced to negotiate the relationship between man and animal. Or we are confronted with the heartbreaking beauty of its natural world, where man is virtually absent." Enwezor, *Snap Judgments*, 12. Not until 2016 did Disney finally feature human characters on the African continent, with its live-action film *Queen of Katwe*.

51. W. E. B. Du Bois argued, "It is a peculiar sensation, this double-consciousness, this sense of always looking at one's self through the eyes of others, of measuring one's soul by the tape of a world that looks on in amused contempt and pity. One ever feels his two-ness,—an American, a Negro; two souls, two thoughts, two unreconciled strivings; two warring ideals in one dark body, whose dogged strength alone keeps it from being torn asunder." Du Bois, *Souls of Black Folk*, 3. Gilroy has expounded on this notion: "Striving to be both European and black requires some specific forms of double consciousness. . . . However, where racist, nationalist, or ethnically absolutist discourses orchestrate political relationships so that these identities appear to be mutually exclusive, occupying the space between them or trying to demonstrate their continuity has been viewed as a provocative and even oppositional act of political insubordination." Gilroy, *Black Atlantic*, 1.

52. Jesse Shipley's work on Ghanaians in the United States explores similar experiences: "Ghanaians abroad are dispersed within broader African American and immigrant communities with competing popular cultures and networks of affiliation. Theories of race and African diasporic cultural ideologies must take account of the internal nuances that intertwine culture, blackness, and nation for first-generation immigrants." Shipley, *Living the Hiplife*, 265.

53. See Russell-Cole, Wilson, and Hall, *Color Complex*; Norwood, *Color Matters*.

54. See Lynn Thomas's "Skin Lighteners" or Jemima Pierre's *Predicament of Blackness* concerning the importance of skin lighteners both on the African continent and in the United States.

55. According to Dominic Thomas, "Individuals or groups may establish connections with other diasporic, immigrant, or refugee structures from sub-Saharan Africa, the Caribbean, Asia, and so forth, and may circulate outside of, or even resist, such community alignments (the Mouride population, for example, in Marseilles, New York, or Los Angeles), preferring instead to navigate autonomously according to the demands and exigencies associated with their dislocated and transplanted status." D. Thomas, *Black France*, 7.

56. Kamari Clarke and Deborah Thomas argue that "we must recognize that the relationship networks among different black communities, and between differently gendered or classed people within particular black communities, are also structured by the same dynamics of power and hegemony that constituted the diaspora itself. . . . It forces us to examine the diasporic 'communities' not as unitary but as divided by issues related to class, gender, sexuality, and generation." Clarke and Thomas, *Globalization and Race*, 13. My research shows how language is also an important divisive issue.

57. Shu-mei Shih demonstrates how the increased recognition of Asian American and Latinx voices has nuanced theorization on the black-white binary found in American race studies. Shih, "Comparative Racialization," 1350–51. The differentiating power of

language seen in my research calls into question the American black-white dichotomy in yet another way.

58. In particular, chapter 1 showed how informants compared themselves to other francophone West Africans, arguing that their French was closer to standard French, in order to establish a competence hierarchy. Some informants even argued that their abilities were superior to the *Français de souche*.

## CHAPTER 3. NEITHER HERE NOR THERE

1. I observed this rhetorical sleight of hand when living in Paris. One day in the Paris metro, I noticed a wanted sign concerning a robbery. The police were looking for *un homme de type africain* (an African-looking man). In this case, *de type africain* was substituted for the term *noir* to avoid using a racial classification in much the same way that a character in Fatou Diome's *La préférence nationale* looks for a *type européen* to tutor her daughter.

2. Faatu's discussion resonates with James Loewen's *Lies My Teacher Told Me*, where he argues that U.S. history textbooks provide students with distorted, Eurocentric, partial treatments of American history.

3. Wekker's *White Innocence*, concerning the erasure of race in Dutch society, offers some insights into what is happening in France. She identifies three paradoxes in Dutch society—failing to identify with migrants, viewing themselves as innocent victims of German occupation, and understating Dutch imperial presence in the world—that contribute to current Dutch racial formation. Because they fail to acknowledge the Dutch role in each of these phenomena, the Dutch are able to profess "white innocence" as well as depict Dutch identity as white. See the introduction, in particular, for more information.

4. As Christine Chivallon notes about the 2001 Taubira Law, "Recent attacks have labelled it as 'une honte' ['a disgrace'] for the country and as a 'loi anti-française' ['anti-French law'], and have given rise to a number of repellent incidents on Twitter." Chivallon, "Representing the Slave Past," 32. See Chivallon, along with Gueye, "Memory at Issue," and C. L. Miller, *French Atlantic Triangle*, for a more thorough discussion of France's attempts to commemorate slavery. It is important to note, however, that the law goes further than U.S. legislation apologizing for slavery. For the wording of these apologies in the U.S. context, see "Apologizing for the Enslavement" and "Concurrent Resolution Apologizing for the Enslavement."

5. In France it is illegal to collect data based on race. Oppenheimer, "Why France Needs to Collect Data." Many people believe that racial classifications are discriminatory. Interviews show how people liken the use of racial categories to practices that happened under the Vichy government: "Classifying people by race would also encourage discrimination, not prevent it, and reduce identity to 'criteria from another era, that of colonial France, or Vichy.' Fadela Amara, a government minister of Algerian origin, went further. 'Our republic must not become a mosaic of communities,' she said. 'Nobody must have to wear the yellow star again.'" *Economist*, "France's Ethnic Minorities." In other words, a mosaic of communities suggests communitarianism. Regarding the notion of French heritage, the phrase *nos ancêtres les Gaulois* (our ancestors the Gauls) was an important slogan during the formation of French nationalism and was even recited in schools in French colonies such as Senegal. See Dietler, "'Our Ancestors the Gauls,'" for an explanation of how this became the case. Diome ingeniously turns the

phrase on its head in the following citation: "Vous m'avez appris à chanter *Nos ancêtres les Gaulois*, et j'ai compris que c'était faux. Je veux apprendre à vos gosses à chanter *Nos ancêtres les tirailleurs sénégalais*, car la France est un grenier sur pilotis, et certaines de ses poutres viennent d'Afrique." (You taught me to sing *Our ancestors the Gauls*, and I understood that it was wrong. I want to teach your kids to sing *Our ancestors the Senegalese infantrymen* because France is an attic on stilts, and some of its beams come from Africa.) Diome, *La préférence nationale*, 89. By referring to this colonial regiment, which was partially responsible for France's victories in both world wars, Diome calls attention to the whitewashing of history and the need to rectify it.

6. For further discussion, see P. Ndiaye, "Pour une histoire des populations noires," and Stille, "Can the French Talk about Race?"

7. Keaton, Sharpley-Whiting, and Stovall problematize the tension between national imaginings of race and lived experiences of racialized beings: "On the one hand, there is evident constitutional and legal discourse of colorblindness in various spheres of French life whereby race has been rejected as a meaningful category, having been discredited as biology and rightly so. Thus, there are, in effect, no French 'racial minorities,' only French people; nor is there an officially recognized identity discourse as there is, for instance, in the United States or the United Kingdom, where one finds terms such as 'Black Americans,' 'African American,' and 'Black British' to express such differentiation. On the other hand, the lived experience of race—more saliently, anti-blackness—belies the colorblind principle enshrined in the universalist-humanist thought upon which the Republic was forged." Keaton, Sharpley-Whiting, and Stovall, *Black France / France Noire*, 2.

8. As Keaton argues, "People of color are supposedly discriminated against because they are 'immigrants' or feared foreigners, not necessarily because they are African or Asian or 'black' (De Rudder, Poiret and Vourc'h 2000). But the fact that a thing is not racially named does not mean it is not racialized." Keaton, *Muslim Girls*, 8. Similarly, Patrick Lozès contends that "[black populations] are most often identified through the reductive prism of 'immigration' and 'integration.' It is skin color that turns a French person into a foreigner and asks him 'to integrate' throughout his life." Lozès, "'Black France,'" 107–8.

9. In the case of France, while immigrants are expected to integrate, the political discourse makes it almost impossible for them to shed the immigrant stigma. For instance, Ineke van der Valk has analyzed the language of French parliamentary debates on immigration and found the following: "Assimilation apparently implies inclusion. The research reported in this article shows, however, that the discourse of the Right on immigration and nationality is characterized by major exclusive features. Similar to the right-extremist Front National, the mainstream Right uses strategies of positive self- and negative other-presentation, associates immigrants with problematic social phenomena and expresses fear about the decline of the French civilization." Van der Valk, "Right-Wing Parliamentary Discourse," 310–11.

10. Elisabeth Mudimbe-Boyi interrogates the concept of *France Noire*, which "situates the Black in a double liminal position: French *but* black, or Black *but* part of France." Mudimbe-Boyi, "Black France," 21. Jean Beaman's work shows how North Africans endure similar treatment, where racial and religious identity precludes national acceptance. In current national identity formation, one cannot be both at once. Beaman, "But Madame," and Beaman, *Citizen Outsider*.

11. Rana, *Terrifying Muslims*; Thangaraj, *Desi Hoop Dreams*. See Butler, *Bodies That Matter*, for her theorizations about the body.

12. It is true that if he dressed in a way that signaled to others that he was Muslim, his religious identity might have been more pronounced in the interview. However, it is important to note that the image of Muslim bodily comportment in the French cultural imaginary is often very different from how many Senegalese Muslims dress. Even in Senegal, which is almost 95 percent Muslim, there is a wide range of dress. See É. Smith, "Religious and Cultural Pluralism," for a discussion of religious and cultural pluralism in Senegal.

13. Lorde, *Sister Outsider*.

14. See Keaton, *Muslim Girls*, for the plight of black Muslims in France and the precariousness of their existence based on the many aspects of their identity.

15. Van der Valk, "Right-Wing Parliamentary Discourse."

16. According to Laurent Dubois, "In the summer of 1998, in the midst of the euphoria surrounding France's World Cup victory, won by a team that symbolized the multicultural mix of France . . . it seemed possible that the Republic might achieve tolerance and coexistence among the different groups that now make up its population. The 'multicoloured' nature of the French team, and the fact that the youth of the *banlieue* saw themselves reflected in the team, was noted by observers. Many repeated the idea that in winning the World Cup, the French team had issued a powerful blow against Le Pen's *Front National* and its restricted vision of France. One commentator wrote: 'Through the World Cup, the French are discovering, in the faces of their team, what they have become, a *République métissée*, and that it works, that we can love one another and we can win' (Castro, 1998)." Dubois, "La République Métissée," 29. Discussions about race and belonging reemerged when France won the 2018 World Cup, and because of social media, these conversations were more global than in previous years. Even before France's tournament win, internet memes joked how France was the only African team left, leading to online debates throughout the African diaspora of whether one should root for France because of the predominance of players of African descent or root against France for continuing to benefit from its colonial past. Walker, "Twitter: 'Africa's Going to the Final.'" See also Pierrot, "Fear of a Black France." The global reflection about national identity and the French national team culminated with a thought-provoking exchange between the ambassador of France, Gérard Araud, and *Daily Show* host, Trevor Noah, which brought into relief the different cultural paradigms with regard to race and society that exist in France and the United States. See Noah, "Trevor Responds to Criticism," and Beauchamp, "Trevor Noah's Feud with France," for more information.

17. Giovanna Zincone, founder and President of FIERI (Forum Internazionale ed Europeo di Ricerche sull'Immigrazione / Forum of International and European Research on Migration), describes the model of reasonable integration put forth by the 1998 Immigration Law (the Turco-Napolitano law) as "not too rigid, not too ideological, nor too pretentious." Zincone, "Model of 'Reasonable Integration,'" 959. Reasonable integration is based on four tenets: interaction based on security, integrity of human rights for undocumented immigrants, full integrity for legal immigrants, and interaction based on pluralism and communication. However, as Salvatore Palidda acknowledges, the Berlusconi government, through the Bossi-Fini law, ensured that Italy's policies would deter the "peaceful integration of immigrants" through a framework of "hostility,

discrimination, and racism." Palidda, "Insertion, Integration and Rejection," 372. Importantly, even before Berlusconi's rise to power, Italy actively discouraged immigrants from settling and integrating. Consequently, the turnover rate is high, with many migrants opting not to stay in Italy for the long run. For more information, see Zincone and Caponio, "Immigrant and Immigration Policy-Making."

18. However, as mentioned in the previous chapter, Christina Lombardi-Diop and Caterina Romeo argue that even if blacks in Italy master the language, they can never truly claim *italianità* and therefore can never fully integrate even if they want to. Lombardi-Diop and Romeo, "Introduction."

19. Bruno Riccio's research has shown how Senegalese migrants proactively contribute to the lack of integration. He contends that Senegalese migrants conform to integrationist policies only superficially, doing what they need to survive in the host country but with one foot firmly planted in their home country: "The lack of attachment to Italy and the transnational mobility of Senegalese contrast with the sedentarist logic on which these practices rely. Senegalese transmigrants in the end are not sufficiently 'disciplined' users: they fit in with, because they are able to bear, the precariousness of reception policies (especially so in Rimini), but they do not conform to the idea of the 'integrating' settler. More specifically, the majority of the Senegalese do not seem to fit the ideal of 'second-stage reception.'" Riccio, "*Toubab* and *Vu Cumprà*," 189. This second-stage reception suggests a desire to root oneself in the host country, most commonly expressed through family reunification. However, very seldom is Senegalese family reunification achieved. Instead, Senegalese immigration is marked by what Riccio deems a third way of integration, which lies somewhere between assimilation and pluralist segregation. Riccio, "*Toubab* and *Vu Cumprà*," 181–87. See also Schmidt di Friedberg, "Le réseau sénégalais mouride en Italie." Furthermore, while Riccio sheds light on a common view of Italy among the Senegalese, he also introduces a complication to my theory when he notes that those who acquire the *permesso di soggiorno* (permit to stay) have the flexibility to move between Italy and Senegal, bringing goods and materials back and forth. Therefore, further research would be prudent to try to understand why the immigration lawyer does not see more Senegalese jumping through the hoops needed to legally and more easily cross national borders.

20. Claire Kramsch has used home as a metaphor with regard to foreign-language learning, arguing that through awareness of different contexts and perspectives, foreign-language learners "try to make themselves at home in a culture 'of a third kind.'" Kramsch, *Context and Culture*, 235. Kramsch has more recently suggested, however, that "third place" as a spatial metaphor seems too static in an increasingly globalized world. She worries that "predicated on the existence of a first and second place that are all too often reified in 'country of origin' and 'host country,' third place can be easily romanticized as some hybrid position that contributes to the host country's ideology of cultural diversity." She has thus reframed third place as symbolic competence where a speaker possesses among other things "an ability to draw on the semiotic diversity afforded by multiple languages to reframe ways of seeing familiar events, create alternative realities, and find an appropriate subject position 'between languages,' so to speak." Kramsch, *Multilingual Subject*, 200, 201.

21. The excerpt uses the following notation: Italian, *Wolof*.

22. Tannen, "What's in a Frame?," discusses negation and expectations.

23. Myers-Scotton, *Duelling Languages*, 478.

24. Gardner-Chloros, *Code-Switching*, 69.

25. The excerpt uses the following notation: Italian, *French*, English, **Wolof/Arabic**.

26. Professore's response to the question about home corroborates what Riccio found in his work: "Transnationally mobile people seem to imply a 'plurilocal' (Rouse, 1991) and more globally 'mobile' conception of home (Rapport and Dawson, 1998). The Senegalese, however, although well organized transnationally, do not develop multiple attachments: their meaning of home does not shift dramatically. Conversely, it seems that their identification with the context of origin helps their transnational organization and strengthens their resistance to an occasionally racist and constraining receiving context." Riccio, "Senegal Is Our Home," 68.

27. See Riccio, "Migranti per il co-sviluppo," or Riccio, "More than a Trade Diaspora," and Carter, *States of Grace*, for studies of Senegalese communities in northern Italy, which have existed there for decades.

28. While there is debate about the racial implications of the phrase, a thread on the translation website www.wordreference.com discusses the term *délit de faciès*. One user argues that "there is definitely a racial overtone in the use and history of the word!!!!! . . . As far as I can remember 'délit de faciès' was an expression born during the 'Guerre d'Algérie' when Arab looking persons were harassed by the police on the sole ground of their racial origin." See "Délit de faciès." Word Reference, 2007–14, http://forum.wordreference.com/showthread.php?t=462835.

29. In the United States, discussions about immigration and integration often entail notions of multiculturalism that emerge from a society founded by immigrants. For instance, Richard Alba and Nancy Foner discuss prevailing discourses: "The United States is sometimes characterized as de facto multiculturalist because it lacks laws and policies that directly promote and shape assimilation and tolerates multiple languages (though their survival times are often short)." Alba and Foner, *Strangers No More*, 21. They mention the importance of settler colonialism in the construction of this image where immigration is closely tied to the national identity of the United States and anyone can benefit from social mobility with enough hard work and perseverance. While one of the purposes of their research is to question this depiction of U.S. multiculturalism, many of the people in my study advance this narrative. Furthermore, New York City's status as an immigrant city and the paragon of multiculturalism plays into how people talk about their experiences with integration.

30. It is true that displaying signs of difference is not always accepted. Attacks on Muslims wearing headscarves or leaving mosques in the United States and England attest to this, especially in the climate of Trumpism and Brexit, respectively. See Khan, "Attacks on American Muslims," and Dodd and Marsh, "Anti-Muslim Hate Crimes Increase." However, there is a sense that Muslims do not stand out as much in large cities in the United States as they would in France.

31. According to Charles Tshimanga, Didier Gondola, and Peter Bloom, "Minority consciousness and activism are perceived as a threat to France's long-proclaimed international humanitarianism precisely because they reveal racial inequalities in a country that purports to be standard bearer of the universal rights of man. This explains the pervading myth that racism in France, as opposed to Britain or Germany, functions in a vacuum, within a race-less society where certain groups are unable to

assimilate or embrace French cultural norms: it is yet another way of creating a climate of racial exclusionism." Tshimanga, Gondola, and Bloom, *Frenchness and the African Diaspora*, 6.

32. *Garding* derives from *garder*, French for "to keep."

33. "Looking diasporic" highlights global citizenship: "It is a self-fashioning that declares one's ability to mobilize foreign styles and thereby define oneself as cosmopolitan. Doing so, I have been arguing, is not an attempt to become a generic world citizen, but a citizen racialized in particular ways." Holsey, "Black Atlantic Visions," 515.

34. As Jesse Shipley has discovered, "For Africans living abroad, feelings of displacement and disjuncture negate cultural and national continuities but also produce new, reflexive ways to identify with a dispersed collective." Shipley, *Living the Hiplife*, 232. See Sharma, *Hip Hop Desis*, for global consciousness of race, and Pierre, *Predicament of Blackness*, for global racial formation.

35. For more information on Du Bois, see D. L. Lewis, *W. E. B. Du Bois*; on Douglass, see Fenton, *Frederick Douglass in Ireland*, and Sweeney, *Frederick Douglass*. With regard to agency in the African diaspora, see Gilroy, *Black Atlantic*, and S. Hall, "Cultural Identity and Diaspora." See Alim, "Translocal Style Communities," for the importance of hip-hop in combating marginalization. The focus on music in transnational spaces is explored in chapter 4.

36. For example, my article on bringing authentic texts such as music to the French-language classroom shows how the hip-hop group Zebda appropriated future president Jacques Chirac's racist political discourse by using his quote about the noise and the smell immigrants produce in the *banlieue*. M. Smith, "Using Interconnected Texts."

37. According to most recent World Bank statistics on remittances, Senegal received more than $2 billion in 2017.

38. This phenomenon of global cosmopolitanism exists in cities all over the world. For example, in his exploration of how the consumption of sports in Shanghai reveals the tension between cosmopolitanism and Chinese nationalism, Eriberto Lozada argues that Chinese cosmopolitanism embodies "an openness to adopting global cultural practices and ideas that also evaluates and critiques China's own positionality to other societies." Lozada, "Cosmopolitanism and Nationalism," 226.

39. The phenomenon of equating Americanness with whiteness has been put in high relief in the era of Trump; however, these interviews took place during Obama's presidency when there was more optimism with regard to the status of black people in the United States.

40. As Amal Ibrahim Madibbo contends, "Recorded history is selective in the sense that it has largely been written from the point of view of dominant peoples. This means that important facts, as well as the voices of the marginalized, were probably not included in the written history." Madibbo, *Minority within a Minority*, 13. For instance, current revisionist history whitewashes America's highly racialized past and present, most notable in the Texas textbook controversy where K-12 textbooks refer to the slave trade simply as migration, downplay the role of slavery in causing the American Civil War, and skirt the issue of segregation and Jim Crow. Schaub, "New Texas Textbooks"; Fernandez and Hauser, "Texas Mother." Similar to "white innocence" in the Netherlands, the United States participates in both "white denial" and "white fragility." Wise, *Between Barack and a Hard Place*; DiAngelo, *White Fragility*. Therefore, differing views of

race in France and the United States have had similar effects on marginalized populations in the two countries: "As these racialist ideologies ossified during colonial expansion, they instilled fears of degeneration and decadence, thus supporting the assimilationist notion of the 'one' that would become central to the constitutions of both France and the United States and that has continued to interfere with the full integration of new migrants." Lionnet, "Continents and Archipelagoes," 1511.

41. There is a long history of seeing racism as an American import. See Stovall, *Paris Noir*, for a discussion of interwar France, when the French noted an increase in what they described as American-style racism.

42. Sarah Fila-Bakabadio argues that "le terme *blackness* émane lui d'un contexte anglophone et particulièrement américain dans lequel il a été racialement construit à travers l'expérience des Noirs aux Etats-Unis" (the term *blackness* emanates from an anglophone and particularly American context in which it was racially constructed through the experience of blacks in the United States). Fila-Bakabadio, "Photographie et géographie corporelle," 23.

43. Abi had been to Spain (nine months), Switzerland, Australia, Denmark, Belgium, the United States, Brazil, the Netherlands (a couple of times), France (three trips), Japan, Italy, and England.

44. Transcription and translation of Abi's speech throughout reflect her use of nonstandard French.

45. The excerpt uses the following notation: French, *French / Spanish*.

46. See Norton, "Language, Identity," and Norton, *Identity and Language Learning*.

47. Spain is similar to Italy in that it had limited colonial holdings in Africa and until recently did not receive large numbers of immigrants. While Abi's experience in Spain was positive, Cameroonian novelist Inongo-vi-Makomé paints a different picture, one similar to Abi's in Italy, arguing, "El negro africano le trae al español la imagen de un ser inferior, de un hombre dominado y, sobre todo, de un pobre! . . . Su color, que va unido a estas condiciones, hace que a primera vista sea despreciado." (The Spaniard sees the black African as an inferior being, a dominated man, and above all, a poor man! . . . His color, which is related to his social position, produces contempt at first sight.) Makomé, *España y los negros africanos*, 104.

48. The excerpt uses the following notation: French, *Italian*, **Spanish**.

49. *Biene* is possibly a mix between the Italian *bene* and the Spanish *bien*.

50. The excerpts in the rest of this section are from the dinner in Queens on July 27, 2014, unless otherwise noted.

51. Similar to Jean Beaman, Bayo Holsey defines black cultural citizenship as "a notion of belonging and community determined not by legal status but instead through other forms of recognition. These forms might include the recognition of shared histories, cultures and tastes, or political commitments." Holsey, "Black Atlantic Visions," 505. This focus on recognition ties into Pierre Bourdieu's symbolic capital. Bourdieu, *Distinction*.

52. This quote is from Charlotte's interview. Twenty-nine-year-old Amadou, who was not at the event in Queens but whom I interviewed several days later, provided a similar perspective: "I was debating about going to France. I had the opportunity to go there. Everybody has the opportunity to go there. But, you know, I heard from people saying that you know racism and police officers always ask your ID everywhere. They give you a hard time."

53. For instance, Joseph recounted a story of being accosted by undercover cops in a Bronx park while he was simply sitting on a bench. He speculated that they assumed he was in possession of weed just because he was black. He added that profiling related to citizenship was usually reserved for people who look Latinx. However, Tiffany Lee calls attention to the erasure of black people from discussions about immigration especially considering how "from 2013 to 2015, Black immigrants made up only 5.4 percent of the undocumented population, yet comprised 10.6 of all newcomers in removal proceedings." Lee, "Black and Undocumented." While none of my informants mentioned experiences with the police with regard to immigration, this does not mean that it is not a concern for black immigrants in New York City in particular and the United States at large. As for Rome, informants noted that the police would sometimes hassle street vendors, of which a large portion are Senegalese, but they did not seem to feel that someone would be asked to prove citizenship for just existing in a public space. However, police can and do ask for identity papers. Furthermore, since immigration laws in Italy make it difficult not only to obtain permanent legal status but also to keep it, many migrants oscillate between states of legality and illegality. Calavita, "Law, Citizenship, and the Construction of (Some) Immigrant 'Others.'"

54. This excerpt is from Charlotte's interview.

55. See O. Kane, *Homeland Is the Arena*, and Stoller, *Money Has No Smell*.

56. In this context, Julien uses the word "Spanish" to describe all Spanish-speaking people and is referring particularly to people with ties to Latin America.

57. Julien highlighted what Stuart Hall has described as "unity within heterogeneity." S. Hall, "Cultural Identity and Diaspora" 235. However, Latinx populations struggle with racial differentiation much like any racially diverse community does. Dzidzienyo and Oboler, *Neither Enemies nor Friends*.

58. Provencher, *Queer French*, 193.

59. Actually, while whites in New York City represent the largest group, at 43.1 percent they do not make up an absolute majority according to the U.S. Census Bureau's "2012–2016 American Community Survey 5-Year Estimates: Quick Facts New York City."

60. Informant "A" could be relying on my identity as an African American as well as other African Americans present to construct this shared narrative.

61. Pierre argues that "a modern, postcolonial space is invariably a racialized one; it is a space where racial and cultural logics continue to be constituted and reconstituted in the images, institutions, and relationship of the structuring colonial moment." Pierre, *Predicament of Blackness*, xii.

## CHAPTER 4. LEVERAGING LANGUAGE

1. People who lost French nationality when former colonies gained independence could apply for "reintegration." See Feldblum, *Reconstructing Citizenship*, for more information.

2. The relationship between breastfeeding and maternal language acquisition has been discussed for centuries. Thomas Bonfiglio provides examples of Dante Alighieri in *De vulgari eloquentia* and Johann Matthäus Meyfart in *Teutsche rhetorica*. The former is one of the first documented examples linking mother tongue to mother's milk: "In musing over the origin of language, Dante is confronted with a problem; if we learn the first

language from our nurses, then from whom did Adam learn his language, since he must have been a 'man without mother or milk' (*vir sine matre, vir sine lacte*) (Cap. 6, 1)?" Meanwhile, the latter states, "Germans do not seek their language from books . . . but instead, suck it, in the cradle, from the breasts of mothers (p. 144)." Bonfiglio, *Mother Tongues and Nations*, 73, 112.

3. Michèle Koven's qualitative research of French-Portuguese bilinguals shows that when people speak different languages, they perform different selves: "Different ways of speaking, within and across languages, create socially and psychologically real effects for people, producing for the same speaker multiple expressions and experiences of socially recognizable selves." Koven, "Two Languages in the Self," 437. This may also be the case for Duudu when he speaks each language; however, he and others like him also put forth another type of self—a Senegalese self recognized through multilingualism.

4. In chapter 1, informants in Paris highlighted what they saw as distrust of and disdain for the English language, which some French people labeled a colonizing force. Ager, "Identity, Insecurity and Image." However, negative opinions were not reserved just for English. In French discourse, the use of any language other than French was seen as problematic.

5. For discussions on competency and multilingualism, see Kachru, "Code-Mixing as a Communicative Strategy," and Grosjean, *Life with Two Languages*. Furthermore, Cecilia Montes-Alcalá has written that code-switching "has been socially stigmatized by monolinguals and bilinguals alike, and . . . is often attributed to illiteracy, lack of formal education, or lack of proficiency in one or both languages." Montes-Alcalá, "Attitudes toward Oral and Written Codeswitching," 218.

6. See McLaughlin, "Dakar Wolof"; Cissé, "Langues, État et société"; Cruise O'Brien, "Langue et nationalité"; Swigart, "Cultural Creolisation"; Swigart, "Limits of Legitimacy"; and Trudell and Klaas, "Distinction, Integration and Identity."

7. For Italy, see various works by Riccio as well as Carter, *States of Grace*; for France, see Bertoncello, *Du Sénégal à Marseille*; for the United States, see O. Kane, *Homeland Is the Arena*.

8. The excerpt uses the following notation: Italian, *French*, **English**, ***Wolof***, Spanish.

9. Conversely, the waiter had used different criteria when he assumed even before I opened my mouth that I could not be Senegalese.

10. The excerpt uses the following notation: French, *English*, **Italian**, Spanish.

11. The excerpt uses the following notation: French, *Italian*, **English**.

12. The excerpt uses the following notation: French, *English*.

13. Paul Ricoeur in *On Translation* has argued that it is through translation that one can best offer linguistic hospitality, something that both Ousseynou and Bouba do.

14. Forty-five-year-old Ndella was born in Dakar but had spent two decades in Paris.

15. The excerpt uses the following notation: Wolof, *French*, **English**.

16. *Torop* is a French loan word, coming from *trop*.

17. *Tubaab*, also written *toubab*, has many meanings. The most common definition is "white person." However, when it denotes a language, it means "French."

18. This excerpt is from a conversation with Ndella and Boubacar on October 27, 2009.

19. The French words used in this exchange (e.g., *bien sûr, anglais, cinq ans, Hollande*) are all words commonly found in Dakar Wolof. Names of European languages and countries entered Wolof through French. Meanwhile, numbers are often expressed in French for convenience since numbers in Wolof can be quite lengthy.

20. The excerpt uses the following notation: Italian, *French*, **non-standard Italian**.

21. *Dispinge* is not a word in standard Italian. *Dipingere* means to paint or describe. It appears he was looking for the word *spingere*, to push.

22. David Crystal shows how the ludic (or playful) function of language is important for language appreciation. According to him, we play with language by manipulating it, making it do what it normally does not do, for our amusement or for the amusement of others. Crystal, *Language Play*, 1.

23. In his work on modernist writers and metropolitan café culture in the Jewish diaspora, Shachar Pinsker demonstrates how cafés have been essential to the construction and maintenance of Jewish identity: "The café is a site of enunciation of identity, lived experience, and contested meanings." Pinsker, "Modern (Jewish) Woman in a Café," 4. W. Scott Haine, Jeffrey Jackson, and Leona Rittner's edited volume explores the concept of café and community: "Cafés are central to intellectual history because the social interaction and solitary introspection within them fulfill vital human needs: nurturing human perceptions with beverages, sights, smells, and sounds these spaces have had a dramatic impact on intellectual history at various points." Haine, Jackson, and Rittner. *Thinking Space*, 3. See Lecoq, "Café," for a discussion of cafés as laboratories.

24. As John Connell and Chris Gibson argue, "Music remains an important cultural sphere in which identities are affirmed, challenged, taken apart and reconstructed." Connell and Gibson, *Sound Tracks*, 117. Simon Frith notes that "music constructs our sense of identity through the direct experiences it offers of the body, time and sociability, experiences which enable us to place ourselves in imaginative cultural narratives." Frith, "Music and Identity," 124.

25. Gilroy, *Black Atlantic*, 81–82.

26. Mahama begins his memoir by describing the era of liberation, which he depicts as "an entire generation of visual art, literature, music, and international cultural exchange [that] was empowered by the electricity of a continent shaking off its oppression." Mahama, *My First Coup d'Etat*, 10. Subsequent citations from this work here are as follows: "Pata Pata," 2; James Brown lyrics, 78; linguistic and cultural diversity, 123.

27. Mahama also highlights transatlantic sartorial exchange: "Black Americans had traded in their blue jeans, suits, and shirtsleeves for batiks, tie-dyes, and dashikis sewn from the popular Ghanaian cloth called 'Angelina.' Meanwhile, we in Ghana had taken to wearing hipsters, miniskirts, and polyester shirts that were left unbuttoned straight down to the navel. As funky as the fashion was, it was merely a by-product; the music was the main event." Mahama, *My First Coup d'Etat*, 123.

28. Taubira, *Mes météores*, 17.

29. Frith, "Music and Identity," 125. Furthermore, in her exploration of cultural production across the Senegalese diaspora, Mahriana Rofheart pays particular attention to how Senegalese literature and hip-hop shape local and global identities: "Authors Aminata Sow Fall, Ken Bugul, and Fatou Diome, as well as several hip-hop artists, have responded to the phenomenon of emigration from Senegal by articulating local as well as global connections—much in the way the Y'en a Marre video delivers a powerfully specific local message on a global stage." Rofheart, *Shifting Perceptions of Migration*, viii.

30. The excerpt uses the following notation: Wolof, *French*, **Italian**.
31. This conversation took place at the Senegalese restaurant on February 12, 2010.
32. Mikhail Bakhtin theorized the notion of heteroglossia to argue that words are historically embedded, conveying previous meanings and associations. He has also contended that speakers transmit an evaluative attitude through their words. See Bakhtin, Holquist, and Emerson, *Speech Genres*.
33. The excerpt uses the following notation: Wolof, *Italian*.
34. This conversation took place at the Senegalese restaurant on April 10, 2010.
35. The excerpt uses the following notation: Italian, *Wolof*, **French**, English.
36. In standard Italian it would be *io sono diventato*.
37. Arabic phrase that has been integrated into Wolof.
38. See Lecoq, "Café," and Pinsker, "Modern (Jewish) Woman in a Café."
39. *Pieds-noirs* were people of French and other European ancestry who were born or lived in French North Africa.
40. The excerpt uses the following notation: French, *English*.
41. *Capter* in this context is slang for *comprendre*.
42. The excerpt uses the following notation: French, *English*. B1: band member no. 1, B2: band member no. 2.
43. Suzanne Romaine marks the distinctions between tag-switching (insertion of a tag, e.g., "you know," "I mean"), inter-sentential switching (switching at the end of a phrase or sentence), and intra-sentential switching (within a phrase or sentence), arguing that each of these is progressively more difficult than the preceding one. Romaine, *Bilingualism*, 10.
44. It is interesting that Abdu says that the word "lyrics" is not translatable in French, even though the term *les paroles* exists. Perhaps he finds this term inadequate.
45. The term evokes the name of the popular hip-hop band "The Roots" as well as Alex Haley's famous book and miniseries on his ancestors' forced migration to the Americas from Africa.
46. In explaining the Markedness Model, Carol Myers-Scotton argues that "speakers use the possibility of making code choices to negotiate interpersonal relationships, and by extension to signal their perceptions or desires about group memberships." Myers-Scotton, *Duelling Languages*, 478.
47. Shipley centers Africa in a transnational discussion of blackness by focusing on what he considers Afro-cosmopolitanism, where investment in different types of cultural production allows people access to a black cosmopolitan world. Holsey's research on Ghanaian transnationalism shows that even for those unable to travel, different forms of cultural production, such as music, allow for what Louisa Schein describes as imagined cosmopolitanism. Shipley, *Living the Hiplife*; Holsey, "Black Atlantic Visions"; Schein "Consumption of Color."
48. The fund-raiser was the same event where Madina's brother Samba felt linguistically inadequate when addressing the crowd in English instead of Wolof.
49. As step coordinator, Ndiaye teaches stepping, a percussive dance that is an integral part of most historically black fraternities and sororities.
50. See Ladegaard, "National Stereotypes and Language Attitudes"; Luján García, *La lengua inglesa en canarias*; and González Cruz and Vera Cazorla, "Attitudes to Language and Culture," for more information. In particular, González Cruz and Vera Cazorla note that the Spanish students they questioned in the Canary Islands preferred learning

British English both because of geographic proximity to Great Britain and the fact that they traditionally learn British English in school. However, the students viewed the United States as *the* world power and the reason why English dominates as a global language. González Cruz and Vera Cazorla also argue that the curriculum should be more sensitive to different varieties of English because student attitudes would most likely change.

51. Fallou Ngom makes a connection between the high percentage of English loan words in cultural registers in Senegal and its relation to American culture, particularly African American culture. For urban youth, English is the language of "modernity and fashion." Ngom, "Social Status," 357. Future research on the reception of American English versus British English in Senegal should explore this phenomenon through a postcolonial lens. Does the fact that British English more readily signifies a postcolonial relationship influence the higher value associated with American English?

52. While viewers hear predominantly SAE through mainstream American media, such as television shows and blockbuster films, they hear AAVE and BSE in American hip-hop and rap. In chapter 1, we saw how AAVE differs from SAE in grammar, vocabulary, and accent. Meanwhile, as Ibrahim notes, BSE "refers to ways of speaking that do not depend on a full mastery of the language. It banks on *ritual expressions* (see Rampton, 1995, for the idea of rituality) . . . which are performed habitually and recurrently in rap." Ibrahim, "Becoming Black," 351.

53. Interestingly, this song was written and sung by both Snoop Dogg and Akon, a Senegalese American hip-hop artist.

54. See Sposet, *Role of Music*, for a rationale and resources for using music in the foreign-language classroom. In addition, studies have recorded the phenomenon of imitating American hip-hop for various purposes. For instance, some Tanzanian rappers rely on imitating American hip-hop to learn to rap: "Mr. II, . . . one of the most popular rappers from Tanzania, explained that he would listen to rap cassettes repeatedly until he could mimic the English lyrics. Though he did not speak English at the time, he would sound out the words until he had a sense of the rhyming and 'flow' of the song." Perullo and Fenn, "Language Ideologies, Choices, and Practices," 24.

55. As Shipley demonstrates in his own research, "Hip-hop represented American coolness . . . [and] provided a Pan-African, global form of inclusion." Shipley, *Living the Hiplife*, 61. Furthermore, my interviewees, in general, seemed to like American hip-hop, listening to artists from a wide variety of genres tied to different regions (e.g., West Coast hip-hop, East Coast hip-hop, southern hip-hop).

56. Shipley explores a similar phenomenon: "For each generation, African American vernacular styles of speech, bodily comportment, and dress have been both signs of global racial affiliation and ways of claiming local distinction (Bourdieu 1984)." Shipley, *Living the Hiplife*, 63.

57. While emulating American rap is important in Senegal, many different genres of rap are being produced, from the socially and politically active music of Keur Gui or of the Journal Rappé's Xuman and Keyti to religious-minded rap, which references *marabouts* and Islamic brotherhoods. See O. Kane, *Homeland Is the Arena*, for more information on the latter.

58. Charles Piot's critique of Gilroy argues for the need to recenter Africa in discussions of the African diaspora. Using his research on cultural practices in northern Togo, he shows that "far from unidirectional, these meanings have circulated promiscuously

from Africa to the Americas and Europe, and from Europe and the Americas back to Africa, thoroughly remaking all parties in the process." Piot, "Atlantic Aporias," 168.

59. For a discussion of protagonists acquiring cultural capital in francophone literature, see D. Thomas, *Black France*, 74. In particular, Thomas considers Laye Camara's *Enfant noir*, Hamidou Kane's *Aventure ambiguë*, and Ousmane Socé's *Mirages de Paris*.

## EPILOGUE

1. The party's name was changed to National Rally (Rassemblement national) in 2018.

2. See Hunt and Wheeler, "Brexit," for information on Brexit; Chrisafis, "Marine Le Pen," on the Far Right's success at the national level; Barry, "Extreme-Right Italian Gunman," for antiblack violence in Italy; Tharoor, "Italy's Election," for a discussion of the Far Right's successes in the 2018 general election; and Squires, "Italy's hardline government," for a discussion of the migrant crisis in Italy.

3. See Stephenson and Knecht, "Trump Bars Doors to Refugees," for information on restrictions placed on some Muslims; Lydia Smith, "Trump-Mexico Border Wall," on the prospects of Trump's border wall dream becoming a reality; Planas and Foley, "Deportations of Noncriminals," on the increase of detainment and deportation of immigrants; Beydoun and Hansford, "F.B.I.'s Dangerous Crackdown," and Irby, "White and Far-Right Extremists," for information on the labeling of activists as Black Identity Extremists; Zhao, "Trump Administration Bans Haiti," concerning Trump's remarks and subsequent ban; Jordan, "Is America a 'Nation of Immigrants'?," for discussion of the changes at the U. S. Citizenship and Immigration Services; Davis and Shear, "How Trump Came to Enforce," for information on forced separation of families in migrant detention centers; Ellis, Hicken, and Ortega, "Handcuffs, Assaults, and Drugs Called 'Vitamins,'" on allegations of abuse, assault, and neglect that minors have reported while in detention facilities; and Jordan and Dickerson, "More than 450 Migrant Parents," on how hundreds of parents have been deported without being reunited with their children.

# Bibliography

*ABC News*. "Paris Riots in Perspective," November 4, 2005. http://abcnews.go.com /International/story?id=1280843.

Adepoju, Aderanti. "Creating a Borderless West Africa: Constraints and Projects for Intra-regional Migration." In *Migration without Borders: Essays on the Free Movement of People*, edited by Antoine Pécoud and Paul Guchteneire, 161–74. Paris: UNESCO, 2007.

Ager, Dennis. "Identity, Insecurity and Image: The Objectives of Language Policy in France and the Francophone World." In Marley, Hintze, and Parker, *Linguistic Identities*, 243–64.

Alba, Richard D., and Nancy Foner. *Strangers No More: Immigration and the Challenges of Integration in North America and Western Europe*. Princeton, NJ: Princeton University Press, 2015.

Alighieri, Dante. *De vulgari eloquentia: 1305*. Edited by Steven Botterill. Cambridge: Cambridge University Press, 1996.

Alim, H. Samy. "Translocal Style Communities: Hip Hop Youth as Cultural Theorists of Style, Language, and Globalization." *Pragmatics: Quarterly Publication of the International Pragmatics Association* 19, no. 1 (2009): 103–27.

Alim, H. Samy, John R. Rickford, and Arnetha F. Ball. *Raciolinguistics: How Language Shapes Our Ideas about Race*. New York: Oxford University Press, 2016.

Allen, Theodore. *The Invention of the White Race*. Vol. 2, *The Origin of Racial Oppression in Anglo-America*. London: Verso, 1997.

Anderson, Benedict R. *Imagined Communities: Reflections on the Origin and Spread of Nationalism*. Rev. ed. London: Verso, 2006.

"Apologizing for the Enslavement and Racial Segregation of African-Americans." H.R. Res. 194. 110th Cong. (July 29, 2008). https://www.govtrack.us/congress/bills/110/hres194/text.

Archibald, James. "La langue citoyenne: Droits et obligations linguistiques des migrants en France et au Canada." In *La langue et l'intégration des immigrants: Sociolinguistique, politiques linguistiques, didactique*, edited by James Archibald and Jean-Louis Chiss, 15–32. Paris: Harmattan, 2007.

Auer, Peter. *Bilingual Conversation*. Philadelphia: John Benjamins, 1984.

———. *Code-Switching in Conversation: Language, Interaction and Identity*. New York: Routledge, 1998.

———. "The Pragmatics of Code-Switching: A Sequential Approach." In Milroy and Muysken, *One Speaker, Two Languages*, 115–35.

Auer, Peter, and Wei Li. "Introduction: Multilingualism as a Problem? Monolingualism as a Problem?" In *Handbook of Multilingualism and Multilingual Communication*, edited by Peter Auer and Wei Li, 1–14. New York: Mouton de Gruyter, 2007.

Back, Les, and John Solomos, eds. *Theories of Race and Racism: A Reader*. London: Routledge, 1999.

Bagguley, Paul, and Yasmin Hussain. *Riotous Citizens: Ethnic Conflict in Multicultural Britain*. Aldershot, England: Ashgate, 2008.

Bailey, Kathleen M. "An Introspective Analysis of an Individual Language Learning Experience." In *Research in Second Language Acquisition: Selected Papers of the Los Angeles Second Language Acquisition Research Forum*, edited by Robin C. Scarcella and Stephen D. Krashen, 58–65. Rowley, MA: Newbury House, 1980.

Baker, Colin. *Foundations of Bilingual Education and Bilingualism*. Clevedon, England: Multilingual Matters, 2006.

Bakhtin, Mikhail M., Michael Holquist, and Caryl Emerson. *Speech Genres and Other Late Essays*. Austin: University of Texas Press, 1986.

Balibar, Étienne. *We the People of Europe? Reflections on Transnational Citizenship*. Translated by James Swenson. Princeton, NJ: Princeton University Press, 2009.

Balibar, Étienne, and Immanuel Maurice Wallerstein. *Race, Nation, Class: Ambiguous Identities*. London: Verso, 1991.

Ball, Rodney, and Dawn Marley. *The French-Speaking World: A Practical Introduction to Sociolinguistic Issues*. New York: Taylor and Francis, 2016.

Barry, Colleen. "Extreme-Right Italian Gunman Shoots 6 African Immigrants in Drive-By Spree: Officials." *Chicago Tribune*, February 3, 2018.

Bauman, R. "An Ethnographic Framework for the Investigation of Communicative Behaviors." *ASHA* 13, no. 6 (June 1971): 334–40.

Bayley, Robert, and Sandra R. Schecter, eds. *Language Socialization in Bilingual and Multilingual Societies*. Clevedon, England: Multilingual Matters, 2003.

*BBC News*. "Key Facts: Africa to Europe Migration." July 2, 2007. http://news.bbc.co.uk/2/hi/europe/6228236.stm.

Beaman, Jean. "But Madame, We Are French Also." *Contexts* 11, no. 3 (2012): 46–51.

———. *Citizen Outsider: Children of North African Immigrants in France*. Oakland: University of California Press, 2017.

Beauchamp, Zach. "Trevor Noah's Feud with France over Race, Identity, and Africa, Explained." *Vox*, July 19, 2018. https://www.vox.com/policy-and-politics/2018/7/19/17590302/trevor-noah-france-french-ambassador-araud-world-cup.

Beydoun, Khaled A., and Justin Hansford. "The F.B.I's Dangerous Crackdown on 'Black Identity Extremists.'" *New York Times*, November 5, 2017.

Belluzzi, Michele. "Cultural Protection as a Rationale for Legislation: The French Language Law of 1994 and the European Trend toward Integration in the Face of Increasing U.S. Influence." *Dickenson Journal of International Law* 14 (1995): 127–673.

Belz, Julie A. "Second Language Play as a Representation of the Multicompetent Self in Foreign Language Study." *Journal of Language, Identity and Education* 1, no. 1 (2002): 13–39.

Ben-Ghiat, Ruth, and Mia Fuller. *Italian Colonialism*. New York: Palgrave Macmillan, 2005.

Berg, Elliot J. "The Economics of the Migrant Labor System." In *Urbanization and Migration in West Africa*, edited by Hilda Kuper, 160–84. Berkeley: University of California Press, 1965.

Berlant, Lauren. "Race, Gender, and Nation in *The Color Purple*." *Critical Inquiry* 14, no. 4 (1988): 831–59.

Bertoncello, Brigitte. *Du Sénégal à Marseille*. Paris: Harmattan, 2009.

Besemeres, Mary. "Different Languages, Different Emotions? Perspectives from Autobiographical Literature." *Journal of Multilingual and Multicultural Development* 25, no. 2–3 (2004): 140–58.

Bhabha, Homi K. *The Location of Culture*. London: Routledge, 1994.

Billig, Michael. *Banal Nationalism*. London: Sage, 1995.

Block, David. *Second Language Identities*. London: Continuum, 2014.

———. *The Social Turn in Second Language Acquisition*. Edinburgh: Edinburgh University Press, 2003.

Blom, Jan-Petter, and John Joseph Gumperz. "Social Meaning in Linguistic Structures: Code-Switching in Norway." In *Directions in Sociolinguistics: The Ethnography of Communication*, edited by John Joseph Gumperz and Dell H. Hymes, 407–34. New York: Holt, Rinehart, and Winston, 1972.

Blommaert, Jan. "From Mobility to Complexity in Sociolinguistic Theory and Method." *Tilburg Papers in Culture Studies* 103 (2014): 1–24.

Blommaert, Jan, and Ben Rampton. "Language and Superdiversity." *Diversities* 13, no. 2 (2011): 3–21.

Bolton, Kingsley. "World Englishes." In *The Handbook of Applied Linguistics*, edited by Alan Davies and Catherine Elder, 369–96. Oxford: Blackwell, 2004.

Bonfiglio, Thomas Paul. *Mother Tongues and Nations: The Invention of the Native Speaker*. New York: De Gruyter Mouton, 2010.

Borrelli, Doris. *Raddoppiamento Sintattico in Italian: A Synchronic and Diachronic Cross-Dialectical Study*. New York: Routledge, 2002.

Bourdieu, Pierre. *Distinction: A Social Critique of the Judgment of Taste*. Translated by Richard Nice. Cambridge, MA: Harvard University Press, 1984.

———. *Language and Symbolic Power*. Translated by Gino Raymond and Matthew Adamson. Edited by John B. Thompson. Cambridge, MA: Harvard University Press, 1991.

———. *Outline of a Theory of Practice*. Translated by Richard Nice. Cambridge: Cambridge University Press, 1977.

Braziel, Jana Evans, and Anita Mannur. *Theorizing Diaspora: A Reader*. Malden, MA: Blackwell, 2003.

Bremer, Katharina, Celia Roberts, Marie-Therese Vasseur, Margaret Simonot, and Peter Broeder. *Achieving Understanding: Discourse in Intercultural Encounters*. London: Longman, 1996.

Brioni, Simone. *The Somali Within: Language, Race and Belonging in "Minor" Italian Literature*. Oxford: Legenda, 2015.

Brown, Jacqueline Nassy. "Black Liverpool, Black America, and the Gendering of Diasporic Space." *Cultural Anthropology* 13, no. 3 (1998): 291–325.

Brubaker, Rogers. *Citizenship and Nationhood in France and Germany*. Cambridge, MA: Harvard University Press, 1992.

Brunot, Ferdinand. *Histoire de la langue française des origines à 1900*. Paris: A. Colin, 1906.

Bucholtz, Mary. "Sociolinguistic Nostalgia and the Authentication of Identity." *Journal of Sociolinguistics* 7, no. 3 (2003): 398–416.

Buggenhagen, Beth. *Muslim Families in Global Senegal: Money Takes Care of Shame*. Bloomington: Indiana University Press, 2012.

Bullock, Barbara E., and Almeida Jacqueline Toribio, eds. *The Cambridge Handbook of Linguistic Code-Switching*. Cambridge: Cambridge University Press, 2009.

Burke, Peter, and Roy Porter. *The Social History of Language*. Cambridge: Cambridge University Press, 1987.

Burstall, Clare. "Factors affecting Foreign-Language Learning: A Consideration of Some Recent Research Findings." *Language Teaching* 8, no. 1 (1975): 5–25.

Butler, Judith. *Bodies That Matter: On the Discursive Limits of "Sex."* New York: Routledge, 1993.

———. *Excitable Speech: A Politics of the Performative*. New York: Routledge, 1997. See esp. introduction, "On Linguistic Vulnerability."

Calavita, Kitty. *Immigrants at the Margins: Law, Race, and Exclusion in Southern Europe*. Cambridge: Cambridge University Press, 2005.

———. "Law, Citizenship, and the Construction of (Some) Immigrant 'Others.'" *Law & Social Inquiry* 30, no. 2 (2005): 401–20.

Calvet, Louis-Jean, and Martine Dreyfus. "The Urban Family: Three Models of Multilingualism." *Plurilinguismes* 3 (January 1992): 29–54.

Camara, Laye. *L'enfant noir*. Paris: Plon, 1953.

Campt, Tina. *Other Germans: Black Germans and the Politics of Race, Gender, and Memory in the Third Reich*. Ann Arbor: University of Michigan Press, 2004.

Canagarajah, Suresh. "Interrogating the Native Speaker Fallacy: Non-linguistic Roots, Non-pedagogical Results." In *Non-native Educators in English Language Teaching*, edited by George Braine, 77–92. Mahwah, NJ: K. Erlbaum Associates, 1999.

Canagarajah, Suresh. *The Routledge Handbook of Migration and Language*. New York: Taylor and Francis, 2017.

Caritas di Roma. *Immigrazione: Dossier statistico*. Rome: Nuova Anterem, 2010.

Carling, Jørgen, Richard Black, and Russell King. "Emigration, Return and Development in Cape Verde: The Impact of Closing Borders." *Population, Space and Place* 10, no. 2 (2004): 113–32.

Caron-Caldas, Suzanne, and Stephen J. Caldas. "A Sociolinguistic Analysis of the Language Preferences of Adolescent Bilinguals: Shifting Allegiances and Developing Identities." *Applied Linguistics* 23, no. 4 (2002): 490–514.

Carter, Donald Martin. *States of Grace: Senegalese in Italy and the New European Immigration*. Minneapolis: University of Minnesota Press, 1997.

Castro, Roland. "Allez la France mondiale." *Libération,* July 10, 1998. http://www.libera tion.fr/tribune/1998/07/10/allez-la-france-mondiale_241583.

Cavanaugh, Jillian R. "A Modern Questione della Lingua: The Incomplete Standardization of Italian in a Northern Italian Town." *Journal of the Society for the Anthropology of Europe* 8, no. 1 (2008): 18–31.

Cazenave, Odile Marie. *Afrique sur Seine: Une nouvelle génération de romanciers africains à Paris.* Paris: L'Harmattan, 2003.

Cazzullo, Aldo. "Kyenge: l'Italia non è un paese razzista." *Il Corriere,* June 13, 2013.

Certeau, Michel de, Dominique Julia, and Jacques Revel. *Une politique de la langue: La révolution française et les patois; L'enquête de Grégoire.* Paris: Gallimard, 1975.

Charbol, Marie. "Château Rouge: A "Little Africa" in Paris? The Users and Usages of a Migrant Commercial Centrality." Translated by Oliver Waine. *Metropolitiques,* May 22, 2003. http://www.metropolitiques.eu/Chateau-Rouge-a-Little-Africa-in .html.

Charry, Eric S. *Hip Hop Africa: New African Music in a Globalizing World.* Bloomington: Indiana University Press, 2012.

Chivallon, Christine. "Representing the Slave Past: The Limits of Museographical and Patrimonial Discourses." In *At the Limits of Memory: Legacies of Slavery in the Francophone World,* edited by Nicola Frith and Kate Hodgson, 25–48. Liverpool: Liverpool University Press, 2014.

Chomsky, Noam. *Aspects of the Theory of Syntax.* Cambridge, MA: MIT Press, 1965.

———. *Syntactic Structures.* The Hague: Mouton, 1957.

Chrisafis, Angelique. "Marine Le Pen Defeated but France's Far Right Is Far from Finished." *Guardian,* May 7, 2017.

Cissé, Mamadou. "Langues, État et société au Sénégal." *Revue électronique internationale de sciences du langage sudlangues* 5 (December 2005): 99–133.

Clarke, Kamari Maxine, and Deborah A. Thomas. *Globalization and Race: Transformations in the Cultural Production of Blackness.* Durham, NC: Duke University Press, 2006.

Clifford, Edward. "Social Visibility." *Child Development* 34 (1963): 799–808.

Club du Sahel. "Mauritania: Restrictions on the 'Return Effects' of Intense and Diverse Migratory Movements." *OECD Emerging Economies,* no. 8 (March 2009): 178–99.

Čmejrková, Světla. "The Categories of 'Our Own' and 'Foreign' in the Language and Culture of Czech Repatriates from the Ukraine." *International Journal of the Sociology of Language* 162 (July 2003): 103–23.

Cohen, William B. *The French Encounter with Africans: White Response to Blacks, 1530–1880.* Bloomington: Indiana University Press, 2003.

Cole, Jennifer, and Christian Groes, eds. *Affective Circuits: African Migrations to Europe and the Pursuit of Social Regeneration.* Chicago: University of Chicago Press, 2016.

"A Concurrent Resolution Apologizing for the Enslavement and Racial Segregation of African Americans." S. Res. 26, 111th Cong. (June 18, 2009). https://www.congress .gov/bill/111th-congress/senate-concurrent-resolution/26.

Connell, John, and Chris Gibson. *Sound Tracks: Popular Music, Identity, and Place.* Critical Geographies. New York: Routledge, 2003.

Connell, R. W., Dean Ashendon, Sandra Kessler, and Gary W. Dowsett. *Making the Difference: Schools, Families and Social Divisions.* Boston: Sage, 1982.

Constant, Fred. "The Invention of Blacks in France." In Keaton, Sharpley-Whiting, and Stovall, *Black France / France Noire,* 103–9.

Cook, Vivian, ed. *Portraits of the L2 User*. Clevedon, England: Multilingual Matters, 2002.

Coppel, Anne. "Les Français et la norme linguistique: Une passion singulière." *Cosmopolitiques* 16 (November 2007): 157–68.

Council of Europe. *Common European Framework of Reference for Languages: Learning, Teaching, Assessment*. 2001. https://rm.coe.int/1680459f97.

Coupland, Nikolas. "Language, Situation, and the Relational Self: Theorizing Dialect-Style in Sociolinguistics." In *Style and Sociolinguistic Variation*, edited by Penelope Eckert and John R. Rickford, 185–210. New York: Oxford University Press, 2001.

Creese, Angela, and Adrian Blackledge. "Translanguaging and Identity in Educational Settings." *Annual Review of Applied Linguistics* 35 (2015): 20–35.

Cruise O'Brien, Donal. "Langue et nationalité au Sénégal: L'enjeu politique de la wolofisation." In *La construction de l'État au Sénégal*, edited by Donal Cruise O'Brien, Momar-Coumba Diop, and Mamadou Diouf, 143–55. Paris: Éditions Karthala, 2002.

———. "The Shadow-Politics of Wolofisation." *Journal of Modern African Studies* 36, no. 1 (1998): 25–46.

Crystal, David. *Language Play*. Chicago: University of Chicago Press, 2001.

Davies, Alan. *The Native Speaker Myth and Reality*. 2nd ed. Clevedon, England: Multilingual Matters, 2003.

Davis, Julie Hirschfeld, and Michael D. Shear. "How Trump Came to Enforce a Practice of Separating Migrant Families." *New York Times*, June 16, 2018.

DeWalt, Kathleen Musante, and Billie R. DeWalt. *Participant Observation: A Guide for Fieldworkers*. Walnut Creek, CA: AltaMira Press, 2002.

DiAngelo, Robin J. *White Fragility: Why It's So Hard for White People to Talk about Racism*. Boston: Beacon Press, 2018.

Dieng, Mame Younousse. *Aawo bi*. Dakar: IFAN Cheikh Anta Diop, 1992.

Dietler, Michael. "'Our Ancestors the Gauls': Archaeology, Ethnic Nationalism, and the Manipulation of Celtic Identity in Modern Europe." *American Anthropologist* 96, no. 3 (1994): 584–605.

Diome, Fatou. *La préférence nationale*. 6th ed. Paris: Présence Africaine, 2001.

Diop, Cheikh Anta. *Nations nègres et culture*. Paris: Présence Africaine, 1954.

Diouf, Mamadou. "The French Colonial Policy of Assimilation and the Civility of the Originaires of the Four Communes (Senegal): A Nineteenth Century Globalization Project." *Development and Change* 29, no. 4 (1998): 671–96.

———. "The Lost Territories of the Republic: Historical Narratives and the Recomposition of French Citizenship." In Keaton, Sharpley-Whiting, and Stovall, *Black France / France Noire*, 32–56.

Dodd, Vikram, and Sarah Marsh. "Anti-Muslim Hate Crimes Increase Fivefold since London Bridge Attacks." *The Guardian*, June 7, 2017.

Doran, Meredith. "Alternative French, Alternative Identities: Situating Language in La Banlieue." *Contemporary French and Francophone Studies* 11, no. 4 (2007): 497–508.

Doughty, Catherine J., and Michael H. Long, eds. *The Handbook of Second Language Acquisition*. Malden, MA: Blackwell, 2003.

Drewelow, Isabelle, and Anne Theobald. "A Comparison of the Attitudes of Learners, Instructors, and Native French Speakers about the Pronunciation of French: An Exploratory Study." *Foreign Language Annals* 40, no. 3 (Fall 2007): 491–520.

Du Bellay, Joachim, and Louis Humbert. *La défense et illustration de la langue française suivie de "De la Précellence du langage françois" par Henri Estienne*. Paris: Classiques Garnier, 2014.

Dubois, Laurent. "La République Métissée: Citizenship, Colonialism, and the Borders of French History." *Cultural Studies*, 14, no. 1 (2000): 15–34.

Du Bois, W. E. B. *The Souls of Black Folk*. New York: Dover, 1903.

Durkheim, Émile. *The Division of Labor in Society*. Glencoe, IL: Free Press, 1933.

Dzidzienyo, Anani, and Suzanne Oboler, eds. *Neither Enemies nor Friends: Latinos, Blacks, Afro-Latinos*. New York: Palgrave Macmillan, 2005.

Earle, Thomas Foster, and K. J. P. Lowe, eds. *Black Africans in Renaissance Europe*. Cambridge: Cambridge University Press, 2005.

Echenberg, Myron J. *Colonial Conscripts: The Tirailleurs Sénégalais in French West Africa, 1857–1960*. Portsmouth, NH: Heinemann, 1991.

Eckert, Penelope, and Sally McConnell-Ginet. "Think Practically and Look Locally: Language and Gender as Community-Based Practice." *Annual Review of Anthropology* 21, no. 1 (1992): 461–88.

*The Economist*. "France's Ethnic Minorities: To Count or Not to Count." March 28, 2009.

Ellis, Blake, Melanie Hicken, and Bob Ortega. "Handcuffs, Assaults, and Drugs Called 'Vitamins': Children Allege Grave Abuse at Migrant Detention Facilities." *CNN*, June 21, 2018.

Ellis, Rod. *Second Language Acquisition*. Oxford: Oxford University Press, 2004.

Enwezor, Okwui. *Snap Judgments: New Positions in Contemporary African Photography*. New York: Steidl, 2006.

Estienne, Henri. *Deux dialogues du nouveau langage françois italianizé, et autrement desguizé, principalement entre les courtisans de ce temps*. Paris: Liseux, 1883.

European Commission. "Europeans and their Languages: Special Eurobarometer 386." June 2012. http://ec.europa.eu/commfrontoffice/publicopinion/archives/ebs/ebs_386_en.pdf.

Fairclough, Norman. *Discourse and Social Change*. Cambridge: Polity Press, 1992.

———. "Global Capitalism and Critical Awareness of Language." *Language Awareness* 8, no. 2 (1999): 71–83.

Faloppa, Federico. *Parole contro: La rappresentazione del diverso nella lingua italiana e nei dialetti*. Milan: Garzanti, 2004.

Fanon, Frantz. *Black Skin, White Masks*. Translated by Charles Lam Markmann. New York: Grove Press, 1967. Originally published as *Peau noire, masques blancs* (Paris: Éditions du Seuil, 1952).

Fassin, Didier. "Politics of the Body and Recognizing Alterity: Fresh Issues Raised by Recent Immigration to France." *Recherches sociologiques* 33, no. 2 (2002): 59–74.

Fassin, Didier, and Éric Fassin. *De la question sociale à la question raciale?* Paris: La Découverte, 2010.

Feldblum, Miriam. *Reconstructing Citizenship: The Politics of Nationality Reform and Immigration in Contemporary France*. Albany: State University of New York Press, 1999.

Fenton, Laurence. *Frederick Douglass in Ireland: The "Black O'Connell."* Cork: Collins Press, 2014.

Ferguson, Charles A. "Diglossia." *Word* 15 (1959): 325–40.

———. "Toward a Characterization of English Foreigner Talk." *Anthropological Linguistics* 17, no. 1 (1975): 1–14.

Fernandez, Manny, and Christine Hauser. "Texas Mother Teaches Textbook Company a Lesson on Accuracy." *New York Times*, October 5, 2015.

Fetterman, David M. *Ethnography: Step-by-Step.* 3rd ed. Los Angeles: Sage, 2010.

Fila-Bakabadio, Sarah. "Photographie et géographie corporelle de l'Atlantique noir." Special issue, *Politique africaine* 136, no. 4 (2014): 21–40.

Firth, Alan, and Johannes Wagner. "On Discourse, Communication, and (Some) Fundamental Concepts in SLA Research." *Modern Language Journal* 81, no. 3 (Autumn 1997): 285–300.

———. "SLA Property: No Trespassing!" *Modern Language Journal* 82, no. 1 (Spring 1998): 91–94.

Fishman, Joshua A. "Bilingualism with and without Diglossia; Diglossia with and without Bilingualism." *Journal of Social Issues* 23, no. 2 (April 1967): 29–38.

———. *The Sociology of Language: An Interdisciplinary Social Science Approach to Language in Society.* Rowley, MA: Newbury House, 1972.

Fletcher, Catherine. *The Black Prince of Florence: The Spectacular Life and Treacherous World of Alessandro de' Medici.* New York: Oxford University Press, 2016.

Flores, Nelson, and Jonathan Rosa. "Undoing Appropriateness: Raciolinguistic Ideologies and Language Diversity in Education." *Harvard Educational Review* 85, no. 2 (Summer 2015): 149–71.

Foucault, Michel. "The Order of Discourse." In *Language and Politics*, edited by Michael J. Shapiro, 108–38. New York: New York University Press, 1984.

———. "Two Lectures." In *Power/Knowledge: Selected Interviews*, edited by Colin Gordon, 78–108. New York: Pantheon, 1980.

Fouquet, Thomas. "Construire la Blackness depuis l'Afrique, un renversement heuristique." Special issue, *Politique africaine* 136, no. 4 (2014): 5–19.

Fouquet, Thomas, and Rémy Bazenguissa-Ganga, eds. "Blackness." Special issue, *Politique africaine* 136, no. 4 (December 2014).

Frith, Simon. "Music and Identity." In *Questions of Cultural Identity*, edited by Stuart Hall and Paul Du Gay, 108–27. London: Sage, 1996.

Gal, Susan. "Multilingualism." In *The Routledge Companion to Sociolinguistics*, edited by Carmen Llamas, Louise Mullany, and Peter Stockwell, 149–56. London: Routledge, 2007.

Gal, Susan, and Judith T. Irvine. "The Boundaries of Languages and Disciplines: How Ideologies Construct Difference. (Defining the Boundaries of Social Inquiry)." *Social Research* 62, no. 4 (1995): 967–1001.

Gambarota, Paola. *Irresistible Signs: The Genius of Language and Italian National Identity.* Toronto: University of Toronto Press, 2011.

García, Ofelia. *Bilingual Education in the 21st Century: A Global Perspective.* Malden, MA: Wiley-Blackwell, 2011.

———. "Education, Multilingualism and Translanguaging in the 21st Century." In *Social Justice through Education*, edited by Tove Skutnabb-Kangas, Robert Phillipson, Ajit K. Mohanty, and Minati Panda, 140–58. New Delhi: Orient Blackswan (formerly Orient Longman), 2009.

García, Ofelia, and Wei Li. *Translanguaging: Language, Bilingualism and Education.* Palgrave Pivot. Basingstoke, England: Palgrave Macmillan, 2014.

Gardner, Robert C. *Social Psychology and Second Language Learning: The Role of Attitudes and Motivation.* London: E. Arnold, 1985.

Gardner, Robert C., and Wallace E. Lambert. *Attitudes and Motivation in Second-Language Learning.* Rowley, MA: Newbury House, 1972.

———. "Motivational Variables in Second Language Acquisition." *Canadian Journal of Psychology* 13 (1959): 266–72.

Gardner-Chloros, Penelope. *Code-Switching*. Cambridge: Cambridge University Press, 2009.

———. "Sociolinguistic Factors in Code-switching." In Bullock and Toribio, *Cambridge Handbook of Linguistic Code-Switching*, 97–113.

Gass, Susan. "Apples and Oranges: Or, Why Apples Are Not Orange and Don't Need to Be; A Response to Firth and Wagner." *Modern Language Journal* 82, no. 1 (April 1998): 83–90.

Gass, Susan M., and Larry Selinker, eds. *Second Language Acquisition: An Introductory Course*. New York: Routledge.

Giddens, Anthony. *Modernity and Self-Identity: Self and Society in the Late Modern Age*. Stanford, CA: Stanford University Press, 1991.

Gillette, Aaron. *Racial Theories in Fascist Italy*. New York: Routledge, 2002.

Gilroy, Paul. *The Black Atlantic: Modernity and Double Consciousness*. New York: Verso, 1993.

———. *"There Ain't No Black in the Union Jack": The Cultural Politics of Race and Nation*. 2nd ed. London: Hutchinson, 2002.

Ginio, Ruth. *French Colonialism Unmasked: The Vichy Years in French West Africa*. Lincoln: University of Nebraska Press, 2006.

Glick Schiller, Nina. "The Centrality of Ethnography in the Study of Transnational Migration: Seeing the Wetland instead of the Swamp." In *American Arrivals: Anthropology Engages the New Immigration*, edited by Nancy Foner, 99–128. Santa Fe: School of American Research Press, 2003.

Goffman, Erving. "Footing." *Semiotica* 25, no. 1–2 (1979): 1–29.

Goldstein, Lynn M. "Standard English: The Only Target for Nonnative Speakers of English?" *TESOL Quarterly* 21, no. 3 (September 1987): 417–36.

Gonzalez, Roseann Dueñas. Introduction to *Language Ideologies: Critical Perspectives on the Official English Movement*, edited by Roseann Dueñas Gonzalez and Ildikó Melis, xxvii–xlvii. Urbana, IL: National Council of Teachers of English, 2000.

González Cruz, Isabel, and María Jesús Vera Cazorla. "Attitudes to Language and Culture in the EFL Classroom: British versus American English?" *Revista de Lenguas para Fines Específicos* 14 (2008): 63–92.

Goudaillier, Jean-Pierre. *Comment tu tchatches! Dictionnaire du français contemporain des cités*. Paris: Maisonneuve et Larose, 1998.

Gramsci, Antonio. *The Southern Question*. Translated by Pasquale Verdicchio. Toronto: Guernica, 2005.

Gray, Herman. *Watching Race: Television and the Struggle for "Blackness."* Minneapolis: University of Minnesota Press, 1995.

Grégoire, Henri. *Rapport sur la nécessité et les moyens d'anéantir le patois, et d'universaliser l'usage de la langue française*. Paris: Imprimerie Nationale, 1794.

Grosjean, François. *Life with Two Languages: An Introduction to Bilingualism*. Cambridge, MA: Harvard University Press, 1982.

Guerini, Federica. "Language Policy and Ideology in Italy." *International Journal of the Sociology of Language* 2011, no. 210 (July 2011): 109–26.

Gueye, Abdoulaye. "Memory at Issue: On Slavery and the Slave Trade among Black French." *Canadian Journal of African Studies / La revue canadienne des études africaines* 45, no. 1 (2011): 77–107.

Gumperz, John J. *Discourse Strategies.* Cambridge: Cambridge University Press, 1982.

———. "On the Linguistic Markers of Bilingual Communication." *Journal of Social Issues* 23, no. 2 (1967): 48–57.

Gunaratnam, Yasmin. *Researching Race and Ethnicity: Methods, Knowledge, and Power.* London: Sage, 2003.

Guthrie, Larry F., and William S. Hall. "Ethnographic Approaches to Reading Research." In *Handbook of Reading Research*, vol. 1, edited by P. David Pearson, Rebecca Barr, and Michael L. Kamil, 91–110. Mahwah, NJ: L. Erlbaum Associates, 1984.

Hagège, Claude. *Le français, histoire d'un combat.* Boulogne-Billancourt: Éditions Michel Hagège, 1996.

Haine, Scott W. W., Jeffrey H. H. Jackson, and Leona Rittner. *The Thinking Space: The Café as a Cultural Institution in Paris, Italy and Vienna.* Farnham, England: Ashgate, 2013.

Hall, Joan Kelly. "(Re)creating Our Worlds with Words: A Sociohistorical Perspective of Face-to-Face Interaction." *Applied Linguistics* 16, no. 2 (June 1995): 206–32.

Hall, Stuart. "Cultural Identity and Diaspora." In *Identity: Community, Culture, Difference*, edited by Jonathan Rutherford, 222–37. London: Lawrence and Wishart, 1990.

———. "The Multi-cultural Question." In *Un/Settled Multiculturalisms*, edited by Barnor Hesse, 209–41. London: Zed Press, 2000.

———. "The West and the Rest: Discourse and Power." In *Modernity: An Introduction to Modern Societies*, edited by Stuart Hall, 184–227. Cambridge, MA: Blackwell, 1996.

Hammersley, Martyn. "Ethnography: Problems and Prospects." *Ethnography and Education* 1, no. 1 (March 2006): 3–14.

Hannerz, Ulf. *Cultural Complexity: Studies in the Social Organization of Meaning.* New York: Columbia University Press, 1992.

Hargreaves, Alec G. *Multi-ethnic France: Immigration, Politics, Culture and Society.* 2nd ed. New York: Routledge, 2007.

Harris, Roxy. "Disappearing Language." In *Literacy, Language and Community Publishing*, edited by Jane Mace, 118–44. Clevedon, England: Multilingual Matters, 1995.

Harris, Roxy, Constant Leung, and Ben Rampton. "Globalisation, Diaspora and Language Education in England." In *Globalisation and Language Teaching*, edited by David Block and Deborah Cameron, 29–46. London: Routledge, 2001.

Harris, Roxy, and Ben Rampton, eds. *The Language, Ethnicity and Race Reader.* London: Routledge, 2003.

Haugen, Einar. "Dialect, Language, Nation." *American Anthropologist* 68, no. 4 (1966): 922–35.

Heath, Shirley Brice. "Ethnography in Education: Defining the Essentials. In *Children in and out of School: Ethnography and Education*, edited by Perry Gilmore and Allan A. Glatthorn, 35–55. Washington, DC: Center for Applied Linguistics, 1982.

Hidalgo, Margarita. "On the Question of 'Standard' versus 'Dialect': Implications of Teaching Hispanic College Students. In *Spanish in the United States: Sociolinguistic Issues*, edited by John J. Bergen, 110–26. Washington, DC: Georgetown University Press, 1990.

Higginbotham, A. Leon. *In the Matter of Color: Race and the American Legal Process.* New York: Oxford University Press, 1978.

Hock, Hans Henrich, and Brian D. Joseph. *Language History, Language Change, and Language Relationship: An Introduction to Historical and Comparative Linguistics.* New York: Mouton de Gruyter, 1996.

Holsey, Bayo. "Black Atlantic Visions: History, Race, and Transnationalism in Ghana." *Cultural Anthropology* 28, no. 3 (August 2013): 504–18.

Hooper, John. "Southern Italian Town World's 'Only White Town' after Ethnic Cleansing." *The Guardian*, January 11, 2000.

Horenczyk, Gabriel. "Conflicted Identities: Acculturation Attitudes and Immigrants' Construction of Their Social Worlds." In *Language, Identity, and Immigration*, edited by Elite Olshtain and Gabriel Horenczyk, 13–30. Jerusalem: Hebrew University Magnes Press, 2000.

Howe, Darin. "Negation in African American Vernacular English." In *Aspects of English Negation*, edited by Yoko Iyeiri, 173–204. Amsterdam: John Benjamins, 2005.

Hunt, Alex, and Brian Wheeler. "Brexit: All You Need to Know about the UK Leaving the EU." *BBC News*, February 26, 2018. http://www.bbc.com/news/uk-politics-32810887.

Hymes, Dell. "The Ethnography of Speaking." In *Anthropology and Human Behavior*, edited by Thomas Gladwin and William C. Sturtevant, 13–53. Washington, DC: Anthropology Society of Washington, 1962.

———, ed. *Language in Culture and Society: A Reader in Linguistics and Anthropology*. Harper International edition. New York: Harper and Row, 1964.

———. "On Communicative Competence." In *Directions in Sociolinguistics*, edited by John Joseph Gumperz and Dell Hymes, 37–65. New York: Holt, Rinehart and Winston, 1970.

———. "Speech and Language: On the Origins and Foundations of Inequality among Speakers." *Daedalus* 102, no. 3 (1973): 59–85.

Ibrahim, Awad El Karim M. "Becoming Black: Rap and Hip-Hop, Race, Gender, Identity, and the Politics of ESL Learning." *TESOL Quarterly* 33, no. 3 (October 1999): 349–69.

INSEE. "Étrangers—Immigrés en 2014: France métropolitaine." 2017. https://www.insee.fr/fr/statistiques/2874036?sommaire=2874056&geo=METRO-1.

———. "La localisation géographique des immigrés: Une forte concentration dans l'aire urbaine de Paris." 2016. https://www.insee.fr/fr/statistiques/2121524.

Irby, Katie. "White and Far-Right Extremists Kill More Cops, but FBI Tracks Black Extremists More Closely, Many Worry." *McClatchy DC Bureau*, January 24, 2018. http://www.mcclatchydc.com/news/nation-world/national/article196423174.html.

Irvine, Judith. "When Talk Isn't Cheap: Language and Political Economy." *American Ethnologist* 16, no. 2 (1989): 248–67.

ISTAT. "Cittadini stranieri. Popolazione residente e bilancio demografico al 31 dicembre 2016: Italia." http://demo.istat.it/.

———. "Cittadini stranieri. Popolazione residente per sesso e cittadinanza al 31 dicembre 2010: Italia." http://demo.istat.it/.

———. "Cittadini stranieri. Popolazione residente per sesso e cittadinanza al 31 dicembre 2016: Italia." http://demo.istat.it/.

———. "The Usage of Italian Language, Dialects and Other Languages in Italy." October 27, 2014. http://www.istat.it/en/archive/136517.

Jaksa, Kari. "Sports and Collective Identity: The Effects of Athletics on National Unity." *SAIS Review of International Affairs* 31, no. 1 (Winter 2011): 39–41.

Jaworski, Adam, and Nikolas Coupland, eds. *The Discourse Reader*. London: Routledge.

Johnson, G. Wesley. *The Emergence of Black Politics in Senegal: The Struggle for Power in the Four Communes, 1900–1920*. Stanford, CA: Stanford University Press, 1971.

Jordan, Miriam. "Is America a 'Nation of Immigrants'? Immigration Agency Says No." *New York Times*, February 22, 2018.

Jordan, Miriam, and Caitlin Dickerson. "More than 450 Migrant Parents May Have Been Deported Without Their Children." *New York Times*, July 24, 2018.

Joseph, John Earl, and Talbot J. Taylor. *Ideologies of Language*. New York: Routledge, 1990.

Kachru, Braj B. *The Alchemy of English: The Spread, Functions, and Models of Non-native Englishes*. New York: Pergamon Institute of English, 1986.

——. "Code-Mixing as a Communicative Strategy." In *International Dimensions of Bilingual Education*, edited by James E. Alatis, 107–24. Washington, DC: Georgetown University Press, 1978.

——. "Standards, Codification and Sociolinguistic Realism: The English Language in the Outer Circle." In *English in the World: Teaching and Learning the Language and Literatures*, edited by Randolph Quirk and H. G. Widdowson, 11–36. Cambridge: Cambridge University Press, 1985.

Kachru, Yamuna. "Monolingual Bias in SLA Research." *TESOL Quarterly* 28, no. 4 (1994): 795–800.

Kane, Cheikh Hamidou. *L'aventure ambiguë*. Paris: Julliard, 1961.

Kane, Moustapha, and David Robinson. *The Islamic Regime of Fuuta Tooro: An Anthology of Oral Tradition*. East Lansing: Michigan State University, 1984.

Kane, Ousmane. *The Homeland Is the Arena: Religion, Transnationalism, and the Integration of Senegalese Immigrants in America*. Oxford: Oxford University Press, 2011.

Keaton, Trica Danielle. *Muslim Girls and the Other France: Race, Identity Politics, & Social Exclusion*. Bloomington: Indiana University Press, 2006.

Keaton, Trica Danielle, T. Denean Sharpley-Whiting, and Tyler Edward Stovall, eds. *Black France / France Noire: The History and Politics of Blackness*. Durham, NC: Duke University Press, 2012.

Keller, Rudolf Ernst. *German Dialects: Phonology and Morphology, with Selected Texts*. Manchester: Manchester University Press, 1961.

Khan, Khizr. "Attacks on American Muslims Are Un-American: Under Trump, They're on the Rise." *Washington Post*, July 21, 2017.

Khouma, Pap. "Io, nero italiano e la mia vita ad ostacoli." *La Repubblica*, December 12, 2009.

——. *I Was an Elephant Salesman: Adventures between Dakar, Paris, and Milan*. Edited by Oreste Pivetta. Translated by Rebecca Crockett-Hopkins. Bloomington: Indiana University Press, 2010. Originally published as *Io, venditore di elefanti: Una vita per forza fra Dakar, Parigi e Milano* (Milan: Garzanti, 1990).

Kinginger, Celeste. "Alice Doesn't Live Here Anymore: Foreign Language Learning and Identity Reconstruction." In Pavlenko and Blackledge, *Negotiation of Identities*, 219–42.

Kington, Tom. "Italy's First Black Minister: I Had Bananas Thrown at Me but I'm Here to Stay." *The Guardian*, September 7, 2013.

Koven, Michèle E. J. "Two Languages in the Self / The Self in Two Languages: French-Portuguese Bilinguals' Verbal Enactments and Experiences of Self in Narrative Discourse." *Ethos* 26, no. 4 (December 1998): 410–55.

Kramsch, Claire. *Context and Culture in Language Teaching*. Oxford: Oxford University Press, 1993.

———. "The Cultural Component of Language Teaching." *Language, Culture and Curriculum* 8, no. 2 (January 1995): 83–92.

———, ed. *Language Acquisition and Language Socialization: Ecological Perspectives*. New York: Continuum, 2002.

———. *The Multilingual Subject: What Foreign Language Learners Say about Their Experience and Why It Matters*. Oxford: Oxford University Press, 2009.

———. "The Privilege of the Non-Native Speaker." *PMLA* 112, no. 3 (1997): 359–69.

Kramsch, Claire, and Anne Whiteside. "Language Ecology in Multilingual Settings: Towards a Theory of Symbolic Competence." *Applied Linguistics* 29, no. 4 (December 2008): 645–71.

Kristeva, Julia. *Revolution in Poetic Language*. New York: Columbia University Press, 1984.

Kubota, Ryuko. "Rethinking the Superiority of the Native Speaker: Toward a Relational Understanding of Power." In *The Native Speaker Concept: Ethnographic Investigations of Native Speaker Effects*, edited by Neriko Musha Doerr, 233–47. New York: Mouton de Gruyter, 2009.

Kuiper, Lawrence. "Perception Is Reality: Parisian and Provençal Perceptions of Regional Varieties of French." *Journal of Sociolinguistics* 9, no. 1 (2005): 28–52.

Labov, William. *Sociolinguistic Patterns*. Philadelphia: University of Pennsylvania Press, 1972.

Ladegaard, Hans J. "National Stereotypes and Language Attitudes: The Perception of British, American and Australian Language and Culture in Denmark." *Language and Communication* 18, no. 4 (1998): 251–74.

Lave, Jean, and Étienne Wenger. *Situated Learning: Legitimate Peripheral Participation*. Cambridge: Cambridge University Press, 1991.

*Le Code Noir: Édit du roi sur les esclaves des îles de l'Amérique* (1680); *Suivi de Código Negro* (1789). Université du Québec à Chicoutimi, 2010. http://dx.doi.org/doi:10.1522 /030168016.

Leconte, Fabienne. "L'identité linguistique des migrants africains en France." In Marley, Hintze, and Parker, *Linguistic Identities*, 117–30.

Lecoq, Benoît. "The Café." Translated by Nancy Turpin. In *Legacies*, vol. 3 of *Rethinking France = Les lieux de mémoire*, edited by Pierre Nora and David P. Jordan, 343–74. Chicago: University of Chicago Press, 2009.

Lee, Tiffany. "Black and Undocumented: 5 Ways We Can Stop Erasing Black Folk from Conversations around Immigration." *The Body Is Not an Apology*, June 24, 2017. https://tinyurl.com/ydgj3hm9.

*Legge* 15 Dicembre 1999, n. 482. "Norme in materia di tutela delle minoranze linguistiche storiche." http://www.camera.it/parlam/leggi/99482l.htm.

Lepschy, Anna Laura, and Giulio Lepschy. *The Italian Language Today*. London: Hutchinson, 1998.

Leung, Constant, Roxy Harris, and Ben Rampton. "The Idealised Native Speaker, Reified Ethnicities, and Classroom Realities." *TESOL Quarterly* 31, no. 3 (Autumn 1997): 543–60.

Lewis, David L. *W. E. B. Du Bois: A Biography*. New York: Henry Holt, 2009.

Lewis, M. Paul. *Ethnologue: Languages of the World*. Dallas: SIL International, 2009.

Lionnet, Françoise. "Continents and Archipelagoes: From E Pluribus Unum to Creolized Solidarities." Special issue, *PMLA: Publications of the Modern Language Association of America* 123, no. 5 (2008): 1503–15.

Lionnet, Françoise, and Shu-mei Shih. *Minor Transnationalism.* Durham, NC: Duke University Press, 2005.

Lippi-Green, Rosina. *English with an Accent: Language, Ideology, and Discrimination in the United States.* New York: Routledge, 1997.

Lipski, John M. "'Partial' Spanish Strategies of Pidginization and Simplification (from Lingua Franca to 'Gringo Lingo')." In *Romance Phonology and Variation: Selected Papers from the 30th Linguistic Symposium on Romance Languages, Gainesville, Florida, February 2000,* edited by Caroline R. Wiltshire and Joaquim Camps, 117–34. Amsterdam: John Benjamins, 2002.

———. *Varieties of Spanish in the United States.* Washington, DC: Georgetown University Press, 2008.

Lloyd, Cathie. "Concepts, Models and Anti-racist Strategies in Britain and France." *New Community* 18, no. 1 (October 1991): 63–73.

Lo, Adrienne. "Codeswitching, Speech Community Membership, and the Construction of Ethnic Identity." *Journal of Sociolinguistics* 3, no. 4 (November 1999): 461–79.

Lodge, R. Anthony. *French: From Dialect to Standard.* New York: Routledge, 1993.

Loewen, James W. *Lies My Teacher Told Me: Everything Your American History Textbook Got Wrong.* Touchstone ed. New York: Simon and Schuster, 2007.

Loi no. 2001-434 du 21 mai 2001. "Tendant à la reconnaissance de la traite et de l'esclavage en tant que crime contre l'humanité." http://www.legifrance.gouv.fr/affichTexte.do?cidTexte=JORFTEXT000000405369.

Loi no. 2005-158 du 23 février 2005. "Portant reconnaissance de la nation et contribution nationale en faveur des Français rapatriés." http://www.admi.net/jo/20050224/DEFX0300218L.html.

Loi no. 94-665 du 4 août 1994. "Relative à l'emploi de la langue française (Loi Toubon)." http://www.legifrance.gouv.fr/affichTexte.do?cidTexte=JORFTEXT000000349929.

Lombardi-Diop, Cristina. "Postracial/Postcolonial Italy." In *Postcolonial Italy: Challenging National Homogeneity,* edited by Cristina Lombardi-Diop and Caterina Romeo, 175–90. New York: Palgrave Macmillan, 2012.

Lombardi-Diop, Cristina, and Caterina Romeo. "Introduction: Paradigms of Postcoloniality in Contemporary Italy." In *Postcolonial Italy: Challenging National Homogeneity,* edited by Cristina Lombardi-Diop and Caterina Romeo, 1–30. New York: Palgrave Macmillan, 2012.

Loomba, Ania. *Colonialism/Postcolonialism.* 3rd ed. New York: Routledge, 2015.

Loporcaro, Michele, and Pier Marco Bertinetto. "The Sound Pattern of Standard Italian, as Compared with the Varieties Spoken in Florence, Milan and Rome." *Journal of the International Phonetic Association* 35, no. 2 (2005): 131–51.

Lorde, Audre. *Sister Outsider: Essays and Speeches.* Trumansburg, NY: Crossing Press, 1984.

Lozada, Eriberto P. "Cosmopolitanism and Nationalism in Shanghai Sports." *City & Society* 18, no. 2 (December 2006): 207–31.

Lozès, Patrick. "'Black France' and the National Identity Debate: How Best to Be Black and French?" In Keaton, Sharpley-Whiting, and Stovall, *Black France / France Noire,* 123–44.

Luján García, Carmen. *La lengua inglesa en canarias: Usos y actidudes.* Las Palmas de Gran Canaria: Departamento de Ediciones de Cabildo de Gran Canaria, 2003.

Mabanckou, Alain. "The Fugitive." Translated by Polly McLean. In *The Granta Book of the African Short Story,* edited by Helon Habila, 200–207. London: Granta Books, 2011.

MacGaffey, Janet, and Rémy Bazenguissa-Ganga. *Congo-Paris: Transnational Traders on the Margins of the Law.* Oxford: James Currey, 2000.

Madibbo, Amal I. *Minority within a Minority: Black Francophone Immigrants and the Dynamics of Power and Resistance.* New York: Routledge, 2006.

Mahama, John Dramani. *My First Coup d'Etat and Other True Stories from the Lost Decades of Africa.* New York: Bloomsbury, 2012.

Maher, Stephanie. "Barça ou Barzakh: The Social Elsewhere of Failed Clandestine Migration out of Senegal." PhD diss., University of Washington, 2015. ProQuest Theses and Dissertations (1758795190).

Makomé, Inongo Vi. *España y los negros africanos.* Barcelona: La Llar del Llibre, 1990.

Managan, Kathe. "Diglossia Reconsidered: Language Choice and Code-Switching in Guadeloupean Voluntary Organizations." *Texas Linguistic Forum* 47 (2004): 251–61.

Marable, Manning, and Vanessa Agard-Jones, eds. *Transnational Blackness: Navigating the Global Color Line.* New York: Palgrave Macmillan, 2008.

Marley, Dawn, Marie-Anne Hintze, and Gabrielle Parker, eds. *Linguistic Identities and Policies in France and the French-Speaking World.* London: Association for French Language Studies in Association with the Centre for Information on Language Teaching and Research, 1998.

Marshall, Thomas Humphrey. "Citizenship and Social Class." In *Citizenship and Social Class,* edited by Thomas Humphrey Marshall and T. B. Bottomore, 3–51. London: Pluto, 1992.

Martin-Jones, Marilyn, and Suzanne Romaine. "Semilingualism: A Half-Baked Theory of Communicative Competence." *Applied Linguistics* 7, no. 1 (Spring 1986): 26–38.

Mathews, Gordon. *Global Culture / Individual Identity: Searching for Home in the Cultural Supermarket.* New York: Routledge, 2000.

May, Stephen. *Language and Minority Rights: Ethnicity, Nationalism and the Politics of Language.* New York: Routledge, 2008.

Mbembe, Achille. "L'Afrique de Nicolas Sarkozy." *Mouvements* 52, no. 4 (2007): 65.

McClintock, Anne. "The Angel of Progress: Pitfalls of the Term 'Postcolonialism.'" *Social Text* 31–32 (1992): 84–98.

McCormick, Kay. *Language in Cape Town's District Six.* Oxford: Oxford University Press, 2002.

McKay, Sandra, and Sau-Ling Wong. "Multiple Discourses, Multiple Identities: Investment and Agency in Second-Language Learning among Chinese Adolescent Immigrant Students." *Harvard Educational Review* 66, no. 3 (1996): 577–608.

McLaughlin, Fiona. "Dakar Wolof and the Configuration of an Urban Identity." *Journal of African Cultural Studies* 14, no. 2 (2001): 153–72.

———. "Haalpulaar Identity as a Response to Wolofization." *African Languages and Cultures* 8, no. 2 (1995): 153–68.

———. "Senegal: The Emergence of a National Lingua Franca." In *Language and National Identity in Africa,* edited by Andrew Simpson, 79–97. Oxford: Oxford University Press, 2008.

McNamara, Francis Terry. *France in Black Africa*. Washington, DC: National Defense University, 1989.

Means Coleman, Robin R. *Say It Loud! African-American Audiences, Media, and Identity*. New York: Routledge, 2002.

Meeuwis, Michael, and Jan Blommaert. "A Monolectal View of Code-Switching: Layered Code-Switching among Zairians in Belgium." In Auer, *Code-Switching in Conversation*, 76–100.

Mela, Vivienne. "Verlan 2000." *Langue Française* 114 (June 1997): 16–34.

Mellino, Miguel. "De-provincializing Italy: Notes on Race, Racialization, and Italy's Coloniality." In *Postcolonial Italy: Challenging National Homogeneity*, edited by Cristina Lombardi-Diop and Caterina Romeo, 83–99. New York: Palgrave Macmillan, 2012.

Menard-Warwick, Julia. "Both a Fiction and an Existential Fact: Theorizing Identity in Second Language Acquisition and Literacy Studies." *Linguistics and Education: An International Research Journal* 16, no. 3 (2005): 253–74.

Merrill, Heather. *An Alliance of Women: Immigration and the Politics of Race*. Minneapolis: University of Minnesota Press, 2006.

———. "Postcolonial Borderlands: Black Life Worlds and Relational Place in Turin, Italy." *ACME* 13, no. 2 (2014): 263–94.

Meyfart, Johannes Matthaeus. *Teutsche rhetorica: Oder, Redekunst: 1634*. Tübingen: Niemeyer, 1977.

Migliorini, Bruno, and T. Gwynfor Griffith. *The Italian Language*. Rev. ed. Boston: Faber and Faber, 1984.

Miller, Christopher L. *The French Atlantic Triangle: Literature and Culture of the Slave Trade*. Durham, NC: Duke University Press, 2008.

———. *Nationalists and Nomads: Essays on Francophone African Literature and Culture*. Chicago: University of Chicago Press, 1998.

———. *Theories of Africans: Francophone Literature and Anthropology in Africa*. Black Literature and Culture. Chicago: University of Chicago Press, 1990.

Miller, Jennifer. *Audible Difference ESL and Social Identity in Schools*. Clevedon, England: Multilingual Matters, 2003.

Milroy, James. "Language Ideologies and the Consequences of Standardization." *Journal of Sociolinguistics* 5, no. 4 (November 2001): 530–55.

Milroy, Lesley, and Pieter Muysken. *One Speaker, Two Languages: Cross-Disciplinary Perspectives on Code-Switching*. Cambridge: Cambridge University Press, 1995.

Ministère de l'Éducation Nationale, République du Sénégal. *Élaboration d'une politique d'éducation de Base de dix ans diversifiée, articulée, et intégrée*, 2014.

Ministero dell'Interno. "Accordo di integrazione per lo straniero che richiede il permesso di soggiorno." 2012. http://www.interno.gov.it/it/temi/immigrazione-e-asilo /modalita-dingresso/accordo-integrazione-straniero-richiede-permesso-soggiorno.

Minnich, Nelson. "The Catholic Church and the Pastoral Care of Black Africans in Renaissance Italy." In Earle and Lowe, *Black Africans in Renaissance Europe*, 280–300.

Moe, Nelson. *The View from Vesuvius: Italian Culture and the Southern Question*. Berkeley: University of California Press, 2002.

Montes-Alcalá, Cecilia. "Attitudes toward Oral and Written Codeswitching in Spanish-English Bilingual Youth." In *Research on Spanish in the U.S.*, edited by Ana Roca, 218–27. Somerville, MA: Cascadilla Press, 2000.

Mudimbe-Boyi, Elisabeth. "Black France: Myth or Reality? Problems of Identity and

Identification." In Keaton, Sharpley-Whiting, and Stovall, *Black France / France Noire*, 17–31.

Murphey, Tim, Chen Jin, and Chen Li-Chi. "Learners' Constructions of Identities and Imagined Communities." In *Experiences of Language Learning*, edited by Phil Benson and David Nunan, 83–100. Cambridge: Cambridge University Press, 2005.

Myers-Scotton, Carol. "Codeswitching as Indexical of Social Negotiation." In *Codeswitching: Anthropological and Sociolinguistic Perspectives*, edited by Monica Heller, 151–86. Berlin: Mouton de Gruyter, 1998.

———. *Duelling Languages: Grammatical Structure in Codeswitching*. Oxford: Oxford University Press, 1993.

———. *Social Motivations for Codeswitching: Evidence from Africa*. Oxford: Clarendon Press, 1993.

Ndiaye, Mandiogou, and Nelly Robin. "Migrants Criminalized while Making the Journey." In *Regional Challenges of West African Migration: African and European Perspectives*, edited by Marie Trémolieres, 175–98. Paris: Organisation for Economic Cooperation and Development (OECD), 2009.

Ndiaye, Pap. *La condition noire: Essai sur une minorité française*. Paris: Calmann-Lévy, 2008.

———. "Pour une histoire des populations noires en France: Préalables théoriques." *Le Mouvement social* 213, no. 4 (2005): 91–108.

Nekvapil, Jiří. "On Non-Self-Evident Relationships between Language and Ethnicity: How Germans Do Not Speak German, and Czechs Do Not Speak Czech." *Multilingua: Journal of Cross-Cultural and Interlanguage Communication* 19, no. 1–2 (2000): 37–53.

Newman, Michael. *New York City English*. Berlin: De Gruyter Mouton, 2015.

Ng, Roxana. "Constituting Ethnic Phenomenon: An Account from the Perspective of Immigrant Women." *Canadian Ethnic Studies / Études ethniques au Canada* 13, no. 1 (1981): 97–108.

Ngom, Fallou. "Linguistic Borrowing as Evidence of the Social History of the Senegalese Speech Community." *International Journal of the Sociology of Language*, no. 158 (2002): 37–51.

———. "The Social Status of Arabic, French, and English in the Senegalese Speech Community." *Language Variation and Change* 15, no. 3 (2003): 351–68.

Ngũgĩ wa Thiong'o. *Caitaani mũtharaba-Inĩ*. Nairobi: East African Educational Publishers, 1980.

———. *Decolonizing the Mind: The Politics of Language in African Literature*. London: James Currey, 1986.

———. *Something Torn and New: An African Renaissance*. New York: BasicCivitas Books, 2009.

Noah, Trevor. "Trevor Responds to Criticism from the French Ambassador—Between the Scenes." *Daily Show*, July 18, 2018. https://youtu.be/COD9hcTpGWQ.

Norton, Bonny. *Identity and Language Learning: Gender, Ethnicity and Educational Change*. Harlow, England: Longman, 2000.

———. "Language, Identity, and the Ownership of English." *TESOL Quarterly* 31, no. 3 (1997): 409–29.

Norton Peirce, Bonny. "Social Identity, Investment, and Language Learning." *TESOL Quarterly* 29, no. 1 (Spring 1995): 9–31.

Norwood, Kimberly Jade. *Color Matters: Skin Tone Bias and the Myth of a Postracial America.* New York: Routledge, 2014.

Oesch Serra, Cecilia. "Discourse Connectives in Bilingual Conversation: The Case of an Emerging Italian-French Mixed Code." In Auer, *Codeswitching in Conversation,* 101–24.

Omi, Michael, and Howard Winant. *Racial Formation in the United States.* 3rd ed. New York: Routledge, 2015.

Oppenheimer, David B. "Why France Needs to Collect Data on Racial Identity . . . in a French Way." *Hastings International and Comparative Law Review* 31, no. 2 (2008): 735–51.

Organisation Internationale de la Francophonie. "La francophonie dans le monde: 2006–2007." https://www.francophonie.org/IMG/pdf/La_francophonie_dans_ le_monde_2006-2007.pdf.

Osumare, Halifu. "Global Hip-Hop and the African Diaspora." In *Black Cultural Traffic: Crossroads in Global Performance and Popular Culture,* edited by Harry Justin Elam and Kennell A. Jackson, 266–88. Ann Arbor: University of Michigan Press, 2005.

Palidda, Salvatore. "Insertion, Integration and Rejection of Immigration in Italy." In *Illiberal Liberal States: Immigration, Citizenship and Integration in the EU,* edited by Elspeth Guild, C. A. Groenendijk, and Sergio Carrera, 357–72. Farnham, England: Routledge, 2009.

Paltridge, John, and Howard Giles. "Attitudes towards Speakers of Regional Accents of French: Effects of Regionality, Age and Sex of Listeners." *Linguistische Berichte* 90 (April 1984): 71–85.

Papastergiadis, Nikos. *The Turbulence of Migration: Globalization, Deterritorialization, and Hybridity.* Cambridge: Polity Press, 2000.

Pavlenko, Aneta. "Autobiographic Narratives as Data in Applied Linguistics." *Applied Linguistics* 28, no. 2 (2007): 163–88.

———. "Poststructuralist Approaches to the Study of Social Factors in Second Language Learning and Use." In Cook *Portraits of the L2 User,* 275–302.

Pavlenko, Aneta, and Adrian Blackledge. *Negotiation of Identities in Multilingual Contexts.* Clevedon, England: Multilingual Matters, 2004.

Pavlenko, Aneta, and James P. Lantolf. "Second Language Learning as Participation and the (Re) Construction of Selves." In *Sociocultural Theory and Second Language Learning,* edited by James P. Lantolf, 155–77. New York: Oxford University Press, 2000.

Pei, Mario. *The Italian Language.* New York: Columbia University Press, 1941.

Penny, Ralph. *A History of the Spanish Language.* 2nd ed. Cambridge: Cambridge University Press, 2002.

Pennycook, Alastair. *The Cultural Politics of English as an International Language.* London: Longman, 1994.

Perullo, Alex, and John Fenn. "Language Ideologies, Choices, and Practices in Eastern Africa." In *Global Pop, Local Language,* edited by Harris. M. Berger and Michael Thomas Carroll, 19–52. Jackson: University Press of Mississippi, 2003.

Phillipson, Robert. *Linguistic Imperialism.* Oxford: Oxford University Press, 1992.

Pierre, Jemima. *The Predicament of Blackness: Postcolonial Ghana and the Politics of Race.* Chicago: University of Chicago Press, 2012.

Pierre, Jemima, and Camille Niauffre. "L'Afrique et la question de la Blackness: Exemples du Ghana." Special issue, *Politique africaine* 136, no. 4 (2014): 83–103.

Pierrot, Grégory. "Fear of a Black France." *Africa Is a Country*, July 8, 2018. https://africasa country.com/2018/07/fear-of-a-black-france.

Piller, Ingrid, and Kimie Takahashi. "A Passion for English: Desire and the Language Market." In *Bilingual Minds: Emotional Experience, Expression and Representation*, edited by Aneta Pavlenko, 59–83. Clevedon, England: Multilingual Matters, 2006.

Pinsker, Shachar. "A Modern (Jewish) Woman in a Café: Leah Goldberg and the Poetic Space of the Coffeehouse." *Jewish Social Studies: History, Culture, Society* 21, no. 1 (2015): 1–48.

Piot, Charles. "Atlantic Aporias: Africa and Gilroy's Black Atlantic." *South Atlantic Quarterly* 100, no. 1 (2001): 155–70.

Planas, Roque, and Elise Foley. "Deportations of Noncriminals Rise as ICE Casts Wider Net." *Huffington Post*, December 5, 2017.

Polanyi, Livia. "Language Learning and Living Abroad: Stories from the Field." In *Second Language Acquisition in a Study Abroad Context*, edited by Barbara F. Freed, 271–91. Amsterdam: John Benjamins, 1995.

Pollett, Andrea. "An Introduction to the Roman Dialect." *Virtual Roma*, February 2004. http://roma.andreapollett.com/S8/dialect5.htm.

Pomerantz, Anne. "Language Ideologies and the Production of Identities: Spanish as a Resource for Participation in a Multilingual Marketplace." *Multilingua: Journal of Cross-Cultural and Interlanguage Communication* 21, no. 2–3 (August 2002): 275–302.

Portelli, Alessandro. "The Problem of the Color-Blind: Notes on the Discourse on Race in Italy." In *CrossRoutes: The Meaning of Race for the 21st Century*, edited by Paul Spickard, 355–64. New York: Routledge, 2004.

Posner, Rebecca. *Linguistic Change in French*. Oxford: Oxford University Press, 1997.

Povoledo, Elisabetta. "Slurs against Italy's First Black National Official Spur Debate on Racism." *New York Times*, June 22, 2013.

Pratt, Jeff C. "Italy: Political Unity and Cultural Diversity." In *The Politics of Recognizing Difference: Multiculturalism Italian-Style*, edited by Ralph Grillo and Jeff C. Pratt, 25–40. Aldershot, England: Ashgate, 2002.

Pratt, Kenneth J. "The Dialect of Rome." *Italica* 43, no. 2 (1966): 167–79.

Price, Stephen. "Comments on Bonny Norton Peirce's 'Social Identity, Investment, and Language Learning': A Reader Reacts. . . ." *TESOL Quarterly* 30, no. 2 (Summer 1996): 331–37.

Provencher, Denis M. *Queer French: Globalization, Language, and Sexual Citizenship in France*. Aldershot, England: Ashgate, 2007.

———. *Queer Maghrebi French: Language, Temporalities, Transfiliations*. Liverpool: Liverpool University Press, 2017.

Prudent, Lambert-Felix. "Diglossie et interlecte." *Langages* 61, no. 61 (1981): 13–38.

Raizon, Dominique. "Chirac revient sur le 'rôle positif' de la colonisation." *RFI*, January 26, 2006. www.rfi.fr/actufr/articles/073/article_41417.asp.

Ramanathan, Vaidehi. *The English-Vernacular Divide: Postcolonial Language Politics and Practice*. Clevedon, England: Multilingual Matters, 2005.

Rampton, Ben. *Crossing: Language and Ethnicity among Adolescents*. London: Longman, 1995.

———. "Language Crossing and the Redefinition of Reality." In Auer, *Code-Switching in Conversation*, 290–320.

Rana, Junaid Akram. *Terrifying Muslims: Race and Labor in the South Asian Diaspora.* Durham, NC: Duke University Press, 2011.

Rapport, Nigel, and Andrew Dawson. "The Topic and the Book." In *Migrants of Identity: Perceptions of Home in a World of Movement,* edited by Nigel Rapport and Andrew Dawson, 3–17. Oxford: Berg, 1998.

Redeker Hepner, Tricia M. *Soldiers, Martyrs, Traitors, and Exiles: Political Conflict in Eritrea and the Diaspora.* Philadelphia: University of Pennsylvania Press, 2009.

Riccio, Bruno. "Migranti per il co-sviluppo tra Italia e Senegal: Il caso di Bergamo." CeSPI, 2006. http://www.cespi.it/it/ricerche/migranti-il-co-sviluppo-tra-italia-e-senegal-il-caso-di-bergamo.

———. "More than a Trade Diaspora: Senegalese Transnational Experiences in Emilia-Romagna (Italy)." In *New African Diasporas,* edited by Khalid Koser, 95–110. London: Routledge, 2003.

———. "Rehearsing Transnational Citizenship: Senegalese Associations, Co-development and Simultaneous Inclusion." *African Diaspora* 4, no. 1 (2011): 97–113.

———. "Senegal Is Our Home: The Anchored Nature of Senegalese Transnational Networks." In *New Approaches to Migration? Transnational Communities and the Transformation of Home,* edited by Nadje Sadig Al-Ali and Khalid Koser, 68–83. London: Routledge, 2002.

———. "Talkin' about Migration: Some Ethnographic Notes on the Ambivalent Representation of Migrants in Contemporary Senegal." *Wiener Zeitschrift für kritische Afrikastudien / Vienna Journal of African Studies* 8 (2005): 99–118.

———. "*Toubab* and *Vu Cumprà*: Italian Perceptions of Senegalese Transmigrants and the Senegalese Afro-muslim Critique of Italian Society." In *The Politics of Recognising Difference,* edited by Ralph Grillo and Jeff C. Pratt, 177–96. Aldershot, England: Ashgate, 2002b.

———. "West African Transnationalisms Compared: Ghanaians and Senegalese in Italy." *Journal of Ethnic and Migration Studies* 34, no. 2 (March 2008): 217–34.

Ricoeur, Paul. *On Translation.* Translated by Eileen Brennan. London: Routledge, 2006.

———. *Reflections on the Just.* Translated by David Pellauer. Chicago: University of Chicago Press, 2007.

Roberts, Sam. "Listening to (and Saving) the World's Languages." *New York Times,* April 29, 2010.

Robin, Nelly. *Atlas des migrations ouest-africaines vers l'Europe, 1985–1993.* Paris: EUROSTAT, 1996.

Rofheart, Mahriana. *Shifting Perceptions of Migration in Senegalese Literature, Film, and Social Media.* Lanham, MD: Lexington Books, 2014.

Romaine, Suzanne. "The Bilingual and Multilingual Community." In *The Handbook of Bilingualism,* edited by Tej K. Bhatia and William C. Ritchie, 385–406. Oxford: Blackwell, 2004.

———. *Bilingualism.* 2nd ed. Oxford: Blackwell, 1995.

Rosa, Jonathan, and Nelson Flores. "Unsettling Race and Language: Toward a Raciolinguistic Perspective." *Language in Society* 46, no. 5 (2017): 621–47.

Ross, Cody T. "A Multi-level Bayesian Analysis of Racial Bias in Police Shootings at the County-Level in the United States, 2011–2014." *PLoS ONE* 10, no. 11, doi: 10.1371/journal.pone.0141854.

Rouse, Roger. "Mexican Migration and the Social Space of Postmodernism." *Diaspora: A Journal of Transnational Studies* 1, no. 1 (1991): 8–23.

Rubin, Donald L. "Nonlanguage Factors Affecting Undergraduates' Judgments of Nonnative English-Speaking Teaching Assistants." *Research in Higher Education* 33, no. 4 (1992): 511–31.

Rudder, Véronique de, Christian Poiret, and François Vourc'h. *L'inégalité raciste: L'universalité républicaine à l'épreuve.* Paris: Presses Universitaires de France, 2000.

Russell-Cole, Kathy, Midge Wilson, and Ronald E. Hall. *The Color Complex: The Politics of Skin Color among African Americans.* New York: Harcourt Brace Jovanovich, 1992.

Sánchez-Pardo, Esther. "Adrift on the Black Mediterranean Diaspora: African Migrant Writing in Spain." *Social Identities* 17, no. 1 (2011): 105–20.

Sarkozy, Nicolas. "Le discours de Dakar de Nicolas Sarkozy: L'intégralité du discours du président de la république, prononcé le 26 juillet 2007." *Le Monde*, November 11, 2007.

Schaub, Michael. "Do New Texas Textbooks Whitewash Slavery and Segregation?" *Los Angeles Times*, July 7, 2015.

Schein, Louisa. "The Consumption of Color and the Politics of White Skin in Post-Mao China." In *The Gender/Sexuality Reader: Culture, History, Political Economy*, edited by Roger N. Lancaster and Michaela Di Leonardo, 471–84. London: Routledge, 1997.

Schieffelin, Bambi B., Kathryn Ann Woolard, and Paul V. Kroskrity, eds. *Language Ideologies: Practice and Theory.* New York: Oxford University Press, 1998.

Schmid, Carol. "The Politics of English Only in the United States: Historical, Social, and Legal Aspects." In *Language Ideologies: Critical Perspectives on the Official English Movement*, edited by Roseann Dueñas Gonzalez and Ildikó Melis, 62–86. Urbana, IL: National Council of Teachers of English, 2000.

Schmidt, Ronald. *Language Policy and Identity Politics in the United States.* Philadelphia: Temple University Press, 2000.

Schmidt di Friedberg, Ottavia. "Le réseau sénégalais mouride en Italie." In *Exils et royaumes: Les appartenances au monde arabo-musulman aujourd'hui*, edited by Rémy Leveau and Gilles Kepel, 301–29. Paris: Presses de la FNSP, 1994.

———. "L'immigration africaine en Italie: Le cas sénégalais." *Études internationales* 24, no. 1 (March 1993): 125–40.

Schumann, John H. *The Neurobiology of Affect in Language.* Malden, MA: Blackwell, 1997.

Schürkens, Ulrike. "Le rôle du français dans un pays en voie de développement: Le Sénégal." *Le langage et l'homme: Recherches pluridisciplinaires sur le langage* 52 (May 1983): 67–75.

Secrétariat Général à l'Immigration et à l'Intégration. "Réforme du contrôle de la connaissance de la langue française par les candidats à la nationalité." October 12, 2011. http://www.alf-auvergne.org/IMG/pdf/reforme_naturalisation.pdf.

Seidman, Irving. *Interviewing as Qualitative Research: A Guide for Researchers in Education and the Social Sciences.* 3rd ed. New York: Teachers College Press, 2006.

Sembène, Ousmane. *La noire de . . .* New York: New Yorker Films, 2001 [1966]. DVD.

———. *Le dernier de l'empire.* 2nd ed. Paris: L'Harmattan, 1985.

———. *Mandabi.* New York: New Yorker Films, 1999 [1968]. DVD.

Semple, Kirk. "City's Newest Immigrant Enclaves, from Little Guyana to Meokjagolmok." *New York Times*, June 8, 2013.

Sene, Fatou K. "Sénégal: Apprentissage de l'anglais en Afrique francophone subsaharienne—Le Sénégal meilleur de sa classe." *Walfadjri*, January 23, 2013. http://fr.allafrica.com/stories/201301250596.html.

Senegal Constitution. Art. I. July 7, 2001. http://www.gouv.sn/-Constitution-du-Senegal -.html.

Senghor, Léopold Sédar. "Le français, langue de culture." *Esprit*, November 1962. http://www.esprit.presse.fr/archive/review/article.php?code=32919.

Sharma, Nitasha Tamar. *Hip Hop Desis: South Asian Americans, Blackness, and a Global Race Consciousness*. Durham, NC: Duke University Press, 2010.

Shih, Shu-Mei M. "Comparative Racialization: An Introduction." Special issue, *PMLA* 123, no. 5 (October 2008): 1347–62.

Shipley, Jesse Weaver. "Aesthetic of the Entrepreneur: Afro-Cosmopolitan Rap and Moral Circulation in Accra, Ghana." *Anthropological Quarterly* 82, no. 3 (Summer 2009): 631–68.

———. *Living the Hiplife: Celebrity and Entrepreneurship in Ghanaian Popular Music*. Durham, NC: Duke University Press, 2013.

Siegal, Meryl. "The Role of Learner Subjectivity in Second Language Sociolinguistic Competency: Western Women Learning Japanese." *Applied Linguistics* 17, no. 3 (1996): 356–82.

Silverstein, Michael. "Monoglot 'Standard' in America: Standardization and Metaphors of Linguistic Hegemony." In *The Matrix of Language: Contemporary Linguistic Anthropology*, edited by Donald Lawrence Brenneis and Ronald K. S. Macaulay, 284–306. Boulder, CO: Westview Press, 1996.

Singh, Rajendra, ed. *The Native Speaker: Multilingual Perspectives*. New Delhi: Sage, 1998.

Skeggs, Beverley. *Formations of Class and Gender: Becoming Respectable*. London: Sage, 1997.

Smith, Étienne. "Religious and Cultural Pluralism in Senegal: Accommodation through 'Proportional Equidistance'?" In *Tolerance, Democracy, and Sufis in Senegal*, edited by Mamadou Diouf, 147–79. New York: Columbia University Press, 2013.

Smith, Lothar, and Valentina Mazzucato. "'Miglioriamo le nostre tradizioni': Gli investimenti dei migranti ashanti nelle abitazioni e nelle imprese ad Accra." *Afriche e Orienti* 6, no. 1/2 (2004): 168–85.

Smith, Lydia. "Trump-Mexico Border Wall: What Is Happening, Who Will Pay for It and What Is the US President Saying on the Border Barrier?" *Independent*, January 10, 2018.

Smith, Maya. "Using Interconnected Texts to Highlight Culture in the Foreign Language Classroom." *L2 Journal* 5, no. 2 (2013): 1–17.

Smith, William Gardner. *The Stone Face*. New York: Farrar, Straus, 1963.

Socé, Ousmane. *Mirages de Paris*. 1937; Paris: Nouvelles Éditions Latines, 1964.

Sòrgoni, Barbara. "Racist Discourses and Practices in the Italian Empire under Fascism." In *The Politics of Recognising Difference*, edited by Ralph Grillo and Jeff C. Pratt, 41–58. Aldershot, England: Ashgate, 2002.

Spears, Arthur K., and Leanne Hinton. "Languages and Speakers: An Introduction to African American English and Native American Languages." *Transforming Anthropology* 18, no. 1 (April 2010): 3–14.

Spielberg, Steven, dir. *The Color Purple*. Burbank, CA: Warner Home Video, 1987. DVD.

Spivak, Gayatri Chakravorty. "Can the Subaltern Speak?" In *Marxism and the Interpretation of Culture*, edited by Cary Nelson and Lawrence Grossberg, 271–313. Urbana: University of Illinois Press, 1988.

Sposet, Barbara A. *The Role of Music in Second Language Acquisition: A Bibliographical Review of Seventy Years of Research, 1937–2007.* Lewiston, NY: E. Mellen Press, 2008.

Squires, Nick. "Italy's Hardline Government Threatens to Pull back from Migrant Rescue Missions." *Telegraph*, June 18, 2018.

Sridhar, S. N. "A Reality Check for SLA Theories." *TESOL Quarterly* 28, no. 4 (1994): 800–805.

"The Status of French in the World." France Diplomatie. Accessed January 31, 2018. http://www.diplomatie.gouv.fr/en/french-foreign-policy/francophony/the-status-of-french-in-the-world.

Staulo, John, ed. *Other Voices: A Collection of Essays on Italian Regional Culture and Language.* Scripta Humanistica. Washington, DC: Scripta Humanistica, 1990.

Stephenson, Emily, and Eric Knecht. "Trump Bars Doors to Refugees, Visitors from Seven Mainly Muslim Nations." *Reuters*, January 27, 2017.

Sterponi, Laura. "Clandestine Interactional Reading: Intertextuality and Double-Voicing under the Desk." *Linguistics and Education* 18, no. 1 (2007): 1–23.

Stille, Alexander. "Can the French Talk about Race?" *New Yorker*, July 11, 2014.

Stoller, Paul. *Money Has No Smell: The Africanization of New York City.* Chicago: University of Chicago Press, 2002.

Stovall, Tyler Edward. *Paris Noir: African Americans in the City of Light.* Boston: Houghton Mifflin, 1996.

———. "Race and the Making of a Nation: Blacks in Modern France." In *Diasporic Africa: A Reader*, edited by Michael A. Gomez, 200–218. New York: New York University Press, 2006.

Swain, Merrill. "The Output Hypothesis and Beyond: Mediating Acquisition through Collaborative Dialogue." In *Sociocultural Theory and Second Language Learning*, edited by James P. Lantolf, 97–114. New York: Oxford University Press, 2000.

Sweeney, Fionnghuala. *Frederick Douglass and the Atlantic World.* Liverpool: Liverpool University Press, 2007.

Swigart, Leigh. "Cultural Creolisation and Language Use in Post-Colonial Africa: The Case of Senegal." *Africa: Journal of the International African Institute / Revue de l'institut africain international* 64, no. 2 (1994): 175–89.

———. "The Limits of Legitimacy: Language Ideology and Shift in Contemporary Senegal." *Journal of Linguistic Anthropology* 10, no. 1 (June 2000): 90–130.

———. "Two Codes or One? The Insiders' View and the Description of Codeswitching in Dakar." *Journal of Multilingual and Multicultural Development* 13, no. 1–2 (January 1992): 83–102.

Talburt, Susan, and Melissa A. Stewart. "What's the Subject of Study Abroad? Race, Gender, and 'Living Culture.'" *Modern Language Journal* 83, no. 2 (June 1999): 163–75.

Tall, Serigne Mansour. "L'émigration internationale sénégalaise d'hier à demain." In *La société sénégalaise entre le local et le global*, edited by Momar-Coumba Diop, 549–78. Paris: Karthala, 2002.

———. "Les investissements immobiliers à Dakar des émigrants sénégalais." *Revue européenne de migrations internationales* 10, no. 3 (1994): 137–51.

Tall, Serigne Mansour, and Aly Tandian. *Regards sur la migration irrégulière des Sénégalais: Vouloir faire fortune en Europe avec des pirogues de fortune.* San Domenico di Fiesole, Italy: European University Institute, 2010.

Tann, Ken. "Imagining Communities: A Multifunctional Approach to Identity Management in Texts." In *New Discourse on Language: Functional Perspective on Multimodality, Identity, and Affiliation,* edited by J. R. Martin and Monika Bednarek, 163–94. New York: Continuum, 2010.

Tannen, Deborah. "What's in a Frame? Surface Evidence of Underlying Expectations." In *Framing in Discourse,* edited by Deborah Tannen, 14–56. New York: Oxford University Press, 1993.

Taubira, Christiane. *Mes météores: Combats politiques au long cours.* Paris: Flammarion, 2012.

Taylor, Robert Bartley. *Cultural Ways: A Concise Introduction to Cultural Anthropology.* Prospect Heights, IL: Waveland Press, 1980.

Thangaraj, Stanley. *Desi Hoop Dreams: Pickup Basketball and the Making of Asian American Masculinity.* New York: New York University Press, 2015.

Tharoor, Ishaan. "Italy's Election is Another Blow to the European Establishment." *Washington Post,* March 5, 2018.

Thomas, Dominic. *Africa and France: Postcolonial Cultures, Migration, and Racism.* Bloomington: Indiana University Press, 2013.

———. *Black France: Colonialism, Immigration, and Transnationalism.* Bloomington: Indiana University Press, 2007.

Thomas, Lynn. "Skin Lighteners, Black Consumers and Jewish Entrepreneurs in South Africa." *History Workshop Journal* 73 (2012): 259–83.

Tognetti, Sergio. "The Trade in Black African Slaves in Florence." In Earle and Lowe, *Black Africans in Renaissance Europe,* 213–24.

Toma, Sorana, and Eleonora Castagnone. "What Drives Onward Mobility within Europe? The Case of Senegalese Migration between France, Italy and Spain." *Population* 70, no. 1 (2015): 65–95.

Tosi, Arturo. *Language and Society in a Changing Italy.* Clevedon, England: Multilingual Matters, 2001.

Trudell, Barbara. "Practice in Search of a Paradigm: Language Rights, Linguistic Citizenship and Minority Language Communities in Senegal." *Current Issues in Language Planning* 9, no. 4 (November 2008): 395–412.

Trudell, Barbara, and Anthony R. Klaas. "Distinction, Integration and Identity: Motivations for Local Language Literacy in Senegalese Communities." *International Journal of Educational Development* 30, no. 2 (2010): 121–29.

Trudgill, Peter, ed. *Applied Sociolinguistics.* London: Academic Press, 1984.

Tshimanga, Charles, Didier Gondola, and Peter J. Bloom, eds. *Frenchness and the African Diaspora: Identity and Uprising in Contemporary France.* Bloomington: Indiana University Press, 2009.

United States Census Bureau, "2012–2016 American Community Survey 5-Year Estimates." Accessed February 28, 2018. https://www.census.gov/.

United States Census Bureau, "2012–2016 American Community Survey 5-Year Estimates: Quick Facts New York City." https://www.census.gov/quickfacts/fact/table/newyorkcitynewyork/POP815216#viewtop.

United States Census Bureau. "2015 American Community Survey 1-Year Estimates: People Reporting Ancestry." Accessed February 28, 2018. https://www.census .gov/.

United States Citizenship and Immigration Services. "The Naturalization Test." 2014. https://www.uscis.gov/us-citizenship/naturalization-test.

van der Valk, Ineke. "Right-Wing Parliamentary Discourse on Immigration in France." *Discourse & Society* 14, no. 3 (2003): 309–48.

Vaugelas, Claude Favre. *Remarques sur la langue françoise: Utiles à ceux qui veulent bien parler et bien escrire.* Paris: Vve J. Camusat et P. Le Petit, 1647.

Verdicchio, Pasquale. *Bound by Distance: Rethinking Nationalism through the Italian Diaspora.* Madison, NJ: Fairleigh Dickinson University Press, 1997.

Vinall, Kimberly. "'Got Llorona?' Teaching for the Development of Symbolic Competence." *L2 Journal* 8, no. 1 (2016): 1–16.

Vitanova, Gergana. "Gender Enactments in Immigrants' Discursive Practices: Bringing Bakhtin to the Dialogue." *Journal of Language, Identity, and Education* 3, no. 4 (2004): 261–77.

Walker, Alice. *The Color Purple.* Orlando, FL: Harcourt, 1982.

Walker, Andy. "Twitter: 'Africa's Going to the Final' after France Beats Belgium." *Memeburn,* July 11, 2018. https://memeburn.com/2018/07/france-african-twitter -world-cup/.

Ward, David. "'Italy' in Italy: Old Metaphors and New Racisms in the 1990s. In *Re-visioning Italy: National Identity and Global Culture,* edited by Beverly Allen and Mary J. Russo, 81–97. Minneapolis: University of Minnesota Press, 1997.

Warner, Tobias Dodge. "The Limits of the Literary: Senegalese Writers between French, Wolof and World Literature." PhD diss., University of California, Berkeley, 2012. ProQuest Theses and Dissertations (1081701616).

Weedon, Chris. *Feminist Practice and Post-Structuralist Theory.* 2nd ed. Cambridge, MA: Blackwell, 1997.

Weinreich, Uriel. *Languages in Contact: Findings and Problems.* 2nd ed. The Hague: Mouton, 1963.

Wekker, Gloria. *White Innocence: Paradoxes of Colonialism and Race.* Durham, NC: Duke University Press, 2016.

Wenger, Étienne. *Communities of Practice: Learning, Meaning, and Identity.* Learning in Doing. Cambridge: Cambridge University Press, 1998.

Wilder, Gary. *The French Imperial Nation-State: Negritude & Colonial Humanism between the Two World Wars.* Chicago: University of Chicago Press, 2005.

Wise, Tim J. *Between Barack and a Hard Place: Racism and White Denial in the Age of Obama.* San Francisco: City Lights Books, 2009.

Woolard, Kathryn, and Bambi Schieffelin. "Language Ideology." *Annual Review of Anthropology* 23 (1994): 55–82.

World Bank. "Bilaterial Remittance Matrix 2017." *Migration and Remittances Data,* April 2018. http://www.worldbank.org/en/topic/migrationremittancesdiasporaissues /brief/migration-remittances-data.

Yano, Yasukata. "World Englishes in 2000 and Beyond." *World Englishes* 20, no. 2 (July 2001): 119–32.

Yule, George. *Pragmatics.* Oxford: Oxford University Press, 1996.

Zarate, Geneviève, Danielle Lévy, and Claire Kramsch, eds. *Précis du plurilinguisme et du pluriculturalisme*. Paris: Éditions des archives contemporaines, 2008.

Zeleza, Paul Tiyambe. "Diaspora Dialogues: Engagements between Africa and Its Diasporas." In *The New African Diaspora*, edited by Isidore Okpewho and Nkiru Nzegwu, 31–58. Bloomington: Indiana University Press, 2009.

Zentella, Ana Celia. *Growing Up Bilingual: Puerto Rican Children in New York*. Malden, MA: Blackwell, 1997.

Zhao, Christina. "Days after 'Shithole' Controversy, Trump Administration Bans Haiti from Applying for Low-Skilled Work Visa." *Newsweek*, January 18, 2018.

Zincone, Giovanna. "A Model of 'Reasonable Integration': Summary of the First Report on the Integration of Immigrants in Italy." *International Migration Review* 34, no. 3 (2000): 956–68.

Zincone, Giovanna, and Tiziana Caponio. "Immigrant and Immigration Policy-Making: The Case of Italy." IMISCOE Working Papers no. 9, 2004. http://imiscoe.org/.

## MUSICAL RECORDINGS

Akon and Snoop Dogg. "I Wanna Love You." Released November 14, 2006. Track 4 on *Konvicted*. Universal. CD.

Baby Izi. "Home Party." Released 2012. https://www.youtube.com/watch?v=Np8h AIOyfGU.

Baloji. "Tout ceci ne vous rendra pas le Congo." Released 2010. Track 12 on *Kinshasa Succursale*. Crammed Discs. CD.

Brown, James. "Say It Loud—I'm Black and I'm Proud." Recorded August 17, 1967–October 18, 1968. Track 1 on *Say It Loud—I'm Black and I'm Proud*. King. LP.

Meek Mill and Young Chris. "House Party." Released October 29, 2011. *Dreamchasers*. Maybach Music Group. Digital download. https://www.youtube.com/watch?v=GKFzPv9vnB8.

# General Index

# Index of Informants